D. Howard Smith was born in Lancashire in 1900 and educated at Accrington Grammar School, Victoria College, Manchester, and London University, where he took a B.D. degree and a B.A. in Chinese. After 20 years as a missionary in North China, he was from 1953 to 1966 Lecturer in Comparative Religion at the University of Manchester, specializing in Far Eastern religions and particularly Chinese philosophies and cults. He is the author of *Pattern in the Mount* and *Chinese Religions*, and was the Sectional Editor for China and Japan in the *Dictionary of Comparative Religion* edited by Professor S. G. F. Brandon.

D1448309

John Morrison

D. Howard Smith

Confucius

Paladin

Granada Publishing Limited
Published in 1974 by Paladin
Frogmore, St Albans, Herts AL2 2NF

First published in Great Britain by
Maurice Temple Smith Ltd
Copyright © D. Howard Smith 1973
Made and printed in Great Britain by
Richard Clay (The Chaucer Press) Ltd
Bungay, Suffolk
Set in Monotype Erhardt

This book is sold subject to the condition that it
shall not, by way of trade or otherwise, be lent,
re-sold, hired out or otherwise circulated without
the publisher's prior consent in any form of
binding or cover other than that in which it is
published and without a similar condition
including this condition being imposed on the
subsequent purchaser.
This book is published at a net price and is
supplied subject to the Publishers Association
Standard Conditions of Sale registered under the
Restrictive Trade Practices Act, 1956.

Contents

Preface   7
Map: China at the time of Confucius   9
Introduction: CONFUCIUS AND CONFUCIANISM   11

Part 1   CONFUCIUS

1. Confucius: his Heritage and his World   21
2. The Man and his Disciples   41
3. The Teaching of Confucius   62
4. The Pre-Han Interpreters of Confucius   89

Part 2   A CONFUCIAN CIVILIZATION

5. The Triumph of Confucianism in the Han Dynasty   117
6. Confucianism and its Rivals: Taoism and Buddhism   136
7. The Revival of Confucianism in the Sung Dynasty   150
8. A Civilization moulded by Confucius   168
9. Confucius and the Modern World   200

Notes   211
Bibliography   233
A Note on Pronunciation   239
Principal Events in the Life of Confucius   241
Table of Dynasties   244
Index   247

Preface

THE rich, and in many ways unique, civilization of China, which developed through more than two thousand years of eventful history, owes more to the impress of Confucius's personality and teaching than to any other single factor. Chinese civilization may truly be called a Confucian Civilization. The influence of Confucius and his teaching not only came to predominate in China, but was powerful also in shaping the social and political life of Korea, Japan and Indo-China. It was through the writings of the early Jesuit Fathers that European scholars were made conversant with the works of this 'Wise Man of the East', and by the eighteenth century Confucian influence was strong in Europe, greatly influencing men like Leibniz and Voltaire. From that time onwards increasing knowledge of Confucianism has led to increasing respect.

In writing this book my aim has been to provide the general reader with a reliable and trustworthy account of the life, teaching and influence of Confucius, and to show how a man, comparatively insignificant and obscure in his own day, came to occupy a supreme place as the Great and Revered Teacher of the Chinese people. The book is not intended for sinologists: consequently I have made no reference in the bibliography to the numerous works in Chinese which I have consulted, nor to articles in journals, general works on comparative religion and encyclopedias from which I have derived much help. Over many years I have studied with immense profit the Confucian classics and other works by Chou dynasty thinkers, both in the original Chinese and in numerous translations in English and French. I am grateful for the help I have derived from both Chinese scholars and from Western sinologists, too numerous to mention individually.

I wish, in particular, to thank Messrs George Allen & Unwin

and Grove Press Inc. for permission to quote extensively from the excellent translation by Arthur Waley of the *Book of Songs*; George Allen & Unwin for permission to quote from Arthur Waley's translation of Confucius; and George Allen & Unwin and George Braziller Inc. for permission to quote from *Buddhism: a Nontheistic Religion* by Helmuth von Glasenapp.

I desire to put on record my indebtedness to my former colleague and friend, Professor S. G. F. Brandon, D.D., who held the chair in Comparative Religion at the University of Manchester. It was at his suggestion and through his encouragement that I undertook the pleasing task of writing this book. I wish to thank Mrs Florence Kirman for the devoted and efficient manner in which she prepared a difficult manuscript for publication. Most of all, I am indebted to my wife, not only for her patience and constant encouragement, but also for reading through the manuscript, offering useful suggestions and advice and for assistance in the preparation of the index. Finally, I desire to express sincere gratitude to the English publisher of the first edition, Mr Maurice Temple Smith, for his unfailing courtesy and encouragement.

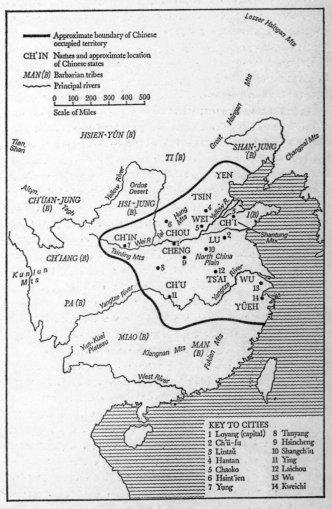

China at the time of Confucius

KEY TO CITIES

1 Loyang (capital)   8 Tanyang
2 Ch'ü-fu   9 Hsincheng
3 Lintzü   10 Shangch'iu
4 Hantan   11 Ying
5 Chaoko   12 Laichou
6 Hsint'ien   13 Wu
7 Yung   14 Kweichi

Approximate boundary of Chinese occupied territory

CH'IN Names and approximate location of Chinese states

MAN(B) Barbarian tribes

Principal rivers

0 100 200 300 400 500
Scale of Miles

Introduction: Confucius and Confucianism

CONFUCIANISM has usually been regarded as an ethico-political system rather than as a religion. For upwards of two thousand years it moulded and shaped the civilization of China and exerted a profound influence upon almost one fourth of the human race, yet its main influence has been humanistic, pragmatical and of this world, and there has been little concern with many questions which, in other great religions, are usually regarded as of first importance. In the main, Confucians have been agnostic as regards the existence of a personal God or of an after-life. Yet it is undeniable that there has always been in Confucianism a strong sense of the spiritual dimension of man and of his close relationship to a spirit-fraught universe. Confucianism in practice has included both religious rituals and religious beliefs, and has made an important contribution to that religious syncretism which evolved into the popular religion of China. As Joseph Needham has written, 'Confucianism was a religion, if you define that as something which involves the sense of the holy, for a quality of the numinous is very present in Confucian temples; but not if you think of religion only as the theology of a transcendent creator-deity.'[1] Confucius (and, indeed, most Confucians since his day) had deep and sincere religious feelings of reverence towards Heaven and an omnipresent spiritual world; he sought to obey the promptings of Heaven and to follow the Way of Heaven through the full realization of that moral nature which he believed to have been conferred upon him by Heaven.

The suggestion has often been made that Confucianism lacks many elements vital to an institutionalized religion. Though it possesses writings which very early came to be regarded as sacred scriptures, it puts no reliance on creeds and dogmas. It has never had a specialized priesthood, or church organization with rules and conditions of membership. Confucianism has been rather a pervasive moral and spiritual teaching, always working through education and example. However, though this is true, Confucianism throughout the centuries has been closely bound up with an elaborate religious cult, the officiants of which were the emperor himself and all the officers of a state administration down as far as the magistrates appointed to county[2] seats. This state cult in its finest manifestation rivalled in dignity, magnificence and splendour the noblest rituals and ceremonies by which, in other world religions, men have honoured their gods. The strict performance of these state rituals was believed to ensure blessing, happiness and prosperity to emperor, land and people, for it was hoped and believed that prayer and sacrifice sincerely offered would merit the continued goodwill of Heaven and the spiritual world. Rituals and ceremonies of an essentially religious nature were performed, not only on a splendid national scale by the emperor on behalf of all the people, but by the magistrates of every county within the Confucian temples that had been erected for that purpose in every major city. Furthermore, the worship and sacrifices to Confucius himself from the beginning of the Christian era, right down to the beginning of the twentieth century, suggest that the religious aspects of Confucianism are by no means negligible.

It is not the aim of this book to attempt a biography of Confucius. In the nature of the case such an attempt would be foredoomed to failure, since what is genuinely known about the events and circumstances of his life is meagre in the extreme, and in process of time has been overlaid by the uncritical and often tendentious writings of hagiographers. It is doubtful if Confucius left behind any writings of his own.[3] What is known about his life and character is gleaned from the writings of his immediate disciples and their followers, or from texts which are known to have come into existence not long after Confucius's death.[4] The earliest extant biography is that found in *The Historical Records* of Ssǔ-ma Ch'ien.[5] This biography appeared in the reign of Han Wu-ti (140–87 B.C.) and is thus some four hundred years after the time of Confucius. It was during the former Han dynasty (221 B.C.–A.D. 6) that Confucianism triumphed over all its rivals and Confucianism was accepted as orthodox doctrine. By this time Confucius had come to be regarded as the great sage-teacher who had lived in the – by then – far-distant antiquity. During the centuries that had intervened hagiographers, genealogists and legendmakers had been busy expanding and amplifying the few genuinely known facts concerning him. Ssŭ-ma Ch'ien commands respect as a historian, but he was a man of his own time, a time when most men accepted without question the marvellous and miraculous, and when myths and legends were regarded as true history. Ssŭ-ma Ch'ien, in writing his life of Confucius, believed many traditions and legends to be perfectly genuine which do not warrant a great deal of trust. Nearly all subsequent historians based their accounts of Confucius on this biography.

Our aim in the first part of this book is to try to account for the unique and distinctive place given to Confucius as the founder of one of the world's greatest systems of religious and philosophical thought. For more than two thousand years, down to the beginning of the twentieth century, Confucius has been regarded preeminently as China's greatest teacher. For most of those two thousand years Confucianism received state recognition, being accepted as the orthodox way of life by scholars and officials throughout the vast Chinese empire. Before that time, when Confucianism was one of many rival philosophies, the greatness of Confucius was being recognized in the writings of Mencius, Hsün-tzŭ and others. In the *Analects* (Lun Yü), which is the earliest and most reliable source for our knowledge of Confucius, though in a late stratum containing the sayings of his disciples,[6] we catch a glimpse of the greatness of Confucius as seen through the eyes of those who loved and followed him. We are told that when men spoke disparagingly of Confucius to his disciple Tzŭ-kung and even suggested that Tzŭ-kung was a better man, the disciple answered, 'Let us take for our comparison the wall round a building. My wall only reaches to the level of a man's shoulder, and it is easy to peep over it and see the good points of the house on the other side. But our master's wall rises many times a man's height, and no one who is not let in by the gate can know the beauty and wealth of the palace that, with its ancestral temple, its hundreds of ministrants, lies hidden within.' Furthermore, whilst other men are likened to hillocks and mounds that can easily be climbed over '. . . it would be as hard to equal our master as to climb up on a ladder to the sky. Had our master ever been put in control of a state or of a great family, it would have been as is described in the words, "He raised them and they stood, he led them and they went. He steadied them as with a rope and they came. He stirred them and they moved harmoniously. His life was glorious, his death bewailed." How can such an one ever be equalled ?'[7] These words were no doubt written down some considerable time after the death of Confucius, but they indicate that after his death his name and fame began to be spread abroad by men who believed that he had no equal.

What was there about this man which distinguished him above others? When we look into the known facts concerning him there seems very little to account for his subsequent greatness. In an age when hereditary power and aristocratic connections counted for so much, this man of humble birth, raised in poverty as an orphan, was never able to exert the influence he hoped for in the affairs of state, even though the state of Lu in which he lived was one of the smallest and weakest of the states which composed the China of those days. Whatever small measure of fame he achieved in his own lifetime was as a scholar and teacher. The success he hoped for as an adviser of princes seems to have eluded him, and he died feeling that in a large measure his life had been a failure. Why then should he have come to exert an influence far greater than any of the princes, nobles and great ministers of his time, whose decisions and actions seemed to be so momentous in their own eyes and in the eyes of the people whom they governed? Why, for instance, should his name and fame be greater than that of the noble and virtuous minister Tzǔ-ch'an of the state of Chêng[8] who was the scion of a noble family? Or why should Confucius have come to take precedence over the famous Duke of Chou[9] who seems to have been the hero whom Confucius himself most admired?

The first part of this book will be an attempt to answer the question why Confucius came to be regarded as China's greatest sage, a teacher beyond compare. To what extent did Confucius accept and absorb the religious, ethical and political sanctions which had for some thousand years been the basis of the developing civilization of China? How far did Confucius seek to modify, change and transform traditional ideas so as to meet the needs of a society in process of change? The period in which Confucius lived the whole of his life was one of political, social and economic change. A system which for hundreds of years had been evolving a closely knit inter-familial structure, in which authority and cohesion were upheld by moral and religious sanctions, was now being challenged by the agnosticism of the thinkers and the brute force of military adventurers. Power had already mostly passed into the hands of the rulers of large states who were independent of a central authority, whilst within the states themselves constant changes were taking place in a power structure as the 'haves' sought to hold on to what they possessed, whilst the 'have nots' strove to wrest it from them. It was the peculiar genius of Confucius to study with patience and zeal the accumulated wisdom of the past as it had been handed down in poetry, history and customary law and ritual. From this wisdom he sought out and found the simple yet fundamental principles on which to organize life on all levels, political, social, within the family and for the individual. He came to believe that there were certain principles of action without which there could be no good life, either for society as a whole or for the individual. It was his genius to state these principles with clarity, and to teach them to a small band of younger men with such warmth and enthusiasm that they not only retained a great affection for him as their revered teacher, but were imbued with a firm conviction that in his teachings lay the panacea for a sick society, and the blueprint for good government, world order, public welfare and peace.

In the second part of this book we examine Confucianism when it had become established in China as the orthodox doctrine by which men's lives were governed, both as individuals and in society, when it was accepted by emperor and people, and had developed into a magnificent, all-comprehensive system. It was found to be applicable to the governing of a great empire, a unique instrument for bolstering up the absolute authority of the emperor and the prestige of the scholar-class who became the officials and administrators of empire. Though it is true to say that by the time of the Former Han dynasty Confucianism had triumphed over all rival ideologies, after the break-up of the Han dynasty Confucianism underwent many vicissitudes. There were times when, under the patronage of various emperors and their courts, Buddhism or Taoism exercised great influence in the state as rival ideologies. Buddhism, in particular, brought to the Chinese such profound philosophical ideas and such convincing interpretations of man's nature, origin and destiny that Confucian scholars were forced to reinterpret and adapt the original teachings of Confucius so as to provide answers to the questions which thoughtful men were posing. In doing this they often attributed to Confucius ideas which had been absorbed from extraneous sources. Many things were accepted as Confucian which were completely at variance with his original teaching. Nevertheless, throughout the centuries, what had been regarded as 'sacred scripture' from Han times, embodying not only the teachings of Confucius himself but more ancient writings on which his teachings had been based, were preserved more or less in the form in which they had been collated and edited by Han dynasty scholars.[10] There was, therefore, always an accessible source of reference, a source to which scholars could return again and again to draw new inspiration and new insights from the fountain-head, and to correct abuses and errors which in process of time had crept in.

It was not, however, till the great neo-Confucian revival of the Sung dynasty (A.D. 960–1279)[11] that Confucianism was firmly re-established as an unassailable orthodoxy. It was then that a galaxy of great scholars reinterpreted the Han dynasty Confucian texts in the light of some thousand years of development in philosophical and religious thought. From that time onwards, whatever the religious predilections personally held by an emperor, the dominant ideology governing China remained Confucian. As far as religion was concerned, an individual might follow his own preference, but the state religion, the state rituals and the morality approved by the state were essentially Confucian. The vast machinery of government, from the magnificent rituals and ceremonies by which the affairs of the state were harmonized with the Will of Heaven to the education and examination of each minor official, was all regarded as appertaining to the Confucian system.

Of all the monarchs who ruled over China throughout her long history it is, perhaps, the Manchu[12] emperor, K'ang Hsi (A.D. 1661–1722) who best exemplifies the ideal of a Confucian ruler. From his early days he strove to become a model Confucian monarch, and set a moral example to his subjects. He became an outstanding Confucian scholar in his own right, and was a generous patron of education and scholarship. During his long reign Confucianism pervaded every aspect of life. The boundaries of the Chinese empire were extended to include as protectorates Korea, Mongolia, Tibet and Taiwan, whilst tribute-bearing missions from many lands streamed to the capital city to acknowledge the authority and supremacy of the Son of Heaven. During this and the two subsequent reigns Confucianism was regarded as being of universal application and not something peculiar to and only applicable to the Chinese. The famous *Sacred Edict*,[13] drawn up by K'ang Hsi and published during his reign, sought to inculcate a Confucian morality among the general populace. Its sixteen injunctions, hung on the walls of all schools in China, and recited twice every month by teachers and their pupils, exalted the twin virtues of filial piety and brotherly love. The official state examinations, based as they were at every level on a knowledge of the Confucian Classics, were the guarantee that all scholar-officials had had a training in Confucian ortho-doxy. The magnificent palaces, temples and altars of the capital city, first conceived of and built by the great Ming emperor, Yung Lo (*d.* 1424), became the setting of impressive ceremonies and rituals which were the hallmark of traditionalism and conserva-tism. Confucianism was accepted as the dominant ideology, a way of life, a system of thought, pervading every aspect of political, social and family life, institutionalized in the state itself.

It will be part of the aim of this book to assess to what extent the complex and highly developed state cult of Confucianism and all that went with it stemmed from the original teaching of Confucius. Would things have been much different if Confucius had never lived? If Confucius could have returned to China in the reign of K'ang Hsi and seen Confucianism as it existed and was practised at that time, how much of all that he saw would he have recognized as his own? How much would have merited his condemnation? Would he have recognized in K'ang Hsi the enlightened monarch, the universal ruler whom, in his own life-time, he had longed to serve?

The teachings of the world's great spiritual and ethical leaders have proved of abiding worth and of perpetual inspiration to millions of people. In this respect Confucius is no exception. His was the inspiration behind the development of one of the richest and noblest civilizations the world has known. As in other religious systems, so in Confucianism, 'the letter killeth, but the spirit giveth life'.[14] Again and again in Chinese history the dead weight of traditionalism, the rigidity of orthodoxy and the meticulous observance of outward form to the neglect of inner sincerity have stifled the living spirit. All too often the voice of free inquiry has been muted, and the search after the good and true, which Confucius himself made his constant endeavour, has been neglected. Fortunately China has never lacked followers of Confucius who, by the nobility of their lives and the integrity of their scholarship, have handed on the true spirit and teaching of their Master to future generations. It can be confidently asserted that this line of true Confucians is by no means exhausted, and that, though on the mainland of China at the present day Confucius is often ridiculed and denigrated, there are still many Chinese scholars whose view of life and incorruptibility of character exemplify the fundamental teachings of China's greatest Sage.

Part I

Confucius

I. Confucius: his Heritage and his World

China of the Shang Dynasty

At the time when Confucius (K'ung fu-tzŭ) was born, in the year 551 B.C., the Chinese people could look back on more than one thousand years of comparatively civilized life as a distinctive and politically organized people. By the middle of the second millennium B.C. the Shang or Yin dynasty was firmly established. Before that time, in the absence of reliable evidence, history gives place to legend. Legends, with which the contemporaries of Confucius were familiar and which must have had some basis in fact, spoke of a Hsia dynasty (traditional dates 2205–1766 B.C.) and before that of semi-divine hero-rulers who had given to the Chinese their distinctive language, their customs, their calendar and the numerous inventions of a civilized way of life.[1]

The Shang dynasty, for which there is abundant documentary and archaeological evidence, seems to have consisted of an upper ruling class of related families and their dependants who acknowledged the overlordship and supreme authority of a king. Below them was a lower stratum consisting of peoples whom they had subjugated, the common people dependent on their masters, tied to the land as serfs, and serving as cultivators of the soil, herders of cattle, domestic servants or artisans and foot soldiers in the armies. The upper classes were the bearers of culture which found its main expression, as we shall see, in their religious and ceremonial practices.

A loose federation of clans, living in the basin of the Yellow River and its tributaries, were united together under a recognized head by the ties of a common ancestry, closely knit kinship through inter-marriage, similar customs and a common language which had already developed a fairly intricate and comprehensive script. By their common action these clans and families had brought under their control a large area of land, but they were constantly exercised in fighting against non-Chinese tribes[2] whom they regarded as barbarians, and in clearing forests, draining marshes, controlling the turbulent rivers, and bringing more and more land under cultivation. It was, perhaps, the common peril and the magnitude of common tasks, which could only be brought to a successful conclusion by united and co-operative effort, which led them to form themselves into a closely knit confederacy under the hegemony of a dominant clan.

Archaeological discoveries made in the early decades of this century have shown very clearly that by the fourteenth and thirteenth centuries B.C. many of the distinctive elements of Chinese civilization and religion were already in being. These were later to form an integral part of the Confucian inheritance. This is particularly true of the religion, both in the predominance of the ancestral cult, and in the close relationship which was to exist throughout the centuries between religion and government. What we understand today as Confucianism, in its more religious aspects, is in large measure a development of ideas and cultic practices which were already in being in the Shang dynasty a thousand years before Confucius was born. Many aspects of Confucianism ante-date Confucius himself. This has always been recognized by Chinese scholars who gave to the Confucian religion the name *Ju Chiao* – 'the religion or the teaching of the Ju'.[3] The *Ju* were the scholar-officials who were the direct successors of the religious experts trained to perform a variety of functions at the great state ceremonies of the Shang dynasty.

In order to understand the origins of Confucianism and of the religion which Confucius himself inherited it is necessary to examine briefly the religious structure of the Shang dynasty, especially as the main elements of Shang religion were taken over into the Chou dynasty (1122–221 B.C.) and continued down to the time of Confucius. Of the religion of the rural peasantry little is known. Their chief concern was with agriculture and the domestication of animals, and their gods were those of the homestead and the hearth, the soil and grain. They worshipped innumerable spirits of deceased men and animals, and the spirits which were thought to animate natural objects. The forces of nature needed to be placated. The animistic beliefs of the peasantry were shared by the slave-owning aristocracy, who, however, as Professor Li Chi has written, observed 'a theocratic religion dominated by excessive devotion to ancestor worship'.[4] As they lived in fortified towns, and were bound together by a kinship system of rights, privileges and relationships, they recognized an obligation to observe an elaborate code of ritual and ceremonial in which every individual had his or her appropriate status. The most important occupations of the nobility were hunting and war on the one hand and the observance of religious and ceremonial duties on the other. Their supreme god, Shang Ti, seems to have been identified with the founder-ancestor of their race. He was thought of as ruling on high, and with him they associated, not only the spirits of their deceased ancestors, but also, as ministering servants, the gods of sun, moon and stars, of rain, wind and thunder, and many other spiritual beings. From him all the noble families traced their descent, but the king was his descendant in a direct line. So, when a king died, he went up to heaven to join his great ancestor, whilst his eldest son now took his place as chief sacrificer and libationer in the ancestor cult. Shang Ti was believed to hold rule over the land and its people. In all matters of importance his will had to be sought, his help and guidance implored, and his goodwill kept. Thus, we see how political power was linked to spiritual power, and government to the maintenance of good relations with the spiritual powers which, at various levels, held sway over the universe and everything within it. This idea became the foundation of sovereignty, and a basic tenet of Confucianism throughout Chinese history.

It was natural that the most important building in the land was the ancestral temple of the royal house. It was there that the weapons of war were stored, and whenever the king engaged in a punitive expedition, either against a recalcitrant lord or against the barbarians, he first sacrificed to his ancestors in this temple and announced to them his plans. It was there that each vassal lord received the insignia of his fiefdom. It was there that representatives of all the noble families met on solemn occasions to participate in the common ancestral cult, at which the king, as head of a great family, offered prayers and sacrifices to the first divine ancestor, Shang Ti, and his numerous associates in the spiritual world. Here, then, we find the origin of the elaborate state cult of Confucianism which, from the Han dynasty onwards, gave magnificent ritual expression to the unity of 'all under Heaven' in one great empire ruled over by a monarch who claimed unique status as 'son of Heaven'. Whilst bearing in mind that Han dynasty scholars, in order to give an aura of antiquity and traditionalism to the political institutions of their own time, gave a false picture of kingship under the Shang and early Chou dynasties, investing antiquity with their own concepts of empire, it would be untrue to assert that the rituals and ceremonials associated with the worship of Heaven and the ancestor cult were a pure invention of Han dynasty scholars and had no basis in the past. The dynastic songs and legends of the *Book of Poetry* (*Shih Ching*) witness to the fact that in Shang and early Chou times there was a highly sophisticated ceremonial life appertaining to the royal court, the worship of Shang Ti and the cult of ancestors. By the time of Confucius the magnificent rituals and ceremonies of earlier times had largely fallen into disuse, owing to the weakness of the dynastic rulers and the usurpation of authority by rival lords. Confucius, with his keen interest in ritual, recognized that much of the colourful ritual of earlier times could have no meaning unless the country was united in allegiance to a supreme head, a state of affairs which only came about two hundred and fifty years after Confucius's death, when Prince Chêng the ruler of the state of Ch'in united the whole of China under his own absolute rule, and took the title Shih Huang Ti (the First Emperor).

Many features of Shang religion were taken over into Confucianism. To assist the king in the correct performance of all his religious functions certain men taken from the ranks of the higher officials received specialized training. The priest-scribes, or *shih*, were selected from members of the royal family itself. Their duty was to record and interpret significant events both in the natural and human spheres, events which were deemed to have a direct bearing on government, and were regarded as warnings or encouragements from the spiritual world. Another class of trained officiants were the 'invokers' (*chu*), scholars who were responsible for the compilation of the prayers which were ceremonially offered to the gods and ancestor spirits. These men became 'masters of ritual', officiating at the state sacrifices, directing the progress of the ceremony, making sure that every word and every act was done in accordance with the prescribed formulae. Finally there were the experts in divination (*wu*) whose duty was to communicate in various ways with the ancestor spirits so as to obtain their commands or their advice. Divination was a very important element in Shang religion.[5] So strong a place has it held in Chinese religion ever since that not only has it always been a main ingredient of popular religion but the *Book of Changes* (*I Ching*), one of the five Confucian Classics, was itself in origin a book of divination, and in later Confucianism became a favourite book on which a whole body of cosmological and philosophical speculation was raised.

The Shang dynasty named their days after cyclical signs, combining signs for the so-called 'ten heavenly stems'[6] with the signs for the twelve double-hour periods into which the Chinese divided their day. They combined these signs to form a sixty-day cycle. They divided the year into twelve lunar periods, interpolating extra days to adjust to the solar year. They paid great attention to astronomical phenomena, and devised a calendar which was of such great importance to an agricultural community that its promulgation, on the advice of experts, was one of the most important duties of kingship. Though Confucius himself seems to have been remarkably free from superstition, Confucianism, when it became the state orthodoxy, took into itself these beliefs in the influence of heavenly bodies and natural phenomena on human life. Among the high government officials were experts in astrology.

As early as the Shang dynasty the main elements of Confucianism as a state cult were already in being, at least in germ. The king exercised important religious functions which were believed to be essential for the well-being of the state. Every territorial magnate had ritual duties of a magico-religious nature to perform on behalf of the territories he governed. Only thus could the fertility of crops and animals be assured, the regularity of the seasons, and the harmonious relationship between Heaven, Earth and man. The country prospered under the constant protection and blessing of a primeval divine ancestor, now raised on high to be supreme god. The king stood to him in a peculiar relationship and consequently possessed a unique religious status.

As in other ancient civilizations the rituals by which the favour of the gods was secured and prosperity assured were focused, as we have already noted, in the person of the king. Yet in China, the pattern of seasonal and symbolic rites which the king undertook to perform on behalf of the land and its people, though originating in a similar chthonic religion to those which developed elsewhere, in which ancestor worship and fertility cults predominated, seems to differ vastly in its development. In early Chinese religion there seems to have been no dramatic representation of the death and rising of a god, no ritual combat to represent the victory of the god over his enemies, no sacred marriage, no triumphal procession in which the king played the role of a god, followed by a train of lesser gods. Ancient China had no equivalent of Osiris, Tammuz, Adonis, Astarte, Cybele and Ceres. Nor does there seem to have been developed in the official cult in China a pantheon of celestial deities such as we find in Indo-European religions. There is a parallel to 'Heaven' (*T'ien*) in the concept of Varuna and Ouranos, but there seem to have been no parallels in Chinese religion to the anthropomorphic deities of the Vedic religion in India – Indra, Rudra, Mitra, Suraya, Ushas, Agni – nor to the personalized gods and goddesses of Greek and Roman religions. Mythological constructions are remarkably absent from early Chinese religion, and this may account, in part at least, for the rationalistic and humanistic tendencies which developed later.

The legacy of the Early Chou Dynasty kings

Some five hundred years before Confucius was born (the traditional date is 1122 B.C.) the last ruler of the Shang dynasty was conquered after long and bitter fighting. A powerful tribe in the west called Chou had earlier pledged their allegiance to the Shang, but having settled down in the Wei valley in modern Shensi, they gradually increased in economic and military strength, and having won over to their side a majority of the Chinese tribes, they decided to make war on their overlords. For a long time the issue of the struggle was in doubt, but finally under King Wu and his illustrious brother, the Duke of Chou, the Chou dynasty was established. The relatively uncultured conquerors from the west were only too glad to take over, at least in its main outlines, the Shang political system and the Shang religion, but they introduced momentous innovations both in politics and in religion, which were to exercise a considerable influence on the life and thought of Confucius. As they are pictured in the historical documents and dynastic odes which were handed down from generation to generation the early Chou kings were ideals of what rulers ought to be. Confucius was brought up to idealize the Kings Wên and Wu and especially the Duke of Chou, who, on the death of his elder brother, made no attempt to seize the throne himself, but acted as regent for his young nephew. Confucius looked back on these early years of the Chou dynasty as an ideal time when the land was united under strong and benevolent rulers, who regarded their high position as a trust from Heaven, ruled in justice and sought the people's welfare and the prosperity and peace of the land. This idealized state is pictured for us in some of the great ceremonial odes which served as hymns to laud the exploits and glorify the characters of King Wên and King Wu, poems that were well known to Confucius and beloved by him:

> Then came king Wên;
> God set right measure to his thoughts,
> Spread abroad his fair fame;
> His power was very bright,
> Very bright and very good.
> Well he led, well lorded,
>
> Was king over this great land.
> Well he followed, well obeyed,
> Obeyed – did king Wên.
> His power was without flaw.
> Having received God's blessing
> He handed it down to grandsons and sons.[7]
>
> Renowned was king Wên,
> Yes, high was his renown.
> He united, he gave peace;
> Manifold were his victories.
> Oh, glorious was king Wên!
>
> King Wên received Heaven's bidding
> To do these deeds of war.
> He attacked Ch'ung;
> He made his capital in Fêng.
> Oh, glorious was king Wên![8]

Terrible in his power was King Wu;
None so mighty in glory.
Illustrious were Ch'êng and K'ang
Whom God on high made powerful.
From the days of that Ch'êng, that K'ang,
All the land was ours.
Oh, dazzling their brightness![9]

Broken were our axes
And chipped our hatchets.
But since the Duke of Chou came to the East
Throughout the kingdoms all is well.
He has shown compassion to us people.
He has greatly helped us.[10]

A truer picture of these semi-barbarous times may be gleaned
from the inscriptions on ceremonial bronzes cast during this
period. Nevertheless, with the advent of the Chou dynasty there
was a considerable advance in ethical thinking. In the lawless
times through which Confucius lived he could look back to these
heroic times of the past and draw inspiration for his own ethical
and political principles.

Undoubtedly the awakened ethical consciousness of the early
Chou rulers grew out of the pressing need to justify their
rebellion, to win and keep powerful friends, and pacify the
people. They had raised the standard of revolt against a dynasty
which had exercised rule for some five hundred years. The last
king of the Shang dynasty is depicted by the Chou propagandists
as licentious and cruel, dissipated and evil. There was probably
some measure of truth in these charges, but though he might
personally be unfitted to occupy the throne he was the legitimate
heir to a long line of illustrious ancestors. He was the direct
descendant of that first-ancestor who had for long been worshipped as a supreme deified spirit. The king was bound by ties
of kinship to the numerous nobles and officers who thronged his
court, a court marked by a level of cultural life far in advance of
that of the rude western tribes who were bent on rebellion. It
was, therefore, an astute move on the part of the Chou conquerors to claim that they were merely instruments in the hands
of the Supreme Deity himself. Shang Ti, because of his care and
concern for the suffering people had called them and raised them
up to carry out His purpose, namely the overthrow of a corrupt

and licentious ruler. Shang Ti had given them a mandate to restore peace, prosperity and justice in the land. This clear mandate to overthrow the Shang and rule in their place they had received from the Supreme Ruler Above (Shang Ti) whose other name was August Heaven (Hao T'ien). Though reluctant to accept, they had not dared to disobey.

I constantly say to myself, Heaven purposed to destroy Yin, as a husbandman [destroys weeds.] How dare I neglect to complete the work of my fields! Heaven seeks in this way to bless me.
His [King Wên's] fame reached up to Shang Ti who blessed him. Heaven therefore bestowed its great command on King Wên to extirpate the dynasty of Yin, to receive its mandate, and take over its territories and people, that they might be well-governed.
It was Heaven who would not let it remain with them. Indeed it would not tolerate their misrule. It assisted us. How could we ourselves dare to aspire to the throne?
Without pity Heaven has brought destruction on Yin, since Yin has lost its mandate to rule, which we of the house of Chou have received.[11]

Thus the early Chou kings justified their rebellion and their seizure of power, but in doing so they established certain vital principles which could in future times be used against oppressive and licentious rulers. These principles were well understood by Confucius, were restated by Mencius, and became an integral part of Confucianism throughout Chinese history. First of all there was the principle that the ruler is the vice-regent of God upon earth, receiving his mandate from God and answerable to God for his actions. Even when, at the time of Confucius, among thinkers and scholars the concept of an all-powerful God above had given place to a depersonalized concept of an over-ruling providence, this idea of the Mandate of Heaven and responsibility to Heaven remained. Secondly, there was the principle that, as God had raised up the Chou kings to rule because of God's kindly and beneficent interest in the common people, a ruler's first concern must be the welfare of the people as a whole. Thirdly, if a ruler neglected his duty and gave himself up to practices which were abhorrent to God, God would show his displeasure. The anger of God would be revealed in crop failures, signs and portents, natural calamities, but above all in the murmurings of the people. As a final measure God himself would take away from the monarch his mandate to rule and confer it on his own appointee, whose duty involved the overthrow and punishment of the ruler who had incurred God's wrath. In the light of these principles no ruler could exercise power solely in the interest of his own family. Power was a trust conferred by God, and could be taken away just as surely as it could be granted.

The early Chou rulers had not only to justify their rebellion. Before them lay the stupendous task of pacifying and reorganizing a vast territory which had been devastated by long and bitter civil war. They had to re-establish some measure of law and order. Under the Shang each territorial magnate had been for all practical purposes sole authority in his own domain, so long as he acknowledged the overlordship of the king. In those early times the administration of extensive territories from one centre was impossible. The states that composed China were divided from one another by large tracts of wild, inhospitable country, by mountain ranges, unnavigable rivers, dense forests and swamplands. Much of the territory was still occupied by non-Chinese tribes. Each territorial ruler had to be given, and was able to assert, a large measure of autonomy. The most the Chou kings could hope to do was to parcel out the newly conquered lands among their allies, relatives and principal retainers, and those members of the defeated Shang confederation who were prepared to come over to their side. Having done this, they needed to strengthen the bonds of loyalty to the throne by every means possible. It was in this attempt to bind the great noble families into a compact confederacy under the hegemony of the Chou kings that some of the most distinctive traits of Confucianism developed.

The system that grew up has been likened to the feudalism that characterized western Europe during the Middle Ages. Though there are points of resemblance, there are also many differences. The noble families which together formed the ruling social class in ancient China were not only very closely connected by intermarriage, but by the recognition of a common ancestry. All the clans and branch clans were united in a common worship at the ancestral temple of their divine progenitor. The Chou royal court and those to whom the House of Chou distributed fiefs personally, thus establishing its own supreme authority, came to accept a belief that they were all descended from a common stock. So, on stated occasions, they assembled together as members of a 'great family' for the purpose of engaging in joint religious celebrations at which they recognized the favours bestowed upon them by the spirit of a common ancestor and at the same time offered to him and to his illustrious living representative their duty and obedience. The cult of ancestors increased in importance under the Chou, and was elaborated into a well-organized system in which the relations between the living and the dead came to be governed by fixed formulae.

The concept of a 'great family' with its main clan and branch clans, the ever-multiplying posterity of a first-ancestor, is very different from that of feudalism. The rites and ceremonies by which the ancestors were worshipped and honoured were manifestations of family and clan solidarity. This solidarity of the whole people was emphasized by the requirement that all the noble houses should be represented at the ancestral feasts of the king. At first Hou Chi, the god of millet, was accepted as the first supreme ancestor of the Chou clans, but in process of time, as the bounds of their rule continually expanded and other large groups were assimilated, the mythical Huang Ti (or Yellow Emperor) came to be thought of as the first progenitor of the Chinese race and the founder of its culture.

The feudalistic nature of the social organization is seen in the right of the Chou kings to grant and renew fiefs, and in the solemn rituals which governed the relations between a lord and his vassal. The feudatories had a duty to attend at court on the accession of a new ruler, and also at certain fixed times in the year. They presented tribute and swore fealty. In times of peace they were obliged to send labourers on projects of common concern, and in time of war they equipped their own units to fight in a joint campaign. They were expected to provide food and accommodation when needed to royal legates or troops. Many of the inscribed bronzes which have come down from the ninth and early eighth centuries B.C. commemorate the conferring of honours by the king on feudatory lords in recognition of loyal services. The inscriptions sometimes quote in detail from the texts of documents of appointment bestowed on a noble or a high official by the ruler on the occasion of the former's visit to court.

Like the king himself, each territorial magnate set up his own ancestral temple in the fortified city where he had his seat. Like the ruler, he too distributed lands within his own fief to loyal ministers, senior officials and military knights in his service. These were all deemed to owe him loyalty and service. It was inevitable that, as many of these nobles grew in strength and as their families increased in numbers, there should develop a spirit of independence. Yet the members of these noble families felt themselves to be bound in a network of intricate relationships in which every person held his or her appropriate station and performed some necessary function. These relationships did not apply either to the barbarian tribes or to the common people. They were a binding moral and religious sanction for the ruling class.

At the time of Confucius, and in the state of Lu in particular, the people looked back some four hundred and fifty years to the famous Duke of Chou. He, more than anyone else, was thought to exemplify in his life and character those virtues of filial piety and loyalty which were to form the basis of Confucian morality. On the death of his elder brother, King Wu, serious rebellion had broken out which the Duke of Chou quelled. He then administered the government as regent on behalf of his nephew, King Ch'êng. Future generations credited the Duke of Chou with creating the system of ritual and music of the Chou dynasty, and placing on a firm foundation the whole of the Chou civilization with its social system, its ethical code and its artistic and cultural life.

It is recorded that the Duke of Chou sent his eldest son, Po Ch'in, to take charge of a large fiefdom in the east in what is now the prefecture of Ch'ü-fu in Shantung. There he founded the state of Lu, where subsequent generations honoured the Duke of Chou as a culture hero. To found this new state of Lu, Po Ch'in took with him only a few members of his own clan, but he took six clan-groups that had belonged to the former Shang–Yin dynasty. These, together with the local inhabitants, formed the bulk of the population of the state. This process of colonization by the founding of new city states marks a stage in the transition from communities based entirely on blood-relationships to communities based on territorial ownership. This inevitably led to great changes of emphasis as regards religion. When senior positions in the government of states came to be held by members of widely different clans, the religious services in the ruler's ancestral temple could no longer act as a bond uniting the whole community, for it was universally recognized that no ancestral spirit would allow participation in his celebrations to any but his own descendants. Each clan maintained its own private worship of its ancestors in the ancestral temple built for its own use. The patron deities of soil and grain, and the territorial deities who inhabited the mountains and rivers, were deemed to be of greater significance in promoting the prosperity of the land and its people than the family worship confined to the ancestral temple of the ruler. In a predominantly agricultural economy, though each lord had his flocks and herds to provide an abundance of animals for the sacrificial feasts, it was the ploughing, sowing, reaping and harvesting of the various types of grain which guaranteed the basic supply of food and drink for nobles and peasants alike. So it was the Earth Altar erected in the suburb of the city for the worship of the spirits of the soil and grain (shê-chi t'an) which became the main focus of worship within a particular territory, and it was the covering over of this altar which signalized the destruction of a fiefdom.

During the Shang dynasty, on the death of a king, it was a younger brother who succeeded to the throne in preference to the eldest son. Under the early Chou kings the law of primogeniture was established in respect both of the royal house and of the five feudal ranks of nobility which were instituted. These correspond roughly to our dukes, marquises, earls, viscounts and barons. Whilst the eldest son of the legal wife had the right to succeed his father, other sons of a deceased king received the title of duke and were given ducal fiefs. The same system operated through the various ranks of the nobility, so that, apart from the eldest son, the members of a succeeding generation were ranked one step lower in the hierarchy. The younger sons of barons became commoners, but being of a class distinct from the peasants who tilled the soil, they sought employment in various ways, as junior officials, household stewards, captains in military service. These gentlemen or knights, as time went on, became a numerous and powerful class in the community.

In the early days of the Chou dynasty, when the territory under Chinese control was continually expanding and new cities were being built, this feudal system worked well, but from the middle of the eighth century B.C. onwards social and economic changes led to a gradual breakdown. By the time of Confucius the system had become completely unworkable. Yet Confucius and the people of his day looked back through the centuries to this period of the early Chou kings and regarded it as an ideal time of peace and prosperity. If one reads through the *Book of Poetry* (*Shih Ching*), in which many of the poems belong to those times, one gains the impression that the standard of material culture was much higher than in subsequent centuries. The nobility enjoyed a rich and artistic social life with leisure to pursue the sports of hunting, archery and charioteering. They dressed in silks, lambswool, rich furs and skins, and adorned themselves with jewels of jade and precious stone. They feasted on bream, tench and carp from the rivers, on venison, roast turtle and bears' paws from the chase. Their farms provided them with meat and poultry, scented herbs, wheat, millet and barley, fruits such as plums, peaches, quince. Some of the poems reveal that the womenfolk had far more liberty and far less restraint than in later times, whilst the peasants and slaves were well-fed, clothed and housed. One poem[12] gives an almost idyllic picture of agriculture, where the master and his eldest son work alongside the headman and the overseer and the men, whose wives bring out the deep food baskets for all to partake. Another poem[13] tells the story of the Lord of Han having audience with the king, bearing his great sceptre of office, and being presented with an embroidered banner, chariot trappings, robes, etc. He provided a feast, 'a hundred cups of clear wine, roast turtle and fresh fish, bamboo shoots and reed shoots'. He took the king's niece to wife and went to meet her with a hundred teams of steeds, each team of eight horses decked with tinkling bells, and when he returned with her and her thronging cloud of bridesmaids, she found that his was a lovely, peaceful dwelling-place in a pleasant but as yet half-tamed land.

> Its rivers and pools so large,
> Its bream and tench so fat,
> Its deer so plentiful,
> And black bears and brown,
> Wild cats and tigers.

So the Lord of Han sent to the court skins of the white wolf, of red panther and brown bear, and having received as his fiefdom all the northern lands, he ruled them as their lord, building walls and digging ditches and apportioning the land to his subordinates. The poems of the *Shih Ching*, which Confucius studied intensively, give the impression of a vigorous, expanding civilization, already possessed of an advanced artistic and ceremonial life.

The Ch'un Ch'iu period

Confucius lived the whole of his life in the latter part of the period known as the Ch'un Ch'iu, which began some two hundred years before his birth and which ended when he died. This period takes its name from the Chinese Classic known as the *Ch'un Ch'iu*, comprising *Chronicles of the State of Lu* from 720 to 489 B.C. The compilation of these chronicles has been attributed, in all probability wrongly, to Confucius. Whatever his responsibility for them may have been – and the matter has been much debated – it is certain that he made a careful study of the history of this period. He made constant reference to it in his own teaching, and many of the events which happened during this period and the men who directed them had a profound influence on his life and work.

In the year 771 B.C. King Yu was defeated and killed by an alliance of barbarian tribesmen with relatives of the queen, who had been set aside because of the king's infatuation with a favourite concubine. The right of the crown prince to inherit was in jeopardy. The rebels looted and destroyed the capital city of Hao, near to the present-day city of Sian in Shensi. When the rightful heir to the throne became king he moved his capital eastwards to Loyang. From that time onwards the power and authority of the Chou kings grew weaker, became nominal and finally ceased to have any importance. The real power devolved upon the heads of the major states, the most powerful of which at any particular time was acknowledged as 'leader' or *pa*. The king was allowed to retain his titles, dignities and religious functions, together with a small and impoverished territory surrounding the capital. Throughout a period of almost incessant warfare the smaller states were gradually absorbed into the larger. Whereas in the eighth century there were some two hundred feudal states in existence, by the time of Confucius their number had been reduced to fifteen. Of these only eleven could truly be called Chinese. Mainly confined to the basin of the Yellow River they formed themselves into a confederacy. Round the periphery were semi-barbarian and culturally backward states, which were able to grow relatively stronger as they expanded outwards and absorbed more and more of the barbarian tribes. The ruler of the powerful state of Ch'in to the north-west claimed to be descended from the ancient sage-emperors of the Chinese, but most of his subjects were barbarians. States to the south, in the basin of the Yang-tzŭ River, and in particular the state of Ch'u, gradually absorbed Chinese culture. They accepted the language and culture and institutions of the Chinese, and became an integral part of the Chinese political system. Towards the end of the sixth century B.C. when Confucius was growing up to manhood, Wu and Yüeh in the south were emerging as powerful states.

Throughout the whole of this period war was endemic. Territories, especially in the central region, were constantly changing hands. High ranking and noble families were being reduced to penury. Sometimes legitimate rulers were murdered in family intrigues or by ambitious military adventurers. Family intrigues within the feudal states were inevitable, when rulers took several wives and concubines and fathered a numerous progeny, whilst ambitious officials and family retainers sought to wrest power from the hands of effete and incapable overlords. Serious efforts were made to bring some order out of chaos. Leagues were formed, solemn treaties drawn up and ratified, and cooperative efforts made to bring recalcitrant states to heel, to repulse barbarian tribes from the north which were making constant inroads on the settled agricultural communities, or to contain the growing aggression and influence of the state of Ch'u to the south. The *Spring and Autumn Annals* (*Ch'un Ch'iu*) record the signing of non-aggression pacts, the ratification of solemn treaties, attempts at arbitration. Though again and again the principles of mutual cooperation and assistance were violated, a semblance of order was maintained and some measure of restraint exercised. This was notably so when Duke Huan of

Ch'i, ably supported by his minister Kuan Chung, made Ch'i into the foremost state (685–643 B.C.). The rapid growth to power of this state was largely due to the fact that Ch'i held monopolies in iron and salt, and began to use iron to improve war chariots and weapons of war. Duke Huan also encouraged scholars to take up residence in his state, greatly improved trade and commerce and gave assistance to neighbouring states when they were threatened by barbarian tribes. For his day he was an enlightened ruler. He sought as far as possible to resolve the quarrels between states without recourse to war. He encouraged the setting up of conferences to discuss points of mutual interest and tried to establish the principle of joint action.[14]

Again, in the years in which Confucius was growing to manhood, a serious and successful attempt was made to bring about a lasting peace. For a long time the smaller central states had suffered terribly as successive wars had been fought over their territories. In the year 546 B.C. when Confucius was five years old, the prime minister of the state of Sung took the initiative in calling a non-aggression conference, and invited the rulers of the various states to renounce war as an instrument of policy.[15] An agreement was reached which paved the way for a peace which lasted some forty years, and when peace was finally broken it was through the aggression of the southern state of Wu, which had not been a party to the original treaty.

Though this period was one of great social upheaval as the feudalistic system declined, it was also a period of dynamic social and economic change. In an age when the struggle for power between states and within states was being carried on almost incessantly and with great ferocity, a man's ability came to count for more than noble birth. A new class was emerging, men who were forced to rely on their own exertions if they were to attain any measure of success in life. These men, known as *shih* and usually translated as 'knights' or 'gentry-scholars', were of noble descent, but had become commoners. As younger sons of the nobility they had acquired some education and training, and they usually inherited enough property or other means of support to ensure that there was no necessity for them to engage in laborious manual toil. They had nothing in common with the peasants. Many of them were ambitious for wealth or fame. Only certain occupations were open to them. Some would accept

37

office under a ruler, gradually winning his confidence and favour by their devotion to his interests, ever hoping that he would generously reward loyal service by a gift of land or by promotion to yet higher dignities. Others found a suitable outlet for their talents by accepting officer status in the armies which every noble family had to maintain if it was not to sink into oblivion. Still others found a way to wealth and fortune by becoming merchants and traders in a period of growing commercial activity. Some became gentry-scholars, who roamed from state to state, willing to sell their services to the highest bidder. For the most part this class of 'knights' was worldly, selfish and ambitious. It had little idealism, but it was the most dynamic group during the period.

Whereas in earlier feudal times both the peasants and the lesser nobility were tied to the service of their prince, the vast social upheaval had brought about a great increase in mobility. There were few restrictions of movement across state boundaries. Soldiers, scholars, merchants were continually on the move. Though the 'five grains' (millet, rice, wheat, hemp and pulse) which provided the staple food and the fermented drink of the people were grown practically everywhere, different districts became famous for certain products and specialized in their production and distribution. The area of present-day Shansi exported lumber, bamboo and precious stones; Shantung produced salt, fish, lacquer, silk and musical instruments; iron was mined in the mountainous parts of Szechuan. It was necessary that there should be a large merchant class to satisfy the cravings of wealthy and noble families for luxuries produced in other areas. By the seventh and sixth centuries B.C. some of the states began to mint their own coinage. Cities increased in size and importance, especially those which were fortunate to be situated on the main trade routes. Within the cities the wants of the wealthy were supplied by hosts of petty officials, servants, soldiers, craftsmen, traders, entertainers. It is estimated that by the end of the fourth century B.C. several Chinese cities had a population exceeding 100,000 and some had several times that number.[16]

In the days of Confucius life in the cities was lively and interesting. A high standard of civilization had been reached. Craftsmen were skilled in the working of jade, semi-precious stones, ivory, bamboo and wood, and also metals such as bronze and brass. The nobility vied with each other in the construction of palatial dwellings. They delighted to strut about clothed in embroidered or brocaded garments, dyed silk or a coarse linen in summer, lambswool, fox-fur or exotic skins in winter. Gems of ivory, jade or semi-precious stones dangled from their waists and tinkled as they walked. They loved to ride in carriages drawn by teams of well-matched horses and furbished with fittings of highly polished bronze or brass. They enjoyed hunting and archery, and at their archery contests everything was conducted in accordance with a strictly organized ritual. At their numerous feasts and festivals they enjoyed a rich variety of food and drink, and were entertained by blind musicians and teams of dancers. Education for their children consisted of poetry, history, music, arithmetic and the rites and ceremonies governing all social and religious relationships. The scholars who crowded the courts of princes not only gave instruction to the younger generation, but were available for counsel and advice on matters of state.

In contrast to the life of the nobility was that of the peasantry. However, it is easy to over-emphasize the evils of their state. They lived a strenuous life with little rest from dawn till dusk and at the beck and call of their masters. They lived for mutual protection in mud- or stone-walled villages, and cultivated the land for their overlords under the supervision of stewards. They grew barley, millet, wheat and vegetables, domesticated numerous animals, especially the pig. Their women-folk engaged in spinning and weaving flax and in the cultivation of the silkworm and the making of silk. Round these communal homesteads were planted mulberry, willow and fruit trees, the favourite fruit being the apricot. Fish and wild game were plentiful. Wine was made from fermented grain flavoured with aromatic herbs. Indigo and various pigments were used as dyes. For variety of food, conditions of labour and general standard of living the peasants of China were probably better off at the time of Confucius than in the closing decades of the nineteenth century of our era.

Such was the world into which Confucius was born. It was a world in which there was a marked division between the nobility and the peasantry, between the privileged, wealthy and cultured who lived under the protection of powerful families, and the toiling masses who served their material needs. But an intermediate class was all the time growing in numbers and importance, men who no longer ranked with the nobility but who could claim noble descent. In this class were many able and ambitious men, ready to seize the opportunities which patronage or chance placed in their hands. It was into this class that Confucius was born.

2. The Man and his Disciples

Ancestry

Of the ancestry of Confucius nothing is known for certain. Long after his death, when his fame had spread throughout China attempts were made to show that he came from a long and illustrious line of forebears stemming from the royal house of Shang. According to the *Historical Records* of Ssŭ-ma Ch'ien, the grandfather of Confucius, named Fang Shu, migrated from the state of Sung and settled in the state of Lu, some sixty miles to the north-east. Sung had been a fiefdom assigned by the victorious Chou to the defeated descendants of the Shang kings. In the *Shih Pên* or *Book of Genealogies*, which recorded the ancestry of the various ducal houses of the time, ten generations separated Confucius from Fu Fu Ho, the legitimate heir to Duke Min of Sung, who, however, yielded his right to rule to Duke Li. Among the names in this genealogy is that of Chêng K'ao-fu, a distinguished scholar who received high honours and was credited with the compilation of the 'Shang Sung' section of the *Book of Poetry* (*Shih Ching*). His son, K'ung Fu-chia, became commander-in-chief of the forces of the state of Sung. Unfortunately the genealogy does not warrant a great deal of trust. The two names between K'ung Fu-chia and Fang Shu appear in no other source, and seem on evidence to have been concocted in the fourth or third century B.C. by some scholar who realized that in this way Confucius could be linked to the illustrious royal family of the state of Sung.[1]

There are absolutely no records concerning Confucius's grandfather and no early work names either his father or mother. The *Analects* (3:15) mentions that Confucius's father lived at a place called Tsou, where Confucius was presumably born. The traditional accounts, concerning which many scholars are extremely sceptical,[2] identify Confucius's father as a valiant officer in the service of the Mêng family, one of the three great families which between them controlled the state of Lu. His name is given as Shu-liang Ho. Confucius's mother was Chêng Tsai, the daughter of a poor and little-known family by the name of Yen. She was bereft of her husband soon after Confucius was born and the fact that the poor, orphaned boy received a good education and later, as a young man, the patronage of the Mêng family suggests that the head of this important family felt some responsibility for the son of a loyal and devoted retainer. Two stories in the *Tso Chuan* relate exploits of Confucius's putative father, Shu-liang Ho, who was a warrior retainer in the service of general Mêng Hsien-tzŭ, a powerful noble of the Mêng family. During the fighting between the Northern League[3] and the state of Ch'u in the year 563 B.C., Shu-liang Ho distinguished himself for valour in an attempt to invest the fortress of Pi-yang which lay at an important junction in a line of water communications between the states of Tsin and Wu. His courage and loyalty at this time seem to have led to his promotion, for seven years later, in 556 B.C., when forces from Ch'i were invading Lu, Shu-liang Ho commanded a detachment of troops which successfully planned and carried out the escape of the head of the noble family of Tsang-sun from his beleaguered fortress of Fang.[4]

It seems, then, that Confucius's father belonged to the growing class of *shih*, men who could not claim to be members of the nobility but who were of noble ancestry. Shu-liang Ho seems to have gained a reputation for bravery and military skill. The fact that he was a soldier, often on the move in the service of his lord, may account for the suggestion of Ssŭ-ma Ch'ien that there was no properly regulated marriage between Confucius's father and mother, and that she came from an obscure commoner's family. She may have been a secondary wife or concubine.

Birth and Upbringing

Concerning the date of Confucius's birth the accounts are confusing. The traditionally accepted date is the year 551 B.C., and this date has become so universally recognized that almost all biographies of Confucius assume that it is correct. But the evidence for a slightly earlier date is strong, and Confucius was probably born in the winter of 552 B.C.[5] The location of the village of Tsou where he was born cannot now be determined, but it was not far from the state capital of Ch'ü-fu, in modern Shantung. Though practically nothing concerning Confucius's childhood and youth is known, there is no reason to doubt that his father died when he was still an infant and he was left in the care of an impoverished mother. In later life he claimed that he had been brought up in humble circumstances, and because of that he had practical experience of those simple, everyday matters which were beneath the notice of the noble-born.[6] We can only surmise how he received his education, but it was certainly a good one. He tells us that when he was fifteen years of age his heart was set on learning.[7] It is probable, therefore, that very early on he showed intellectual promise and was allowed to join a private school set up by the Mêng clan for the education of their numerous children. However that may be, the formative years of his development were between the ages of fifteen and thirty, that is from 538–523 B.C. We can deduce the nature of his education from his own deepest interests in later life. He had made a thorough study of the *Odes* and the *Historical Documents* which were available, together with the ritual code which was considered to be immensely important for the regulation of all social life and relationships. He had taken a keen interest in and had a deep appreciation of music. He revealed a love of archery and fishing. It is probable that much of his early education was acquired when he was a junior official in the administration, keen and ambitious, with access to books, and encouraged by his seniors to study them. In those days books were bulky, being written by means of a stylus on bamboo strips which were bound together with leather thongs. Such libraries as existed would be mainly confined to the homes of the nobility or to the offices of state administration.

Mencius tells us that Confucius was at one time a mere clerk attached to the state granaries, and that he was later appointed to keep check on the pasture-lands belonging to the state. In these posts he showed his diligence by the accuracy of his reckoning and by his care to see that the sheep and cattle were fat and healthy.[8] At the age of nineteen Confucius married, but of his wife and family we know practically nothing. He had an elder half-brother who, according to tradition, was lame; this made it necessary for Confucius to act as head of the family, and as such he was instrumental in finding a suitable husband for his niece.

He had a son and a daughter, but his son predeceased him and seems to have been somewhat of a disappointment to his father.

Confucius undoubtedly grew up with an ambition to play a role in practical politics, yet he seems to have been temperamentally unfitted to achieve any marked success as a statesman. In an age when courts were places of intrigue and men won the favour of princes by flattery and sycophancy, Confucius was out of place, for he could be mordant in criticism, and his blunt honesty and native uprightness were a reproach to the devious politicians with whom he had to associate. He turned more and more to study, and to the teaching of younger men, a task for which he proved to be eminently fitted. His great gifts as a teacher soon came to be recognized, especially by those who were privileged to become his disciples.

Formative Influences

At fifteen I set my heart on learning. (*Analects*, 2:4)

During the childhood of Confucius and throughout the formative years between the ages of fifteen and thirty, events both within the state of Lu and in the larger world outside were helping to mould the thinking of the young scholar. In terms of power and influence the state of Lu was small and weak in comparison with the strong and powerful states of Tsin, Ch'i and Ch'u. It lay far to the east of the central plain where the Chou kings, shorn of temporal power, still carried out those ritual and religious functions by which the ancient cultural heritage was sustained. The royal territory was small, the royal court impoverished, but tradition was strong and the cultural links with a glorious past were tenacious.

The territories of Lu were less than 20,000 square miles in extent and its population was probably less than one million. Though its duke could claim direct descent from the famous Duke of Chou, the state, when compared with Chêng and Wei, was culturally backward and undeveloped. Lu had fallen on evil days. Throughout the childhood and youth of Confucius, government was in the hands of three great baronial families, called Mêng-sun, Shu-sun and Chi-sun, all descended from an earlier ruler of Lu, Duke Huan. The heads of these three families had seized power from the legitimate ruler, and were constantly jockeying for ascendancy over each other. Nearly all the important offices of both civil and military administration were considered to be the hereditary prerogatives of members of the three families. They formed an oligarchy, and treated the legitimate ruler as a mere puppet. This usurpation of power formed the pattern for a process which continued down through the various ranks of the nobility, and which was gradually destroying the great hereditary families and leading to a state of complete anarchy. It was in these conditions that the young Confucius was working out, in the light of his studies of ritual and history, those principles which were to form the basis of his ethico-political teaching.

Whilst showing a keen interest in the affairs of his own state of Lu, Confucius, as was natural for any intelligent young man, was also deeply influenced by the events and personalities in the wider field of interstate relationships. He was extremely fortunate in that he grew up during a period when a serious attempt was being made to bring interstate rivalries to an end and procure a lasting peace. In the year 546 B.C. when Confucius was still a child, a famous minister of the comparatively weak state of Sung was successful in calling together an interstate peace conference at which an armistice between the two main rival state coalitions was agreed. Though this armistice broke down in less than ten years, a comparatively peaceful state of affairs was maintained throughout Confucius's childhood and youth. A number of wise and worthy administrators were controlling policy in the city states of the central plain. Among them was a political adviser called Shu Hsiang who, though not in office, was extremely influential in the state of Tsin. Yen Ying, the principal statesman of Ch'i, was both a scholar and a gentleman, and as such was highly regarded. But the most important of all was Tzŭ-ch'an, the prime minister of Chêng, who died in 522 B.C. when Confucius was twenty-nine years old. All these able scholars had been born into the nobility, but into families that had lost much of their former power and grandeur, and were therefore not so much concerned with the power struggle. The fame and popularity of Tzŭ-ch'an spread far beyond the limits of the small state of Chêng. He was the first to produce a codified law which he had inscribed on bronzes, so that they remained as permanent and exact evidence of the law which all citizens were expected to obey. This action brought criticism from conservative scholars who saw in it a departure from tradition. They also criticized Tzŭ-ch'an's newly introduced economic policies, but when they resulted in a great increase in productivity and greater well-being in the state, the criticism soon turned to approval. Confucius, according to the *Analects*, regarded Tzŭ-ch'an with great esteem and said of him, 'In him were to be found four of the virtues that belong to the Way of a true gentleman. In his private conduct, he was courteous; in serving his master, he was punctilious; in providing for the needs of the people, he gave them even more than their due; in exacting service from the people he was just.'[9] Again, he speaks of him as 'a kindly man'.[10] Of Yen Ying he said, 'he is a good example of what one's intercourse with one's fellow men should be. However long he has known anyone, he always maintains the same scrupulous courtesy.'[11]

The years in which Confucius was growing up to manhood were marked by a growth of scepticism in religion. In ancient China religion had been the cement that bound societies in loyalty to a common ancestor spirit, and it was an essential element in government. Whenever a city state was founded the first concern was the building of the ancestral temple, and thereafter religious ceremonies were carried out there at regular intervals and were deemed necessary for the well-being of the state. The nobles who ruled over these states acknowledged the overlordship of a king because they believed that he was the appointee of Heaven and served the Will of Heaven. But by the middle of the first millennium B.C. interstate rivalries had so weakened the power of the central authority that the king was no more than a puppet of ambitious and powerful nobles. Yet, in spite of constant appeals to Heaven and the meticulous performance of the prescribed rituals, Heaven seemed to be indifferent and gave no help. Within the various states illustrious families sank to ruin, their ancestral temples destroyed, whilst ambitious retainers or upstart adventurers took their place. Yet the most urgent appeals to the ancestor spirits brought no response. Might triumphed over right. Treaties ratified by the most solemn oaths in the presence of the spirits and the ancestors were broken with impunity. In such a state of affairs it was no wonder that men felt that they could place no faith in their gods and ancestor spirits. The sanctions of religion were no longer capable of controlling the relationships between men.

Though undoubtedly among scholars and thinkers there was a growth of scepticism, it was not so much a denial of the existence of a supreme power known as Heaven (*T'ien*) as a growing feeling that the Way of Heaven was far above men's comprehension. It was certainly not something that could be discovered by magical arts and practices, by star-gazing, by divination through the tortoise shell and the milfoil stalks.[12] Heaven's will was surely not revealed in solar eclipses, the movements of wind and rain and the strange and unusual phenomena of nature. In a sense, it was their recognition of the greatness, the power and the majesty of Heaven as something 'wholly other' which was causing thinkers to question the validity of those cultic practices which were designed to cause Heaven to interfere in human affairs. The point is well illustrated in the account in the *Tso Chuan*[13] of a violent typhoon followed by a destructive fire which raged through four states in central China bringing havoc and panic in the year 524 B.C., when Confucius was twenty-seven years old. According to the account, the event had been predicted the previous year by the master of divination in the state of Chêng, and he had urged the prime minister to try and avert the calamity in the usual way by continual sacrifices. This Tzǔ-ch'an refused to do, saying, 'Heaven's way is far removed: it is man's way that is near to us.' Here Tzǔ-ch'an does not deny Heaven's Way. He simply declares that what Heaven ordains is beyond human understanding and beyond human powers of interference. No amount of prayer and sacrifice will avert the typhoon if it has been ordained, but what a statesman can do is to direct human efforts so that there will be some mitigation of its effects. Here, no doubt, we see the seeds of rationalism, and a growing belief that the most worthwhile activity of a statesman is to concentrate on bringing about human well-being. It is surely too narrow an estimate of Confucius's attitude and beliefs concerning religion to say that he divorced ethics from religion and taught a humanism in which there was no room for transcendental values. It is true that when Confucius emerged from those formative years as a fully fledged thinker there was no place in his system for an anthropomorphic T'ien or Shang Ti. He had, also, no positive teaching concerning life after death. He repudiated the irrational beliefs in ghosts and prodigies. Yet one cannot study his teachings as they have come down to us through the records of his disciples without being acutely conscious that he was fundamentally a 'religious' man. He believed in transcendental values, in love and righteousness as cosmic virtues, in the Way of Heaven as directive of the Way of Man. He also possessed a real concern that sincerity should motivate men's actions whenever they sought to express their religious feelings in the cultic practices of those times. The spirits should be approached with reverence, and all forms of worship should be performed with the utmost care and attention.

Maturity

> At thirty I had planted my feet firmly upon the ground.
>
> *(Analects*, 2:4)

As we have seen, during his early manhood Confucius was employed in minor offices in the state of Lu. The salary from his employment allowed him to live as a gentleman in reasonable comfort, for when he was still in his early twenties, and after the birth of his son, his mother died, and we are informed that Confucius went to much trouble and expense to find out where his father had been buried and to have both father and mother interred together in the same grave at a place called Fang where his grandfather had originally settled. He then followed the customary practice of mourning, a practice which he no doubt strictly observed, for later on when his disciple Tsai Yü asked about the three years' mourning and expressed the opinion that one year ought to be quite enough, Confucius reproved him severely, and reminded him that for three years a child is utterly dependent upon his parents for everything.[14] A deep affection for and a dutiful conduct towards his mother is probably reflected in many of the sayings in the *Analects* about the necessity for filial conduct, a theme to be taken up by later Confucians, until the supreme virtue of filial piety came to be exaggerated beyond all reason.

Confucius was undoubtedly ambitious. He had prepared himself for service to the state by years of study, and the older he grew the more convinced he became that good government could only be administered on the lines which he set down in his teachings. But there was little or no possibility of his being appointed to high office. All the important posts were reserved for members of the nobility. The class of gentlemen or knights to which Confucius belonged no doubt did most of the governmental work, but over them were the Great Officers of court whose positions were mainly hereditary. It seems likely that Confucius did attain to the rank of 'leader of the knights' which gave him rank immediately below that of the Great Officers.[15] In any case Confucius was unfitted by temperament to serve under the ruthless and selfish men who held the real power in Lu. He was far too blunt and outspoken in his criticisms of those whose conduct did not accord with propriety and justice. When he was reaching maturity, although the office of prime minister in the state of Lu was filled by Chao-tzŭ of the Shu-sun family, the real power was wielded by the chieftain of the Chi-sun family, Chi Ping-tzŭ by name, who exercised a *de facto* domination over the government. The Duke of Lu was a helpless puppet in his hands. In 517 B.C., when Confucius was thirty-six years of age, the duke was so impoverished that he could not even pay for the musicians and dancers who normally performed at the ancestral celebrations. On the other hand, so powerful and rich was the head of the Chi-sun family that he engaged a full team of eight rows of eight dancers for a highly formal ceremony in his ancestral temple, a ceremony which was the prerogative of the royal house of Chou. This usurpation of a ritual which was a royal prerogative was condemned by Confucius in no uncertain terms. Speaking of the head of the Chi family on this occasion he said, 'If this man can be endured, who cannot be endured!'[16] Such bluntness would hardly commend him to the man who, more than anyone else in the state, had power to further his interests.

Various factions in the state of Lu devised a plan to curtail the power of Chi Ping-tzŭ and to restore the rightful authority of Duke Chao of Lu, but when it came to a final reckoning the other two great baronial families rallied to the support of the Chi family and the duke had to flee into exile in Ch'i, where he remained for seven years before he died. During this period Chi Ping-tzŭ acted as regent and took to wearing the ornamental jewels of office. It is probable that Confucius's first excursion beyond the borders of his own state was a result of these disorders. No credence can be given to the story of an earlier visit of Confucius to the court of Chou in the city of Loyang in present-day Honan (where he is said to have learned about the ceremonial and the maxims of the founders of the dynasty, walked over the grounds set apart for the great sacrifices to Heaven and Earth and inspected the pattern of the *Ming T'ang* or Hall of Light) or to that of his meeting with Lao-tzŭ, the reputed author of the *Tao Tê Ching*.[17] It may be that opposition to the policy and behaviour of Chi Ping-tzŭ and loyalty to his duke made it politic for Confucius to withdraw from Lu for a time. How long he stayed in Ch'i we do not know, but it was in Lin-tzê, the large, rich and progressive capital of Ch'i, that Confucius was able to study the ancient and beautiful Shao music and dance as executed by a carefully chosen band of musicians attached to the court of Ch'i.[18] Here, too, he learned much about the famous hero-statesman Kuan Chung. He seems to have remained in Ch'i for some considerable time, and to have received hospitable treatment from a duke who was ever ready to attract to his court learned and gifted men. According to the *Analects*,[19] Duke Ching of Ch'i sought his advice concerning government, and seems to have wished to retain his services. He wanted to assign to Confucius the revenues of a town called Lin-chu, but Confucius declined the gift on the grounds that he had not performed services to warrant acceptance, and such advice as he had been permitted to give had not been taken. We are told that later on the duke was dissuaded by his minister Yen-ying from assigning to Confucius the fields of Ne-ch'i, and it is interesting to note the grounds given for Yen-ying's advice, that Confucius was 'impractical, conceited, set a high value on ceremonial and had many peculiarities'.[20]

When the Duke of Ch'i tired of Confucius the latter returned to Lu, and some fifteen years passed before he received official governmental employment. It was during this period that he established himself as a teacher and began to attract a growing number of disciples. Mêng Hsi-tzŭ, a nobleman of the Mêng family, had left instructions before his death that his sons Mêng I-tzŭ and Nan-kung Ching-shu should take instruction from Confucius in ritual. Other youths of noble family undoubtedly studied under him, but the majority of his students were drawn from that rising class of knights to which he himself belonged, men whose primary objective was to train for service either at court or within some noble family as stewards and principal retainers. They were troubled years and Confucius was fortunate to be an onlooker of political events. In 509 B.C. Duke Chao died in exile in a little border town in Ch'i and his brother, Duke Ting, succeeded to his position. The real power remained with Chi Ping-tzǔ until his death in 505 B.C. Then factional strife within the Chi family led at length to the seizure of power by a retainer called Yang Huo. For three years he held despotic control of the state, but he became over-presumptuous and plotted the murder of the head of the Chi family, Chi Huan-tzǔ. In the civil strife which resulted he was defeated and fled to Ch'i, taking with him the hereditary state treasures. There is an account in Book Seventeen of the *Analects*[21] of Yang Huo's desire to get Confucius to take office, and of Confucius's reluctance to do so, for though he could not condone the conduct of the Chi family in usurping the authority of the Duke of Lu, neither the character nor the brutal actions of Yang Huo could merit his approval. A different situation arose, however, when Kung-shan Fu-jao, warden of Pi, the chief stronghold of the Chi family, rose in revolt against his master. Confucius was with difficulty restrained by his disciple Tzǔ-lu from accepting the invitation of Kung-shan Fu-jao because he genuinely believed that this rebel against his lord intended to restore the Duke of Lu to his rightful position.[22] According to the accepted morality of the times a retainer owed implicit obedience to his overlord, but when that overlord was himself in revolt against his superior the whole system of moral responsibility was in danger of breakdown. Confucius has been much criticized for his attitude, but his aim was the restoration of peace and good government, and he believed that, given a suitable leader who would genuinely take his advice, the desired results might be attained.

Soon after Yang Huo had been defeated and had fled to Ch'i Confucius received his first official appointment of any standing as chief magistrate of the town of Chung-tu in Lu. This probably took place in or about the year 501 B.C. when Confucius was fifty years of age. At that age he entered the class known as *Ai* or 'elders', and was given the rank of 'senior officer'. He was then promoted to be assistant superintendent of works. The head superintendent was a member of the Mêng family. Later still he received office under the minister of crime. Mo-tzŭ, Mencius and the *Tso Chuan*[23] all aver that he was actually appointed as minister of crime, but this is extremely unlikely as the office was normally held by the head of one of the noble families, related to the duke, and was in all probability hereditary.

Confucius in Office

It was during the years between 501 B.C. and his leaving his native state (probably in 495 B.C.) that Confucius exerted considerable influence over governmental affairs in Lu. This is not in any way the result of his being entrusted with high office. His intellect and learning had gradually won him recognition. Several of his disciples had been given important posts within the Chi family, and it was probably their importunity, together with the friendship of Chi K'ang-tzŭ, who in 492 B.C. succeeded to the headship of the Chi family, that opened the way for Confucius to be given official recognition, even though it was little more than a sinecure. In the year 499 B.C. he was among those who accompanied the Duke of Lu on a state visit to Ch'i, but the story in the *Tso Chuan*[24] which records how Confucius thwarted a plan to kidnap the duke, and by his clever statesmanship forced Ch'i to restore lands previously taken from Lu, has all the marks of fiction, and is regarded as false by most Chinese scholars. It is from Mencius that we learn that Confucius took office under Chi Huan-tzŭ, who died in 492 B.C.[25] and the *Analects* suggests that Confucius had reached a rank and position in which he expected to be consulted on important governmental business, but was nevertheless overlooked. Occasionally he was called upon to advise Duke Ting who died in 495 B.C.[26] There is no record of the real dictator, Chi Huan-tzŭ, ever having consulted him. Although considered to be of late date, the record given in *Analects* 16:2–3, gives a fair indication of the frustration which Confucius must have felt at this time as he observed the usurpation of power by those who were unworthy, and the 'Way' which he proclaimed being flouted on every hand. It may be true that the occasion which sparked off Confucius's decision to leave Lu was indeed a present by Ch'i to the court of Lu of female courtesans and their acceptance by Chi Huan-tzŭ,[27] but the real reason for his leaving was surely the inward conviction that he possessed political ideals and political wisdom which, if acted upon, would lead to the restoration of a united China under one supreme head. Consequently, he felt he had a duty to spread his message as widely as possible before he died.

Exile from Lu

Convinced that there was little chance of ever realizing his ideals of government within the state of Lu, Confucius, at about the age of fifty-six, resigned office and set out in search of a ruler who would give practical expression to his teachings. His journeyings lasted at least ten years, and during that time he passed through many states and experienced chequered fortunes. In those days there were few or no restrictions on travel between one state and another and the chief danger was that of lawlessness. There was great mobility of population, merchants, soldiers, fortune-hunters, scholars moving from one state to another. In some of the wealthier states the rulers gained a measure of fame and notoriety by attracting to their courts scholars, musicians and craftsmen, and were willing to offer rich rewards to distinguished scholars who were prepared to make their services and advice available when needed. As for Confucius, very little is definitely known of these years of travel except that he seems to have spent a good deal of the time in the neighbouring state of Wei, was able to accomplish very little and eventually returned to his native state a disappointed man. These years did, however, demonstrate Confucius's own unswerving fidelity to his principles, and the loyalty and affection of the small band of disciples, some of whom accompanied him and others who, being in office in Lu, smoothed the way for his return.

Those who accompanied him included Yen Hui, Tzǔ-lu and Tzǔ-kung, and, travelling in a convoy of carriages, Confucius and his followers were welcomed by the princes of the states he visited and invited to be guests at their courts. In Wei he lodged with a worthy officer called Yen Ch'ou-yü.[28] He took office under Duke Ling, a worthless and dissipated man, and was supported by the public treasury. After a fairly brief stay in Wei he travelled south to Ch'ên, on his way passing through Sung where Huan T'ui, the minister of war in Sung and elder brother to one of

Confucius's disciples, called Ssŭ-ma Niu, tried to assassinate him. Confucius had to travel through Sung in the dress of a private man[29] and arrived in Ch'ên in considerable distress. There he lodged with Ching-tzŭ, the minister of works, and had an audience with the minister of crime[30] at which the latter tried to get Confucius to criticize the conduct of the late Duke Chao of Lu, something which Confucius would not do. How long Confucius remained in Ch'ên and in the small neighbouring state of Ts'ai is not known, but a long period elapsed before he is heard of again, once more residing in Wei in the year 484 B.C. By this time Duke Ling had been dead for some years, and his grandson, Duke Chu, was nominal ruler though the real power was in the hands of the minister K'ung Yu. K'ung Yu honoured Confucius and saw to it that he had a government stipend.[31] About this time messengers came from Lu asking Confucius to return.[32]

The Closing Years

The return of Confucius to his own state of Lu in the eleventh year of Duke Ai and in the sixty-ninth year of his own life seems to have been by invitation of the head of the Chi family, Chi K'ang-tzŭ, who was prevailed upon to send messengers with the customary presents. Several of Confucius's disciples were by this time prominent in the service of the state. In 488 B.C. Tzŭ-kung had acted as ambassador to the state of Wu and had distinguished himself. In 484 B.C. Jan Ch'iu was appointed steward of the Chi family and commander of one of its bands of soldiers. Fan Ch'ih acted as his lieutenant. It was in this year that an army from Ch'i invaded Lu, and Jan Ch'iu used his forces to such effect that the invading army had to retire.[33] Towards the end of 482 B.C. one of the officers of Ch'i murdered his duke, and Confucius urged upon Duke Ai the duty of punishing the offender, but Confucius's advice was rejected. It is clear from the *Analects* that at this time Confucius held rank immediately below that of the Great Officers, and had access both to the duke and to the heads of the three baronial families who held the real power.[34] Oppressive taxes levied by Chi K'ang-tzŭ had to be collected by his steward, Jan Ch'iu, who could, however, have resigned his post rather than take part in an unrighteous and iniquitous act of oppression.

He preferred the fruits of high office to the principles of right and justice as taught by his former teacher, and so we have the only instance of a disciple being publicly repudiated by Confucius.[35]

Though, during the last years of his life, Confucius gathered round him a new group of disciples, and seems to have spent much time in the study of many of the ancient texts, collating material and information which he had probably collected during his extensive travels, he had to face sorrow and bereavement, disappointment and calumny. He seems to have been deeply affected by the deaths of those he loved. After his return to Lu the death of his only son[36] was followed by the death of his favourite disciple, Yen Hui.[37] In 481 B.C. Ssŭ-ma Niu died in tragic circumstances[38] and in the following year Confucius lost his oldest disciple, the bold and outspoken Tzŭ-lu.[39] At court he was disparaged by the head of the powerful Shu-sun family,[40] and the hatred of a crowd of mean people brought anxiety to his heart.[41]

Of Confucius's death there is no trustworthy account. The account given in the *Record of Rites* (*Li Chi*)[42] and copied by Ssŭ-ma Ch'ien is inconsistent with his character. In the *Ch'iun Ch'iu* there is only a brief statement under the sixteenth year of Duke Ai, 'Summer, a day in the fourth month, Confucius died.'

Confucius the Man

What kind of man was Confucius, this man who for more than two thousand years occupied a supreme place as the undisputed teacher of the most populous country on earth? Of the physical appearance of Confucius nothing reliable is known. According to the *Shih Chi* he was exceptionally tall and of striking appearance, possessing great dignity. As traditionally depicted by later times he was of ungainly appearance and decidedly unattractive, with a prominent bump on his forehead, large pendulous ears and prominent front teeth. He was certainly not the perfect saint nor the super-human sage whom later admirers made him out to be. Nor was he the haughty, hypocritical, ambitious, place-seeking stickler for the minutiae of ritual pictured by anti-Confucian polemicists of the centuries immediately following his death. There is no doubt that some Confucians as early as the time of

Mo-tzǔ had gained for themselves an unenviable reputation for worldliness and personal ambition, but their behaviour in no way reflected that of Confucius himself.

In the pages of the *Analects* we can still see pictured the man as he appeared to that intimate circle of disciples who loved him, and many of his recorded sayings reflect the kind of man he was. This picture of him, supported also by several passages in *Mencius* and the *Li Chi*, reveals a humane and lovable person, not perfect by any means, but with excellent and noble qualities.[43] Henri Maspero and Waley consider that Chapter 10 of the *Analects* is a ritual treatise portraying the ideal gentleman, but even in this chapter there are passages which seem to refer definitely to Confucius.[44]

From the *Analects* we get the impression of someone who knew himself to be descended from noble stock, and consequently always strove to live and act as a true gentleman, a man of fine feeling and of discriminating taste. Respectful himself, he demanded respect from others; courteous, he was never obsequious; dignified and firm, he remained affable. Although at court and at all state functions he was punctilious as to his deportment, within the intimate circle of his disciples he was cheerful, relaxed, informal, kindly and patient. With them he did not remain aloof, but he could be pungent and highly critical of conduct which he deemed inappropriate to a gentleman. He was no ascetic and enjoyed comforts and pleasures in moderation. Physical comfort, status and wealth were to be enjoyed but should not primarily be sought after and certainly never to the detriment of one's own personal integrity and virtue.

Confucius had a passionate love of learning and sought to inculcate it in others. He loved music and devoted much time to its study. He himself played a kind of lute, and loved also to join in informal singing. He was also fond of outdoor sports such as archery, fishing and charioteering. He obviously appreciated elegance, beauty, good breeding and good manners. He had a strongly developed sense of humour. Many of the recorded sayings in the *Analects* can only be properly understood as light-hearted repartee in intimate conversation with the disciples. He was also a man of deep sympathy with the poor and the distressed, someone of keen sensibility and strong emotions who felt deeply the loss by death of disciples and friends.

Confucius, as depicted in the *Analects*, is a very charming character, and his charm lies in his intense humanity. Modest and sincere, he sought to live up to his own ideal of what a true gentleman should be, and was always ready enough to admit that he had still far to go and much to learn.

The Teacher and his Disciples

In the extant literature that can be dated to a time prior to Confucius there is no mention of the establishment of schools except for training in archery. Such schools are mentioned in inscriptions on bronze vessels.[45] We can, however, infer that there was a class of professional teachers and schools of a kind. A large body of educated men were needed for the day-to-day administration of the states, to keep the archives, chronicle events and to be available to guide and advise rulers in respect of the elaborate ritual and ceremonial of religious and court life. Books, though bulky and cumbersome, were numerous. Noble families engaged private tutors for their children and it is probable that, as in later times, the children of near relatives and of important retainers were allowed to take part in the lessons. Young men in office would be given training by their superior officers. Confucius, however, was the first person in Chinese history of whom it is definitely known that, acting in a purely private capacity, he founded a school, taking as his students men from all grades of society, and training them for government office. But his real aim was much more than that. He sought to give them a thorough and broadly based education in the liberal arts. He tried to stimulate in them his own passionate love of learning. Above all, he insisted on inculcating a strict morality as the essential prerequisite of a good life and a good society. He claimed[46] that he never rejected even the poorest student who could bring no better present as school fees than a bundle of dried meat, and in making this claim he was perhaps tacitly criticizing those teachers whom he had known whose chief concern was to stand well with their employers and gain a good salary. Through the men whom he took as pupils Confucius hoped gradually to restore the virtuous type of government which he believed to have been exemplified by the sage-kings of antiquity who, with the aid of upright ministers, ruled over a happy and contented people.

Tradition credits Confucius with having over seventy disciples and their names have been recorded, more than half of them belonging to Confucius's own state of Lu. Actually only some twenty are named in the *Analects*, and of these only a few are prominent either because they are depicted as conversing with Confucius and asking him questions, or because they were chiefly responsible for disseminating his teachings after his death, becoming the founders of Confucian schools. Only two or three of those named are known to have come from noble families: Mêng I-tzǔ and his brother Nan-kung Ching-shu, and Ssǔ-ma Niu of Sung. The majority came from the class of *shih*, to which Confucius himself belonged, and their chief aim was to gain sufficient education and training to fit them for government service.

It is generally believed that the disciples of Confucius fall into two groups, an older group who were trained by him in the years before he set out on his journeyings, and a younger group who studied with him after he finally returned to Lu as an old man in or about the year 484 B.C. Tzǔ-lu was the oldest of his disciples, being only some seven years younger than Confucius. Forceful, impetuous, warm-hearted, upright, he yet lacked those qualities of wisdom and unselfish goodness which made Yen Hui the favourite of his master. There were times when Tzǔ-lu was bold enough to reprove his master or to advise him strongly to refrain from action which Tzǔ-lu thought inadvisable.[47] In great contrast to him was Yen Hui, whose poverty never clouded a cheerfulness of spirit and an eagerness to go all the way with his master. Tzǔ-kung also figures among the older group of disciples and is often mentioned in the *Analects*. He was a man of sound judgement, eloquent and pleasing, with marked political acumen so that he eventually rose to exercise a considerable influence in inter-state diplomacy in the years between 495 and 468 B.C. These three accompanied Confucius on his travels and willingly shared his privations and dangers. Tzǔ-lu and Yen Hui both died before Confucius and Confucius grieved especially over the loss of Yen Hui.[48] Tzǔ-kung and another disciple, Jan Ch'iu, were both recommended by Confucius to Chi K'ang-tzǔ for service with the Chi family,[49] but whereas Jan Ch'iu was prepared to give higher preference to the fruits of office than to the teaching of his master, and was disowned by Confucius,[50] Tzǔ-kung always remained loyal and was the one who acted as master of ceremonies when the disciples carried out the customary mourning rites for their master.[51]

Of the group of disciples who came to study under Confucius towards the end of his life several of them are remembered because it was principally through them that the teachings of Confucius were disseminated throughout the Chinese states, and various schools of Confucianism came into being. The *Han Fei-tzǔ* states that there were eight different schools of Confucianism stemming from different teachers, of whom three were disciples of Confucius in his lifetime. Those most responsible for preserving and spreading the teaching after Confucius's death were the disciples Tzǔ-yu, Tzǔ-chang, Tzǔ-hsia and Tsêng-shên. Mencius recounts a curious story that after the death of the master Tzǔ-yu, Tzǔ-chang and Tzǔ-hsia, considering that another disciple called Yu-jo most resembled Confucius, wished to make him the head of the Confucion movement and accept him as master, but they dropped the idea when they found that Tsêng-shên was averse to it.[52] Tzǔ-yu and Tzǔ-hsia were especially noted for their culture and learning,[53] and Tzǔ-hsia had a school of his own[54] training some pupils to become tutors to kings, and he himself late in life became tutor to the Marquis Wên of Wei. Tsêng-shên was undoubtedly a man of great personal integrity, who had imbibed the main principles of his master's teaching and himself had many disciples. He possessed great influence in propagating the teachings of Confucius. The great Sung dynasty Confucianist, Chu Hsi, suggested that while Confucius himself was responsible for the first section of the *Great Learning*, Tsêng-tzǔ wrote the rest, whilst other scholars have attributed the *Classic of Filial Piety* to him. Though both these ascriptions are now considered to be erroneous, they do witness to the importance and influence of Tsêng-tzǔ in the Confucian tradition.

Summary

It is a curious fact that many modern Chinese scholars seek to minimize the place and influence of Confucius in the revolutionary process which was changing social, economic and political patterns which had continued for centuries. Whilst admitting his ability as a teacher, they set him down as a dyed-in-the-wool conservative who was seeking to bolster up a fast-decaying feudalism which had worked well enough five centuries before but which had in Confucius's day already become an anachronism. They represent Confucius as hankering after a fancied golden age of antiquity. They picture him as a rather pathetic figure, completely out of place in the rude power politics of the age and preaching an ethic which sought to perpetuate the inequalities inherent in the relationships of ruler and subject, father and son, husband and wife, elder and younger. Regarding him from the standpoint of a so-called democratic and socialist state, they denigrate him as a reactionary and the upholder of privilege and status. They fail to see how far-reaching and revolutionary in the context of his own time were the ideas which he promulgated, how humane were his sympathies, and how fundamental were the measures by which he proposed to cure the evils of his day and establish a way of life in which all men could find deep satisfaction.

It is equally curious that so many modern Chinese scholars try to divorce Confucian ethics altogether from religion. They regard the ethical system of Confucius as purely humanistic and fail to see that his whole ethical philosophy stems from a pure yet humble faith in the essential 'rightness' of the universe, and in a full assurance that above man there is a cosmic will which is ever working for righteousness and peace.

These scholars present us with a travesty of the real Confucius. Only a powerful and indeed unique personality could have won for himself so completely the affection, devotion and loyalty of disciples who were determined that a message so universally rejected by the ruling powers in Confucius's own lifetime should, after his death, be spread through the whole of the Chinese world. Only one whose ideas were profoundly relevant to the times could have become the acknowledged founder of a system of thought which spread so rapidly that it established itself over all its powerful rivals in spite of vigorous attempts to destroy both it and its advocates. Only teachings which had in them something of universal validity and appeal could provide the ideological basis for a united Chinese empire and for a civilization which was to grow and flourish through two thousand years.

We can now turn from this brief account of the man and his disciples to consider his contribution to religious, ethical and socio-political thought. In doing so we shall, I hope, uncover the reason why Confucius is ranked among the very greatest of the world's teachers.

3. The Teaching of Confucius

ETHICAL concepts lie at the heart of Confucius's thinking. He was first and foremost a moral philosopher. He taught[1] that the goal for the individual is the development of personality until the ideal of a perfect man, a true gentleman, a sage, is reached. On the other hand his goal for society is universal order and harmony under the rule of a perfect sage. Scholars will no doubt continue to differ as to whether or not it is possible to have a satisfactory ethic without a religious or metaphysical basis. Many leading Confucians have claimed that the teaching of Confucius was purely humanistic. Some have even gone so far as to say that he was in fact anti-religious. In contrast to Judaism, Christianity and Islam, where ethics has always been firmly linked to religion, it was, they affirm, the divorcement of ethics from religion which produced the Confucian system. They point out that Confucius never discussed such questions as the immortality of the soul or the existence of God, nor did he discuss natural science or the origin and nature of the universe. His philosophy was purely concerned with humanity and human relationships, and there is in his teaching no philosophy of nature or of the cosmos.

It is my belief that in this interpretation of Confucius, so commonly accepted by Chinese and Western scholars alike, there are two fundamental errors. In the first place, the fact that Confucius was no metaphysician does not in any way invalidate the truth that his reaction to what he believed the universe to be was fundamental to his ethics. He lived in an age before great metaphysical questions were being raised and attempts made to answer them. In his day beliefs concerning the nature of the universe were naïvely and uncritically accepted, but it was universally assumed that the universe is fundamentally well-ordered and beneficent to man. The ancient religion, with its anthropomorphic concepts of an over-ruling providence, was a powerful influence and only here and there were voices raised to question the majesty and supremacy of August Heaven and the authority of the ancestor-spirits. The fact that Confucius exhibited scepticism as regards the superstitious beliefs of the general populace in the activities of ghosts and spirits is no argument that he was anti-religious. That he refused to discuss the question of survival after death, and was reluctant to talk about T'ien (Heaven) indicates that, like the Buddha, he saw no point in interminable discussion on questions for which there could be no certain answer. This suggests that on some points at least Confucius was prepared to live by faith rather than by sight. There is really not a scrap of real evidence to show that Confucius was anti-religious. All the evidence points the other way. He always spoke of T'ien with profound reverence. He claimed that he prayed to T'ien, enjoyed T'ien's protection, and was himself commissioned to his task by T'ien.[2]

In the second place, Confucius inherited a religious tradition which had behind it more than a thousand years of development, a religion closely associated with the functioning of government and with family and which pervaded every aspect of life. It was a religion rich in ritual and ceremonial observances, and the evidence of the earliest records concerning Confucius indicates that he was meticulous in observing the customary rites, sought to understand their inner meaning and purpose, and was indignant with those who showed indifference or an obvious lack of sincerity in their performance.[3]

While I freely admit that Confucius was not primarily a religious teacher, it is my conviction that he was a deeply religious man. The assurance that his own 'power of virtue' (Tê) was born of Heaven and that he had a Heaven-sent task to perform gave him strength to triumph over his disappointments and face with equanimity both hostility and neglect. One Chinese scholar[4] has suggested that Confucius's thought begins with human life and reaches up to the Way of Heaven (T'ien Tao). I would suggest, rather, that the Way of Heaven is fundamental to Confucius's ethical thought and the foundation of his ethical system in which he works out the basic principles for his Way of Man (Jên Tao).

Confucius was essentially a man of his own time and the product of the cultural tradition which he inherited. It is foolish to denigrate him because the egalitarian, socialistic and democratic ideas of much later times are absent from his teaching. He was no revolutionary except in the sense that the ideas of a germinal thinker are always liable to bring about revolutionary changes and initiate social processes which have a cumulative effect long after their originator has died. He refused any claim to originality, believing himself to be simply one who sought to perpetuate all that was best in the accumulated wisdom of ancient times. Four elements of Chou civilization formed essential elements of his ethical system.

The first I have already mentioned. It was the religion in which belief in, worship of, and sacrifice to a supreme deity was linked to a profound reverence for the ancestor-spirits. The overruling providence of Heaven, its majesty, benevolence and righteousness, are constant themes in the poetry and historical documents which refer to the founding of the Chou dynasty and with which the student Confucius was familiar. In those documents, T'ien or Shang Ti is pictured as supreme over the cosmos and all other spiritual beings. T'ien or Shang Ti takes a keen interest in human life and welfare. In the same documents the character of the Duke of Chou is set forth as an example of a true nobleman, and Confucius realized that the one thing above all others that characterized the nobleman was his understanding of the Decree of Heaven (*Analects*, 20:3). The mean man, on the other hand, does not know the Decree of Heaven and so does not fear it (*Analects*, 16:8). Consequently, he lacks reverence for the teaching of the Holy Sages. The belief that life and destiny are ordained by Heaven, so strongly inculcated in the ancient religion, may result in the fatalism that was shown by some of Confucius's contemporaries, and which Mo-tzŭ condemned in the attitude of the Confucians of his day,[5] but Confucius's own views were not fatalistic. He firmly believed that men had power to choose or reject Heaven's appointments. When, a generation later than Confucius, the philosopher Mo-tzŭ stressed that the benevolence and righteousness of Heaven are the ultimate source and justification for human virtues, we can be almost certain that, in this respect if not in others, he was teaching what he had learned in his Confucian upbringing and was echoing the belief of Confucius himself.

Secondly, society centuries before the time of Confucius had been organized on the basis of family. In the early days of the Chou dynasty fiefs had been allotted to the feudal lords in a system of planned colonization. These feudal lords, linked to one another and to the royal house by marriage ties, took their families, retainers, peasants, artisans and soldiers to form self-sufficient colonies based on an agricultural economy and governed from well-fortified walled cities. These large family groupings of the nobility were preserved only so long as the relationships of parents to children, brothers to brothers, and masters to servants were effectively controlled. Consequently the virtues of filial piety and brotherly affection were the *sine qua non* for the continued existence and well-being of the family. Confucius recognized that unless the intimate relationships of family life were controlled by *jên* (love) and *i* (righteousness) there could be neither filial piety nor brotherly affection and the family as a social unit would inevitably disintegrate. In the history of his own time there were innumerable instances of families falling to ruin because of the lack of these virtues. *Jên* and *i* became the foundation of Confucius's *jên tao* (way of man), and *jên* came to occupy a primary place in his thinking as the greatest of all virtues and indeed the summation of all virtues.

In the third place, the practical needs of an agricultural economy, and especially the pressing tasks of clearing forests, controlling rivers, draining marshes and founding new settlements, emphasized the importance of mutual friendliness and assistance. The fact that new settlements were often pushed forward into territories occupied by hostile non-Chinese tribes meant that the very existence of many communities depended upon cooperative effort and on loyalty and obedience to the leader. In such a situation it came to be generally recognized that community interests must triumph over individual selfishness and greed, and that even more important than efficiency were the virtues of loyalty, reciprocity, faithfulness, love and justice. When, by the time of Confucius, rivalries and jealousies were tearing society apart, when ancient loyalties were giving place to self-aggrandizement and brute force, it was good to recall a more hopeful era when the king's power and authority were everywhere recognized throughout the states, when mutual assistance could be called upon in time of need and when men stood loyally by their pledged word.

In the fourth place, the harmony and peace necessary for the development of a rich and happy communal life were seen to be promoted best by careful regulation of all human relationships. The Chinese of ancient times were no more peace-loving than any other people. Among the chief occupations of their nobility were hunting and war. It was found possible to control a quarrelsome and aggressive nobility by means of a strict adherence to a code of conduct detailed enough to cover all the normal relationships of life, a code of conduct in which everyone had his or her recognized status and position. Very early in their history the Chinese developed an inordinate interest in what was called *li*, that is, the rules and rituals and properties appropriate for all occasions. These rituals, when accompanied by pageantry and music, had a strong civilizing influence. It is true that at first the *li* were thought not to extend to relationships with barbarians or with the common people, but they did control and keep within bounds the intercourse between the numerous families of the nobility. Ritual and music were the essential manifestations of culture. Behaviour according to ritual was the outward mark of a gentleman. Music, which included miming and dancing, was a powerful stimulus to the community spirit, whether in the solemn seasonal and family festivals, or in the rhythmic chanting which usually accompanied arduous communal labours. Confucius, we know, made a special study of ritual and music, and these, together with literature, history and ethics, made up the material for his own teaching.

Thus, the ethical and social teaching of Confucius grew out of his recognition that the great advance in prosperity, social organization and culture which characterized the early centuries of the Chou dynasty had come about largely because ethical values had been recognized as the cement of family and state. It is foolish to condemn Confucius because he made no attempt overtly to overthrow the existing order which has been called feudalistic and reactionary. The early Chou feudalism was already beginning to break down before Confucius was born, but it was to be a long time before another political pattern evolved to take its place. When the ties which had for long held society together were no longer considered to be binding, though, relatively speaking, the individual had more freedom, society was brought near to chaos. In the days of Confucius it was family quarrels and the usurpation of authority by younger sons, ministers, officials and disloyal servants which were the chief cause of the civil wars which brought untold misery to the common people. In such a situation it was understandable that Confucius sought to uphold the existing order by insisting on a respectful obedience to parents, loyalty to one's ruler and absolute sincerity in the performance of social and religious duties. Confucius cannot be blamed because he failed to see that the stirring and troublous times in which he lived were the first beginnings of a momentous change in which, after more than two hundred years of war and carnage, the old feudal type of society which had worked so well in the past would give place to a united empire and to a political system in which men of ability, regardless of heredity and noble birth, might hope by effort and scholarship to rise to eminence. What we need to remember is that it was his teaching and the school which he founded that, more than any other single factor, set in motion the revolutionary idea that it was men of character and scholarship who formed the true aristocracy, and that laid down the guiding lines of a system of training in character and scholarship which in due time produced an élite body of men capable of administering the affairs of a vast empire.

If there is one concept which is central to the teaching of Confucius it is that of 'The Way' (*tao*), though as Confucius never attempted to define it we can only understand it in the light of his philosophy considered as a whole. The Chinese character *tao* originally meant a path, a road or a way. A road is a way provided for men to travel on in order to reach a certain goal or destination.[6] In the *Analects* the character as used by Confucius is given an ethical connotation. It is the 'way' a man *ought* to travel because it is ordained by Heaven that he should walk in it. It is, fundamentally, 'the Way of Heaven' and only becomes 'the Way of Man' because all wise and good men follow it by seeking to conform their conduct to the ordainment of Heaven. It was the 'way' which Confucius himself had learnt as he sat at the feet of the sages of ancient times. It is a 'way' which Confucius taught, and in doing so emphasized love, righteousness, propriety and wisdom which became the cardinal virtues of the Confucian ethical system. It is the 'way' which all men must follow if they are to attain human perfection, for Heaven had not only provided the 'way' for men to walk in, but had endowed man with a nature which was fundamentally good.

It is because this concept of 'the Way of Heaven' is central to Confucius's teaching that his supreme ideal of manhood is the *Shêng Jên*. The *Shêng Jên* were the holy sages of ancient times who, having followed the 'way' to its goal, had attained divine status. But for Confucius the importance of the sage-kings of ancient times was not in this attainment, but that they had put into actual practice the 'way' in political and social life, and so had provided a standard of behaviour, an authentic and external code of conduct for all men to follow. Confucius considered this ideal to be so far above a struggling imperfect mortal such as himself that he took the term *chun-tzŭ* as a practical ideal towards which to strive. The *chun-tzŭ* were, in the first place, the princely descendants of rulers and nobles, but Confucius used the term of all men who were of noble or princely character and behaviour. The term can best be translated as 'gentleman' or 'noble-minded man'. All men who earnestly seek to follow the 'way' are *chun-tzŭ*, and the virtues which Confucius taught are those which are exemplified in the character and conduct of a true gentleman.

The training which Confucius tried to give his followers was aimed at producing noblemen in this sense of nobility of character, men who would be able to take their place in any society because an inner serenity and poise were reflected in moderation and good manners. He hoped that his pupils would be honoured with positions of responsibility and trust because of their sincerity, loyalty, uprightness and accordance with propriety, because they were men who would act in obedience to the dictates of conscience and the promptings of a humane and just mind.

Fundamental Ethical Concepts

We turn now to a more detailed examination of the ethical concepts which lie at the heart of Confucius's thinking.

Jên

Of all the virtues which characterize a true gentleman, *jên* is supreme in the teaching of Confucius. In the *Analects* he is represented as using the term more than forty times, and a study of these usages clearly demonstrates what he meant by the term. The character has been variously translated as love, goodness, benevolence, man-to-man-ness, human-heartedness, kindness. In the usage of Confucius, *jên* is the greatest of all virtues and, in fact, the summation of all virtues. It is indeed, as Waley has pointed out,[7] 'a sublime moral attitude, a transcendental perfection attained only by legendary heroes, but not by any living or historic person'. It is the highest perfection of goodness, such as only a holy sage can attain, and yet all men may strive after it and reach some measure of attainment. Wise men covet it, for its possession is more important than life itself (*Analects*, 4:1–6; 7:29; 15:8, 34).

If *jên* is so important, what are the methods suggested by Confucius for its attainment? He teaches that only by strenuous moral effort can one hope to increase in *jên*, and such moral effort involves self-cultivation, love towards others, and the continued practice of goodness. All men act according to their nature, but one's nature, though bestowed by Heaven is, as it were, nature in the raw. It may be too aggressive or too yielding, too easily exalted by joy or cast down by sorrow, too introvert or extrovert, insensitive or over-sensitive. The partialities of one's nature need to be corrected so as to reach a harmonious balance. This can only be done by self-cultivation, so as to attain mastery over self. But to practise this self-cultivation implies a standard, a measure of what is right. Such a measure is supplied by what is generally accepted as fitting, and that is *li* or the *mores* of polite society. This is what Confucius meant when he taught that *jên* is self-denial and a return to propriety (*li*) (*Analects*, 12:1).

But *jên* also consists in loving others (*Analects*, 12:21). This love for others is made evident by the virtues of loyalty and consideration, for loyalty consists in the entire devotion of oneself to the best interests of another, and consideration consists in never doing to others what one would not wish done to oneself. Qualities of loyalty and consideration will not breed any resentment either in family life or in social affairs and so the virtue of *jên* will be extended to others.

Yet it is only by constant practice of *jên* that one learns to appreciate more and more the ideal of perfect goodness and the difficulty of its attainment. Confucius knew full well that virtue does not grow in a vacuum, but only by benevolent conduct in the practical affairs of everyday life. The perfection of personality lies in acting always with reverence and respect, displaying in all the varied relationships of life courtesy, liberality, faithfulness, diligence and kindness.

Though *jên* is the leading ethical concept in Confucius's thought, the sum of all virtues, in the formation of the character of the ideally 'princely man' it stands with many other essential qualities which Confucius stressed again and again in his teaching.

I, RIGHTEOUSNESS OR JUSTICE

Soon after the death of Confucius, the philosopher Mo-tzŭ was exalting *i* or righteousness as a cardinal virtue, claiming that Heaven is righteous and loving and that it is the will of Heaven that all men should copy Heaven by seeking themselves to be righteous. He went on to claim that only the 'worthy' were fit to be given charge of government.[8] Still later, the Confucian Mencius taught that righteousness is a principle which belongs to man's nature, needing, however, to be given full development. It is something that a good man cherishes and holds on to even in preference to life itself. 'I like fish, and I also like bears' paws. If I cannot get both together, I will let the fish go, and take the bears' paws. So I like life, and I also like righteousness. If I cannot keep the two together, I will let life go, and choose righteousness. I like life indeed, but there is that which I like more than life; and therefore I will not seek to hold it by any improper means.'[9] What had Confucius himself to say concerning righteousness and what criteria had he for deciding what was righteous or just? An investigation of the usages in the *Analects* reveals that, according to Confucious, righteousness is thought of as what is fitting, right, seemly. Confucius does not try to give an abstract definition of righteousness. Men learn to distinguish between what is righteous or unrighteous in the concrete situations of life, and they find that righteousness is a quality displayed in the character and conduct of the *chun-tzŭ* or noble-hearted man, whose inner nature is motivated by *jên* and whose outward conduct accords with *li*.

Confucius never refers to a fixed or unchangeable law, or to a divine fiat which lays down what men can or cannot do in any particular circumstance, because he realizes that what is fitting on one occasion may be inappropriate to another. He does suggest, however, that there emerges within a civilized society a generally accepted standard of what human conduct ideally ought to be. The righteous man is one who both inwardly and outwardly strives to approximate to that standard, and, according to Confucius, men have always before them the example of the truly righteous sages of ancient times.

The nearest that Confucius ever comes to explaining what he means by righteousness is when he connects it with the 'Way' (*Tao*). Confucius had no doubts that the 'Way' of governing a country so as to produce the greatest well-being and happiness of the people was the way which was fitting and right and therefore righteous, and such was the 'way' of the ancient sages. So he said, 'When the Way prevails in your land, count it a disgrace to be needy and obscure. When the Way does not prevail, count it a disgrace to be rich and honoured' (*Analects*, 8:13). Confucius insists that a love for learning from the righteous way of the ancient sages is fundamental, for without such learning all the excellent virtues degenerate into great evils: the good lack discernment, the learned lack principles, those who like to make promises bring injury to others, candour becomes rudeness, courage results in turbulence and constancy leads to recklessness (*Analects*, 17:8). We can infer that in this passage of the *Analects*, when Confucius is speaking of 'learning' he means 'learning righteousness', because in another passage concerning the virtue of courage he says, 'A gentleman puts righteousness above everything. If a gentleman possesses courage but lacks righteousness, he will cause disturbances; if a common man possesses courage but lacks righteousness, he will become a thief' (*Analects*, 17:23).

In two places in the *Analects* Confucius is reported as saying that there is one thread running through all his way of life (*Analects*, 4:15; 15:2), but he seems to have left his disciples to deduce for themselves what it was. His disciple Tsêng-tzǔ, when asked what this fundamental principle was, explained it as 'loyalty and consideration'. Was Tsêng-tzǔ right? He speaks of two virtues, not one, virtues which Confucius undoubtedly prized very highly. If Confucius had meant to single out one thing which might be said to run like a thread through all his life and teaching, it was surely the pursuit of righteousness. So it was that when Tzǔ-kung summed up his master as one whose aim is to learn and retain in the mind as much as possible, Confucius made it quite clear that there was more to it than that (*Analects*, 15:2). His learning is concerned with what is right and fitting, and with what accords with the Way, that is, with righteousness. And this can be illustrated from several passages: 'The basic disposition of a true gentleman is righteousness, which he puts into practice according to ritual (*li*) modestly setting it forth and faithfully bringing it to completion' (*Analects*, 15:17); 'I have heard the saying, "They dwell in seclusion in order to seek the fulfilment of their aims, they practised righteousness in order to extend the influence of their way", but I have never seen such men as these' (*Analects*, 16:11); 'What gives me sorrow is the thought that I have failed to cultivate my moral power, and have not fully investigated what I have learnt, that I have failed to respond to righteousness when I have heard of it, and failed to reform what was unworthy' (*Analects*, 7:3); 'To apprehend what is righteous and not to do it is cowardice' (*Analects*, 2:24); 'A gentleman, in his dealings with the world, is prejudiced neither for nor against; he simply seeks to accord with righteousness' (*Analects*, 4:10).

Undoubtedly, Confucius's views on righteousness were greatly influenced by the behaviour of the princes and politicians of his day, whose chief aims in life seemed to be wealth and rank, and who were prepared to use any and every means to attain them. To cultivate a love of righteousness would act as a restraining influence upon a gentleman. A good man is one who 'when he sees a chance of gain asks himself, is it righteous' (*Analects*, 14:13; 16:10); 'To attain wealth or rank by unrighteous means is as far from me as a floating cloud' (*Analects*, 7:15). Confucius did not disdain rank or wealth. He seems, in fact, to have had a hankering after political influence and power, and he certainly enjoyed the good things of life. He was no recluse or ascetic and had no belief in self-denial merely as a discipline. Rank and wealth must be refused only if their acceptance is incompatible with righteousness.

Hsiao T'i, FILIAL PIETY AND BROTHERLY LOVE

Though the virtues of filial piety (*hsiao*) and brotherly love (*t'i*) occupy a very important place in the teaching of Confucius, he added little to what was already firmly accepted. In the pre-

Confucian literature the duty of filial piety is a recurring theme because in the ancient patriarchal society, organization into clans and families and the grading of the members of a family into a hierarchy in which each had his or her recognized function and status was of great importance. Each family was a social unit, largely self-contained and self-governing, and though in theory the head of the family could demand and enforce implicit obedience and in all family disputes acted as a final court of appeal, yet in practice it was recognized that the maintenance of the family in mutual helpfulness and harmony depended upon conceding to each and every one his or her rights as a person and treating everyone with dignity and fairness.

Confucius recognized that these virtues of filial piety and brotherly affection, learned within the bosom of the family, were of great importance to good government, and that there was an analogy between family and state. When someone asked him why he was not in public service he replied that to be filial and affectionate to one's brothers was contributing to good government, and in itself an important service to the state (*Analects*, 2:21).

In what, according to Confucius, does filial piety consist? It is far more than just seeing to it that one's parents are well provided for, or taking from them the burden of hard work, or making sure that their wants are a first priority (*Analects*, 2:6–8). It is to live and act in such a way that the parents have no cause for anxiety except as regards one's health. It is to obey them so long as their demands accord with what is right. A filial son has the right and duty to remonstrate gently if he believes his parents to be in the wrong, but he must always be deferential (*Analects*, 4:18). Yet his first obedience is to propriety (*li*), that is, to those accepted rules of behaviour which are regarded as right and proper. When parents are alive, he must serve them according to propriety; and when they die, he must bury them and sacrifice to them according to propriety (*Analects*, 2:5). The teaching of filial piety and brotherly affection is fundamental in the training of the young, for correct behaviour beyond the confines of family is but an extension of these virtues, which Confucius calls the root of goodness (*jên*).

In the following centuries Confucians came to place more emphasis on filial piety than Confucius had done, so that by the end of the third century B.C. it was exalted in some Confucian schools to be greatest of all virtues, as for instance in the *Classic of Filial Piety* and in several chapters of the *Book of Rites* (*Li Chi*).[10]

Chung-Shu, LOYALTY AND CONSIDERATION

While filial piety and brotherly affection were primary virtues inculcated within the family, loyalty (*chung*) and consideration (*shu*) were considered by Confucius to be of fundamental importance to those engaged in public life. When his disciple Tsêng-tzŭ was asked what was the one thing which linked together like a thread all Confucius's teaching, he replied, 'Our master's way is simply this: loyalty and consideration' (*Analects*, 4:15). When, on another occasion, Confucius was asked by Tsŭ-kung if there was one word which might act as a principle of conduct throughout life Confucius replied, 'Maybe the word "consideration" (*shu*), do not do to others what you would not desire them to do to you' (*Analects*, 15:23). By loyalty, Confucius meant to serve with all one's heart unfeignedly, and by consideration he meant to put oneself in the place of others. Nevertheless, at a time when implicit loyalty to one's prince, whether right or wrong, was a sure way to promotion and success, Confucius always stressed that loyalty to one's own principles is more important than loyalty to a human master. He recognized that wealth and rank are desirable, but must be relinquished if they can only be retained by forsaking one's principles; whilst poverty and obscurity, however hateful, must be accepted for righteousness' sake. A noble character is never prepared to part company with goodness (*jên*) (*Analects*, 4:5), and is as concerned to discover what is right as lesser men are concerned with their pay (*Analects*, 4:16). He will not seek to escape from poverty by doing wrong (*Analects*, 7:11), and late in life Confucius roundly condemned his disciple, Jan Ch'iu, because he was prepared to prove his loyalty to the head of the Chi family by collecting unjust taxes (*Analects*, 11:16). Probably one main reason why Confucius never attained to any considerable position of power or influence in political life was because he absolutely repudiated wealth and rank obtained by wrong means and was prepared to find contentment, if need be, with 'coarse food, water to drink, and a bent arm for a pillow' (*Analects*, 7:15).

According to Confucius, perfection of personality could only be attained by the cultivation of good manners so that, in whatever society a gentleman might be, he would behave with kindness and courtesy and due consideration for others. For this purpose he taught that two studies were invaluable. One was the study of the rules of right conduct, that is conduct appropriate for all occasions as set down in various guides to etiquette for the nobility, which later on were produced in book form in the *Chou Li*, *I Li* and the *Li Chi*. The other was the study of music which came to occupy quite an important place in Confucian education, as it did in the education system of Greece. Confucius was well aware that man's emotional nature is strong, always demanding outlets and incapable of being totally suppressed. Men's behaviour is governed by a mind in large measure motivated by love and hate, joy and depression, fear, jealousy, anger, tenderness, compassion. Two things are necessary. The first is to bring about an inner harmony of the mind so that each emotion, as it arises, is given a fitting outlet. No emotion must be allowed unbridled expression, but one must seek to cultivate a balanced harmony within the mind itself. In this pursuit the melodies, harmonies and rhythms of music are of great value, and in the process of character-training there were few things that could match the disciplined coordination of an orchestra or the rhythmic and balanced movements of a formal ritual dance. Confucius was well aware that there was music which encouraged licentiousness and frivolity, and so condemned the songs of Wei and Chêng,[11] but he recognized the importance of music as an instrument of education, as a subject, which when rightly taught, promoted virtue. The second thing necessary is to bring external restraints upon men's conduct so that they do not exceed what is deemed to be fitting and right. This is the function of the study of propriety, the rites and ceremonial, the usages of polite society (*li*).

The term *li* signifies one of the most important concepts in Confucian ethics.[12] It is made up of two elements, one representing influence coming down from Heaven, and the other, which gives the pronunciation, representing a sacrificial vessel. Originally the term was used for 'religious rites', but the concept was soon broadened to include all habitual, customary and socially accepted rites, yet even up to modern times the term often refers to rites of a religious nature. Nevertheless *li* came to include all the customary regulations and acknowledged practices which govern social relationships. It was important in government and partook of the nature of law. As Dubs writes, '*li* may be translated by religion, ceremony, deportment, decorum, propriety, formality, politeness, courtesy, etiquette, good form, good behaviour, good manners, the rules of proper conduct'.[13]

As we have already seen,[14] in the time of Confucius there were, practically speaking, only two occupations open for those sons of the nobility who were given the rank of 'knights' or 'gentlemen'. They could either enter government service in the political or administrative field, or they could hope to carve out for themselves a career in military service. In both cases they were bound by rigid formalities and court etiquette which gradually spread into the common life of the educated classes. *Li* came to represent all those external observances of morality which were considered to be binding on all gentlemen, that is, the manners and ceremonial of polite society, but it also included the regulations of government. It is used in both these senses by Confucius in the *Analects*. 'The master said, We know in what way the Yin modified *li* when they followed upon the Hsia. We know in what way the Chou modified *li* when they followed upon the Yin' (*Analects*, 2:23). 'When they [parents] are alive, serve them according to *li*. When they die, bury them according to *li*, sacrifice to them according to *li*' (*Analects*, 15:10). The chief aim of Confucius's teaching being the perfection of personality, he laid great emphasis on manners, on external deportment, on the restraints of propriety which are evidenced in one's disposition and conduct as regards others and in one's cultural standing.

Emphasis on Education

Confucius has always been regarded primarily as a teacher, and, as we have already seen,[15] he seems to be the first in Chinese recorded history to have established a private school in no way connected with the courts of the nobility. He himself laid great emphasis on study and the search for knowledge and held an important theory regarding the method of study which is succinctly stated in *Analects*, 2:15: 'To learn, and not to think over [what one has learnt] is useless; to think without learning is dangerous.' Here Confucius is emphasizing the utter futility of learning by rote or memorizing the lessons which the accumulated wisdom of the past has to teach without turning over in the mind what one has learnt in order to discover its true meaning and how to apply it to present needs and circumstances. Knowledge results from thought which systematizes and harmonizes the innumerable facts and experiences which the process of learning brings to one's notice. On the other hand, there is great danger in allowing the mind to indulge in purely subjective meditation and fantasies which have no basis in objective reality and practical experience. Confucius taught that a gentleman should be widely learned in all the elements of culture, but should know how to bring all this learning under the restraining influence of ritual (*Analects*, 6:25). He claimed that a man was fit to be a teacher who could so reinterpret the learning of former times as to apply it to the problems of the present (*Analects*, 2:11).[16] The process of learning leads to the assimilation of knowledge, which is futile and useless until, by pondering on what one knows, one learns to apply that knowledge to the practical affairs of life.

Since the aim of study is the attainment of knowledge, one has to be sure of what one knows and what one does not know. It is just as important an aspect of knowledge to know that there are things that one does not know as to be aware of the things that one does know (*Analects*, 2:17). It is probable that Confucius believed that there were realities beyond human understanding and therefore beyond the scope of human enquiry. It is certain that there were topics he was reluctant to discuss because he knew that he had no certain knowledge concerning them. Thus, Tzŭ-kung is reported to have said of him, 'We are permitted to hear our master's views concerning culture and the manifestation of goodness, but he will tell us nothing about the nature of man or the ways of Heaven' (*Analects*, 5:12).

Confucius himself had an inordinate love of learning. Speaking of himself he said, 'I have listened in silence and noted what was said. I have never grown tired of learning, nor wearied in teaching others what I have learnt' (*Analects*, 7:1). 'To be a sage or a perfectly good man, how dare I claim such qualities? Still, I can claim that the practice of them has never been distasteful nor have I tired of teaching others' (*Analects*, 7:33). The practice of the 'Way' was both the fundamental principle and the goal of education, and the practice of the 'Way' involved the cultivation of those virtues which we have already underlined.

Confucius's principles of education may be summed up in what he said in *Analects*, 7:6: 'Set your mind upon the "Way", firmly lay hold of every right attachment, trust in goodness [*jên*], find your relaxation in the arts.' For him, the purpose of education is primarily the development of character. The acquisition of knowledge is important but secondary. A good teacher encourages his pupil to make the practice of the Way his target. He seeks all the time to show that there is practical merit in training the mind to love virtue. He holds up the perfect Way of the sages as the ideal to strive after, an ideal for the mind to hold on to. He encourages his pupil to lay hold on every right attachment, so that he constantly and unremittingly practises the cardinal virtues until they become habitual. He trusts in goodness, the sum of all virtues, and believes that only by striving to attain goodness does one approximate to what a human being ought to be. He comes to manifest a quality of life that is in harmony with what is right, and so fulfils the obligations of his humanity. Beyond all this, but secondary to it, a wide field of study is open to him: the arts of writing, arithmetic, manners, music, archery, charioteering, etc., the arts in which all gentlemen sought proficiency. In fact, Confucius recognized that training in these arts had a powerful influence on the development of character. The moral emphasis in Confucius's teaching is shown in his statement that 'a young man's duty is to behave well to his parents at home and to his elders when abroad, to be cautious in making promises and punctual in keeping them, to have kindly feelings towards everyone, but to seek the intimacy of the good. If, when all this is done, he has any energy to spare, then let him study the polite arts' (*Analects*, 1:6). Always, with Confucius, training in character and deportment is fundamental. A knowledge of culture and of the fine arts is undoubtedly useful and assists in the production of a well-rounded and balanced personality, but it is a secondary and not the primary aim of a teacher.

Confucius was the first teacher in Chinese history to make absolutely clear what were the principles and ideals of his system, principles and ideals which were to dominate all future education in China. He stamped the educational system of China with the enduring marks of his own personality, ideas and ideals. Perhaps nothing has done more to mould and shape the pattern of Chinese culture throughout more than two millennia than this educational system. It is a system which has often been riddled by evils and abuses, but fortunately there has always been before the eyes of Chinese scholars the actual words of Confucius to recall them again and again to fundamental principles and high ideals.

Teaching Material

When Confucius founded his school, the *Odes*, *Historical Documents*, *Ritual* and *Music* provided this basic teaching material.[17] We do not know to what extent these were in book form at the time of Confucius. We do know that the use of books was extensive. Confucius informs us that when teaching these classics he was careful to use the correct pronunciation and not the dialect of the state of Lu (*Analects*, 7:17). He often discussed the *Odes* with Tzŭ-kung and Tzŭ-hsia, was distressed that his disciples made so little effort to study them (*Analects*, 17:9) and concerned that his own son should make progress in their study (*Analects*, 16:13; 17:10). He saw in the Ritual (*Li*) the principles and rules which govern cultured society: 'If you do not study the Ritual,' he said, 'you will find yourself at a loss how to take your stand' (*Analects*, 16:13); 'Without the prescriptions of the Ritual courtesy becomes tiresome, caution becomes timidity, daring becomes turbulence and inflexibility becomes hardness' (*Analects*, 8:2).

Confucius was passionately fond of music and spoke of the music which, according to tradition, had been composed for the accession to the throne of the legendary Shun. To his way of thinking this music was perfectly beautiful and good. When he went to the capital of the state of Ch'i and heard this music for the first time played by a competent orchestra we are told that for three months afterwards he did not know the taste of meat (i.e. did not notice what he was eating). He said, 'I did not believe that such perfect music existed in Ch'i' (*Analects*, 7:13). When he returned from his exile in Wei to his native state of Lu, he set himself the task of separating the songs of the court (*ya*) from the great ancestral hymns (*sung*) (*Analects*, 9:14). He regarded music as a discipline of study essential for the development of virtue: 'Stimulate men with the Odes, establish them with the Ritual, perfect them with Music' (*Analects*, 8:8). He recognized the value of poetry in stirring the emotions and strengthening the will, the value of ritual in establishing a man's conduct, and the value of music in perfecting the moral nature.

Teaching Method and Aims

Confucius showed his genius as a teacher in the methods which he used to develop the ability and intelligence of his pupils. In dealing with their questions he took account of the differences in their dispositions. He had little patience with the dullard and the lazy, insisting that a student must not only be eager to learn but willing to cooperate with his teacher by giving earnest application to the subject. Waley's translation of *Analects*, 7:8, is instructive: 'The master said, "Only one who bursts with eagerness do I instruct; only one who bubbles with excitement, do I enlighten. If I hold up one corner and a man cannot come back to me with the other three, I do not continue the lesson."'

For Confucius, the most important aspect of education was the silent, pervasive influence of the personality and character of the teacher, so that on one occasion he said, 'I would much rather not have to talk.' Whereupon his disciple, Tzǔ-kung, said, 'If our master did not talk, what should we disciples have to pass on?' Confucius replied, 'Heaven does not speak; yet the four seasons run their course thereby. Heaven does not talk' (*Analects*, 17:19). Among his students he made no distinction between wealthy and poor, noble and commoner, and that at a time when class distinctions were regarded as of paramount importance. The poorest came to him without being turned away (*Analects*, 7:7) and Yen Hui, probably the poorest of all who came to him for instruction, was his favourite disciple.

According to Confucius, the supreme aim of education is to produce the perfected sage. That was his ideal and he had no doubts that in the past history of the race there had been such men, but he always refused to accept that designation for himself or, indeed, for any of his contemporaries. It remained for subsequent ages to speak of him as the Divine Teacher and the

Perfect Sage, co-equal with Heaven and Earth. As that ideal seemed to be so far beyond the reach of possibility, he concentrated upon producing 'gentlemen' or 'noble-minded men' (*Chun-tzŭ*), an ideal which all men might reasonably strive after. 'A divine sage I cannot hope ever to meet. The most I can hope for is to meet a true gentleman' (*Analects*, 7:25): the word here translated as 'gentleman' is *chun-tzŭ*. Originally, the term designated the noble-born as opposed to the commoner, but Confucius enlarged the connotation of the term to embrace all who sought to practise virtue. The marks of a *chun-tzŭ* were goodness, wisdom and courage: 'The ways of a true gentleman are three. I myself have met with success in none of them. For he that is really good (*jên*) is never unhappy; he that is really wise is never perplexed; he that is really brave is never afraid' (*Analects*, 14:30). The three virtues of goodness, wisdom and courage were considered by Confucius to be most important for the perfecting of personality. The good are self-disciplined and love others. They rejoice in the Way of Heaven and are confident in their destiny. They burn with desire for peace, always seeking reconciliation between the self and others and, having no cause for anxiety, they possess an inward joy. The wise are conversant with the laws which govern affairs. They know how to distinguish between right and wrong, good and evil, and so they are able to come to a clear and unperplexed judgement in every kind of situation. The brave show a fearless disregard for difficulty or danger in upholding what they know to be right.

In training his pupils to become gentlemen in the sense which I have indicated, Confucius had always before his mind the needs of society and government. The aim of his system of education was to supply the right kind of people to assist in the administration of government. According to his ideas only the perfect sage was competent to exercise supreme rule in the land, but men of virtuous character were needed to assist in the administration which was becoming more and more difficult and complex. Thus Confucius's educational policy was linked to his political ideas, and one of the supreme aims of Confucianism ever since has been to produce a constant supply of the right kind of men to carry out government office. The training which Confucius gave was to equip men with competence in practical affairs, and there is no doubt that Confucius himself craved a place in government and believed himself possessed of qualities which would prove of inestimable value to a virtuous ruler. He was obviously disappointed that his merits went unrecognized: 'Am I indeed to be forever like a bitter gourd that is only fit to hang up but not to eat?' (*Analects*, 17:7); Mencius says of Confucius that when he went three months without being employed by some ruler, he looked disappointed and unhappy.[18]

Confucius exalted virtue (*tê*) as the foundation of government. 'He who rules by moral force [*tê*] is like the pole-star, which remains in its place while all the lesser stars do homage to it' (*Analects*, 2:1). Government should be in the hands of those who practise virtue first themselves, then the people will follow. We are told that when Chi K'ang-tzŭ, who exercised the real power in the state of Lu, asked Confucius about government, he replied, 'If you desire what is good, the people will at once be good. The virtue of a ruler is like the wind. The virtue of the people is like grass. When the wind passes over it, it cannot but bend' (*Analects*, 12:19). 'If a ruler himself is upright, all will go well even though he does not give orders. But if he himself is not upright, even though he gives orders, they will not be obeyed' (*Analects*, 13:6). Confucius believed that the sullenness, resentment and uncooperative attitude of the people, together with the extensive growth of lawlessness, were the direct result of the greed and licentiousness of the rulers. According to him virtue in a ruler is of practical importance in the government of a state. The way to gain the respect and obedience of the people is for the ruler to set an example: 'Approach them [the common people] with dignity and they will respect you. Show piety towards your parents, and kindness towards your children and they will be loyal to you. Promote those who are worthy, train those who are incompetent; that is the best form of encouragement' (*Analects*, 2:20); 'Raise up the straight and elevate them over the crooked, and the people will support you' (*Analects*, 2:19); 'In dealing with the aged, be a comfort to them; in dealing with friends be of good faith with them; in dealing with the young, cherish them' (*Analects*, 5:25); 'It is by deeds of righteousness that men extend the influence of their way' (*Analects*, 16:11).

We have already seen that ritual and music were considered by Confucius as essential in the training of character, so that his pupils might understand and follow the manners and ceremonials of polite society. He also stressed their importance in government. He noted the fact that when the Yin dynasty overthrew the Hsia, and the Chou the Yin, on each change of dynasty the rituals had been greatly modified to suit the new situation (*Analects*, 2:23), and he lamented the fact that so little evidence concerning the rituals of the former Hsia and Yin dynasties had been preserved by their descendants (*Analects*, 3:9).

In the *Classic of Filial Piety* (*Hsiao Ching*) Confucius is recorded as saying, 'For changing the people's manners and altering their customs, there is nothing better than music; for securing the repose of superiors and the good order of the people, there is nothing better than the ritual'.[19]

As a method of promoting good government, Confucius proposed a careful attention to the use of words, that they should be used correctly and with greater precision so that when we speak of a prince, a minister, a father or a son, these words should have a definite connotation in men's minds, and action should accord with what the name implies. A prince should act in a way expected of a prince, and so also with minister, father, son, etc. (*Analects*, 12:11; 13:3). One of the evils in the political life of those times was that feudal princes were usurping the powers and privileges of the king, whilst officers and retainers in great families were usurping the authority of their lawful lords (*Analects*, 16:2).

Confucius had something to say regarding the financial and economic aspects of government. He recognizes that the wealth of a country depends more on the people than on the ruler. When the masses of the people have plenty, the ruler shares in that plenty, but when they have not enough to eat, he too has not enough for his needs (*Analects*, 12:9). Even a country that is relatively poor and sparsely populated will find a sufficiency of both goods and men if things are properly apportioned and the people are living in mutual peace and harmony (*Analects*, 16:1). In a well-populated country, the first aim of government should be the enrichment of the people and when that is done, they should be given instruction (*Analects*, 13:9). For the duty of government is to see that there is a sufficiency of food, adequate armaments for defence, and that it possesses the confidence of the people, but of these the most important is the confidence of the people, because a government which loses a people's trust is itself lost (*Analects*, 12:7). A good ruler attends strictly to the business of administration, is careful to fulfil whatever promises he makes, is economical in expenditure, cares diligently for his people and uses the labour of the peasants on government service only at those times of the year when they can best be spared from their agricultural tasks (*Analects*, 1:5).

It was, I believe, the growing recognition that the practical application of the teaching of Confucius would result, not only in the perfecting of individual character but in the promotion of a harmonious and well-governed state, which led to its final establishment as the orthodox system suited to the Chinese nation. In this great system of thought, love and goodness were the motive force governing all the other ethical concepts, the Way of Heaven being a first principle directing the activities of human life. For Confucius the art of politics is born in ethics. His political thought finds its starting-point in virtue. The motive power of progress in human life lies in seeking to know the ordinances of Heaven, and then learning to accept them with obedience, so that one finally comes to the point where they have become so much a part of one's nature that one can now follow freely the dictates of one's own heart.

We are told that Confucius never took for granted anything of which he was not absolutely sure, that he was never over-positive, obstinate or egotistic (*Analects*, 9:4), and that he was humble enough to discuss with the simplest peasant any question which was sincerely raised (*Analects*, 9:7).

Confucius's ethical philosophy is rooted in humanism. His emphasis is on being a man, but nevertheless a man whose fundamental nature is recognized to be ordained by Heaven. His emphasis is more on practice than on book learning, on the study of virtue rather than knowledge, on teaching a man to become a gentleman rather than an erudite scholar. He was suspicious of artful words and an ingratiating manner, of the loquacious and the boastful. His ideal pupil was Yen Hui who 'had a great love of learning', who strove 'never to boast of his good qualities nor of the trouble he took on behalf of others' and who was 'capable of occupying his whole mind for three months on end with no thought but that of goodness' (*Analects*, 5:25; 6:2; 6:5).

Confucius's Religious Thought

When we examine the *Analects*, which is, after all, our primary source for knowledge of Confucius, we are struck by the absence of any specifically religious teaching. We find no discussion of the spiritual and very little that goes beyond the practical affairs of everyday life. Questions concerning the Way of Heaven, the nature of man, the existence and functioning of spiritual beings, survival after death and so on were topics commonly discussed in Confucius's day, if we are to accept the evidence of the *Tso Chuan*,[20] and they occupy the mind of the philosopher Mo-tzŭ,[21] who lived only a generation after Confucius. Yet concerning all these subjects Confucius was remarkably reticent. He refused to discuss the Way of Heaven or the nature of man (*Analects*, 5:12). He never talked of prodigies or spirits (*Analects*, 7:20). When asked by Tzŭ-lu how one should serve the *manes* of the ancestors and other spiritual beings, he suggested that men's first duty is to serve the living (*Analects*, 11:11).

Owing to the paucity of material in the *Analects* many Chinese scholars have concluded that Confucius was not a religious man. We can learn very little from the *Analects* as to Confucius's religious thought. Unfortunately, there can never be any certainty that recorded sayings of Confucius in later works truly reflect his thought. As with the Gospels in the *New Testament*, sayings are attributed to the Master which, on reflection, one realizes could only have reached their present form at a much later time. If we are to believe the *Doctrine of the Mean* (*Chung Yung*), Confucius taught that there are intelligent spiritual beings to whom men owe reverent worship.

In the *Record of Rites* (*Li Chi*) we are told that the disciple, Tsai Wo, asked Confucius, 'I have heard the names *kuei* and *shên*, but I do not know what they mean.' 'The master said, "The [intelligent] spirit is of the *shên* nature, and shows that in fullest measure; the animal soul is of the *kuei* nature, and shows that in fullest measure."'[22] A generation after Confucius, Mo-tzŭ, who, we must remember, had been trained in boyhood in a Confucian school, criticized the Confucians of his day because of their belief that Heaven is without intelligence and the spirits of the dead are without consciousness. He also rebelled against their determinist attitude, and rejected their teaching concerning fate (*ming*). He not only stressed the righteousness and benevolence of Heaven, but spoke of the Will of Heaven. It might be argued that the Confucians of Mo-tzŭ's day reflected more truly the attitude of Confucius to these questions than did Mo-tzŭ, the rebel. But that is not certainly so. It is true that in the *Analects* Confucius is never recorded as speaking of the Will of Heaven (*T'ien chih*), but he does refer several times to the Way of Heaven (*T'ien tao*) and to the decree of Heaven (*T'ien ming*). The question arises, did Confucius use this word *ming* in the same determinist way as it was used by the Confucians who opposed Mo-tzŭ? Did he regard *ming* as an inexorable fate against which men may struggle in vain, a decree of Heaven which completely rules out the freedom of the will? There are passages in the *Analects* which might suggest that Confucius did accept this completely deterministic view. 'The master said, "If Heaven ordains that the Way shall prevail, then the Way will prevail. But if Heaven ordains that the Way should perish, then it needs must perish"' (*Analects*, 14:38). But more often than not, the sense in which Confucius uses the word *ming* leaves the way open for human choice and human freedom. Heaven's *ming* is something which men may choose to disobey, but at their peril. It is something that men seek to understand in order to conform their lives to it. Thus, it is a guiding principle for life, a standard to follow in all one's activities.

It is, I think, necessary to make a clear distinction between the concept of *ming* as a preordained fate from which there is no escape and as a decree of Heaven which men choose or reject of their own free will, but by choice of which a man fulfils the purpose of his being. It is in this latter sense that Confucius usually thinks of the decree of Heaven, and there are places where *T'ien Ming* may be fairly translated into English as 'the Will of Heaven'. Thus, 'he who does not understand the decree of Heaven cannot be regarded as a true gentleman' (*Analects*, 20:3); 'A gentleman fears the decree of Heaven, whereas a small man has no fear of it because he does not understand it' (*Analects*, 16:8); 'At fifty I knew what were the decrees of Heaven' (*Analects*, 2:4).

The decree of Heaven (*T'ien Ming*) and the Way of Heaven (*T'ien Tao*) are mutually related, for the Way is what Heaven has ordained. Again it is difficult from the few references in the

Analects to be sure as to what Confucius meant by Heaven (*T'ien*). Did he think of Heaven in purely naturalistic terms as an ever-revolving and amoral system? 'Heaven does not speak; yet the four seasons run their course thereby, the multitude of creatures are born thereby. Heaven does not speak!' (*Analects*, 17:19). Or did he think of Heaven as a great over-ruling power, exercising a moral control over the universe, either in anthropomorphic terms as a personal spirit, or as a supreme abstract principle? There are sayings of Confucius which suggest that he believed in Heaven as an objective reality, and even possessing qualities which we usually regard as appertaining to personality: 'Heaven it was that gave birth to the virtue that is in me' (*Analects*, 7:22); 'The master said, "Greatest as lord and ruler was Yao. Sublime indeed was he. There is no greatness like the greatness of Heaven, yet Yao could copy it"' (*Analects*, 8:19); 'When king Wên perished, did that mean that culture [*wên*] ceased to exist? If Heaven had really intended that such culture as his should disappear, a latter-day mortal would never have been able to link himself to it as I have done. And if Heaven does not intend to destroy such culture, what have I to fear from the people of K'uang?' (*Analects*, 9:5); 'The truth is, no one knows me . . . but the studies of men here below are felt on high, and perhaps, after all, I am known; not here, but in Heaven' (*Analects*, 14:37); 'In pretending to have retainers when I have none, whom do I deceive? Do I deceive Heaven?' (*Analects*, 9:11). If we bear in mind that Confucius had inherited a religion which had come down from the time of his great hero, Chou Kung, when *T'ien* was equated with *Shang Ti* and not only worshipped by the practice of elaborate rituals and sacrifices, but conceived of in anthropomorphic terms, even though we may credit Confucius with being an agnostic, his agnosticism is that of a religious man. Though in general he refrained from discussing fundamental religious questions, his essential humanism was linked to a reverent regard for what is transcendental. His obvious pleasure in religious rituals (*Analects*, 3:9, 15, 17), his emphasis on the ritual mourning for rulers and parents (*Analects*, 14:43; 17:21), his reverent attitude as regards the customary sacrifices (*Analects*, 3:10, 11, 12), all point to a belief in the value of religious rites to society and to the individual, so long as they are observed with sincerity and moral earnestness.

We cannot do better than end this chapter with a quotation from a recent book by Helmuth von Glasenapp. He writes:

Though it is often stated that Confucius was a philosopher and moralist, not a religious teacher, this is not quite true. Such a judgement is based on the assumption of a religion being exclusively the more or less emotional type of occidental creeds . . . Confucius did not lay down a concise dogmatic teaching about gods and spirits and their relation to men, nor about the nature of life after death, supernatural events, etc. But there is no justification for considering him irreligious on these grounds. Confucius's thought was formed in accordance with his time and his country; he accepted the ancestor cult as obligatory, believed in the efficacy of sacrifices and rites, and therefore in the necessity of their observance. This shows sufficiently that he is not to be considered only as an ethical or political theorist, but also as a religious thinker. Though he was not the founder of a new religion, he certainly is the renovator of an existing one. To Confucius, Heaven was the one and highest world principle. He took Heaven to be a personal being, but saw in it not so much a god who arbitrarily, by means of miracles and revelations, interferes with the course of history and with individual life; rather he considered it to be the regulator of the eternal, cosmic moral law which rules all things in heaven and on earth and keeps them in order.[23]

4.   The Pre-Han Interpreters of Confucius

CONFUCIUS died in the year 479 B.C. at the age of seventy-three. There is no reason to doubt the short notice of his death given in the *Tso Chuan*.[1] Under the sixteenth year of Duke Ai of Lu it records that 'in summer, in the fourth month on the eighteenth day, K'ung Ch'iu died'. The much more detailed account given in the *Li Chi*[2] and copied by Ssǔ-ma Ch'ien in his life of Confucius in the *Historical Records (Shih Chi)* is quite untrustworthy and inconsistent with the character of Confucius as portrayed in the *Analects*. It is quite possible, as is hinted in the *Tso Chuan*, that Duke Ai of Lu, when he heard of the death of the old philosopher-teacher, did as a matter of form send his condolences, but that he should have composed a song of mourning for Confucius in the following extravagant terms is incredible, 'Merciful Heaven, thou hast no compassion upon me, in that thou hast not left me the one aged man fitted to protect me, the Unique One, during the period of my rule. Full of mourning I am in my pain! O woe! Father Ni! Now I no longer have anyone who could serve me as a model.'[3] Such words must be attributed to some later hagiographer. We may be quite sure that Duke Ai did not regard the death of Confucius as being of any great consequence in the affairs of the state. Confucius had been disappointed towards the end of his life in that he had not been accorded the recognition and respect which would have been his had he held public office, and which his disciples felt he richly deserved. At one time, shortly before his death, when Confucius was critically ill, Tzǔ-lu caused some of his disciples to pretend that they were official retainers such as Confucius would have been entitled to had he held office. When Confucius regained consciousness and understood what was going on around him, he reproved Tzǔ-lu with the words, 'How like Yu [Tzǔ-lu] to go in for this sort of imposture! In pretending to have retainers when I have none, whom do I deceive! Do I deceive Heaven? Not only would I far rather die in the arms of you disciples than in the arms of retainers, but also as regards my funeral – even if I am not accorded a state burial, it is not as though I were dying by the roadside.'[4]

The probability is that Confucius died in comparative obscurity, but the small band of disciples, led by Tzǔ-kung, not only ministered to him throughout his last illness but saw to it that he had a decent burial and that all the necessary funeral and mourning rites according to the custom of those days were scrupulously observed. We are informed by Mencius,[5] followed by Ssǔ-ma Ch'ien, that the disciples mourned for three years, the period customary for parents and rulers, and that after they separated Tzǔ-kung built himself a hut by the grave mound and continued to mourn for three years more. It is unlikely that the disciples observed strictly the rules for deep mourning which would have kept them out of public life for a long period, but it is reasonable to believe that the disciples, as they were able, assembled at the grave of Confucius at certain times and seasons of the year and there offered sacrifices to his *manes*. As generation succeeded generation and Confucius came to be more widely honoured, it became customary for Confucians in the state of Lu to continue these rites, and the time came when a temple was erected in his honour and sacrifices made at regular seasons of the year. We are told that the founder of the Han dynasty, though he despised the Confucian scholars and treated them contumaciously, when passing through Lu in the year 196 B.C. visited the tomb of Confucius and sacrificed an ox.[6] By the time of Ssǔ-ma Ch'ien scholars gathered there 'and practised the rites of a communal banquet and held a great archery contest at the grave', 'to contemplate his chariot, his garments and his ceremonial implements' and 'to perform the rites of his house'.[7]

When Confucius died no one could have foretold that within a few generations of his death his teachings would have spread their influence throughout the states which composed China, and that scholars would be proud to call themselves Confucians and spend their efforts in interpreting and enlarging upon his moral and political philosophy. The germinal ideas which are so tersely expressed in various passages in the *Analects* were soon to be taken up and expanded in Confucian works of abiding worth and significance. In this chapter it is our aim to try and trace the process by which a humble scholar and earnest teacher was transformed into the Divine Sage, the uncrowned King, the co-equal of Heaven and Earth. It was a process by which a few simple ethical and political ideas were elaborated and enlarged until they became the ideological system of a great empire, exercising a dominant influence over almost every aspect of life for more than two thousand years.

Chinese scholars have been faced with almost insuperable difficulties as they have sought to make a critical assessment of the early stages of the development of Confucianism, and to adjudge the date and provenance of early Confucian literature. All the early Confucian literature has been preserved to us as a result of the work of Han dynasty scholars. After nearly three centuries of political unrest and almost unremitting warfare there followed a short period of tyrannical despotism when Confucianism was under a cloud, its scholars persecuted and its literature proscribed. Much of the ancient literature was condemned to be burnt.[8] It became an almost superhuman task to collect, edit and publish in an acceptable form all the Confucian lore that could be recovered, much of it dependent on the memories of old scholars. Even as regards that primary source for Confucius and his teaching, the *Analects*, it had been preserved in two different recensions, one from the state of Lu and the other from the neighbouring state of Ch'i, and the problems of authenticity increased when, about 150 B.C. a third copy was discovered when demolishing the wall of a house which had been occupied by Confucius's descendants, a copy written in an ancient script which was unreadable to most scholars. When, therefore, we take any pre-Han literature and use it to illustrate the development of Confucian thought in the period subsequent to his death, we need always to bear in mind the fact that all this literature was preserved by scholars who, however honestly they sought to preserve the original texts which had been produced centuries before, were not only confronted with textual problems of great magnitude such as copyists' errors, transpositions of material, passages which were indecipherable or even lost, but who were themselves inevitably biased in their judgement by the fact that over those intervening centuries, Confucianism had grown into a complex organization of which every contributing part found its justification in so far as it could be actually attributed to Confucius himself.

It is possible, I believe, to become too sceptical so as to leave practically nothing which can be indisputably attributed to Confucius himself. We need constantly to bear in mind that it is not possible positively to declare that any particular passage found in works subsequent to Confucius, purporting to be the actual words of Confucius and usually preceded by the phrase 'The Master says' is in fact to be attributed to him. It is, however, possible to state quite categorically that after Confucius's death his teachings were taken by some of his close disciples and disseminated to an ever widening circle. In this respect we can accept the account given by Ssŭ-ma Ch'ien[9] that, after Confucius's death, his numerous disciples scattered and travelled among the feudal states. The important ones became teachers and ministers of the feudal lords, the lesser ones became friends and teachers of the officials or went into retirement and were no longer seen. These teachings of his became the inspiration of such works as the *Ta Hsüeh*, the *Chung Yung*, *Mencius* and *Hsün-tzŭ* and the *Hsiao Ching*, works which were recognized as being in the Confucian tradition, expounding or enlarging upon important elements in his teaching. Sometimes in these works theories are developed or arguments adduced which go far beyond anything envisaged by Confucius himself, but nevertheless these are works which would never have seen the light of day if their authors had not grown up in the school of Confucianism. Furthermore, as the teachings of Confucius became widely known they roused the opposition and criticism of these who believed that there were better ways of establishing the good life for the individual and for society. It was during the troubled times known to us as the period of the Warring States (403–221 B.C.[10]) that Confucianism contended with many rival philosophies for the minds and the allegiance of princes. When ethical, social and political philosophies arose associated with the names of Mo-tzŭ, Yang Chu, Lao-tzŭ, Chuang-tzŭ, and when many schools of thought developed, Taoists, Logicians, Legalists, etc., they all had to take account of Confucius's teaching, if only to rebut it. Often, rightly or wrongly, they embellished their own writings with sayings of Confucius or anecdotes concerning him in an attempt to justify their own arguments.

It was undoubtedly the example and inspiration of Confucius which led scholars throughout the disturbed period of the Warring States to take a deep interest in the poetry, historical documents and the customary rituals and ceremonies of former times. It was their work which, after much editing, finally emerged in the Han dynasty as the *Confucian Classics*. Even if, as seems likely, Confucius himself wrote none of these *Classics* we do well to call them the *Confucian Classics* because their compilation owes so much to his inspiration.

It is sometimes assumed that great advances in the realm of ideas can only take place in times of peace and under stable government, when philosophers, scientists, artists and writers have abundant leisure to pursue undisturbed their creative activities. In China as in other countries this has not proved to be true. Again and again, times of turmoil and disturbance have been marked by great developments in thought, whilst, as soon as a dynasty has become firmly established, there have been pressures for conformity to a state-recognized orthodoxy, and deviation has been discouraged. In spite of the turbulence and almost incessant warfare throughout the period of the Warring States, there emerged a whole galaxy of first-rate thinkers and several rival ethico-political or philosophical systems developed. Throughout that period the feudal lords were bent on self-aggrandizement, and the more powerful among them undoubtedly had dreams of subjugating the rest and creating a united empire. The more astute, realizing the immense value of having about them fertile and creative thinkers, men with ideas and policies, encouraged noted scholars to settle at their courts, flattering them with marks of respect and bribing them with titles and emoluments. In this there was both opportunity and danger for the scholar. There was opportunity for learned Confucians to encourage the practical application of the fundamental principles of Confucianism. There was danger lest the exalted positions and rich prizes now open to scholars trained in the Confucian tradition should tempt them to become sycophants and hypocrites. We see both these tendencies at work: the first is seen in Mencius, who declared that life itself was of less account than righteousness and was prepared to reprove rulers in no uncertain terms; the second is seen in those Confucians whom Mo-tzŭ castigates, men whose main interest was in ceremonies, music, elaborate funerals and an agnostic belief in Fate.

During this period schools, developed on the lines originated by Confucius, produced a constant stream of trained scholars. These men were allowed to move freely from state to state, and their services were eagerly sought. Debate between rival schools of thought was encouraged at some of the feudal courts, and these debates seem to have aroused great interest. In spite of war – and perhaps in part because of it – there was an expanding economy and a growth of large cities. The lot of the poor peasantry, as Mo-tzŭ shows, was wretched and hopeless, as their sons were recruited to swell the armies and their produce sequestered to meet insatiable demands. But for the educated man the times, though dangerous, were filled with opportunity and challenge. There were Confucian scholars who had a penetrating understanding of the teaching of Confucius which led them to develop their own distinctive philosophies. Such men were the authors of the *Chung Yung*, the *Ta Hsüeh*, *Mencius* and *Hsün-tzŭ*. These works immeasurably enriched Confucianism and added greatly to the esteem in which Confucius was held, but they alone would never have produced the authoritative and orthodox Confucianism of the Han dynasty, which skilfully incorporated into its system elements taken from Mo-tzŭ, the Taoists, the Legalists, together with the cosmological theories of the Yin-Yang and Five Elements [11] schools. In fact, as we shall see later (pp. 125–32), the Confucianism of the Han dynasty was an amalgam of ideas and theories culled from many sources. Some of these ideas were alien to all that Confucius had stood for, but in process of time they were given the imprimatur of his name.

We have already had occasion to refer to the *Ta Hsüeh*, *Chung Yung*, *Mencius*, *Hsün-tzŭ* and the *Hsiao Ching*. It is generally accepted that these works were all composed by Confucians during the Warring States period even though extensive additions were made to some of them at a later period. All of them were destined to play an important role in the developed Confucianism of later times. Each of them placed special emphasis on some aspect of Confucian teaching which appeared to be, in the eyes of the author, of supreme importance. In this way germinal themes which are only briefly stated in the *Analects* were taken up and developed in a more positive, systematic and logical way. Taken together these works give a fairly comprehensive conspectus of the meaning and message of Confucius.

The Ta Hsüeh[12]

The *Ta Hsüeh* or *Great Learning*, traditionally ascribed to Tsêng-tzŭ, one of the greatest of the personal disciples of Confucius, was probably written by some unknown Confucian scholar about the middle of the fourth century B.C., a date suggested by the fact that the essay form in which the book is written did not develop in China much before the middle of that century. The author is a typical Confucian in that he bases his teaching on the conviction that men can be appealed to by reason, that they can be moved by the force of example, and bettered by education. He also believed that it is possible to persuade those who possess power and authority to exercise virtue and seek righteousness, and above all to consider as of paramount importance the welfare of their people. Perhaps the author reveals a too shallow and optimistic estimate of human nature. Certainly he was a good man with high ideals; in all likelihood he was a tutor to princes and composed the book in order to encourage them to become model rulers.

The author saw Confucius first and foremost as an educator, the educator of men for positions of responsibility, power and trust. 'The Way of learning to be great' is therefore his theme, and he follows Confucius in the belief that education must be chiefly concerned with the cultivation of character and the attainment of personal excellence. Personal excellence rests on the cultivation of conscientiousness and consideration for others, the two aspects of human-heartedness (*jên*). He who would be great so as to bear the responsibilities of government must strive after the attainment of three things: to manifest the shining power of moral personality; to exercise love to all the people; to be content only with the highest good. For it is by making goodness the supreme aim of life that one attains tranquillity of mind, equanimity, serenity of life. It is only when the mind is truly tranquil that one can begin to deliberate, and so learn to distinguish between what comes first and what comes last, what is internal and what is external, what is fundamental and what is secondary. Thus, one becomes sure of the main aim of life, and of the processes by which that aim might be achieved.

The author, in stressing the Confucian emphasis on learning, seeks to show that the cultivation of one's personal life is fundamental to the well-being of family and state and the pre-condition of that universal peace which all men profess to desire. But the cultivation of the personal life depends upon the mind being freed from all bias, partiality and prejudice, and on the will being purposive, sincere and without self-deception. These results cannot be attained without the discipline of learning, the kind of learning by which one gains a penetrating insight into the meaning of things, a wide and extensive knowledge and a deep understanding on which one can hope to make true judgements. To quote Professor W. T. Chan,[13] the *Ta Hsüeh* 'gives the Confucian educational, moral and political programs in a nutshell' and 'is the central Confucian doctrine of humanity (*jên*) in application'.

The true worth of this little classic soon came to be recognized so that it was incorporated in the *Li Chi* or *Book of Rites*[14] and later became an essential textbook in the Confucian system of education. What is even more important is that its central teachings were recognized as being based on and inspired by the message of Confucius himself.

The Chung Yung[15]

Though the *Ta Hsüeh* and the *Chung Yung* are usually coupled together, and both were probably written about the same time, they represent very different aspects of Confucian teaching. Whereas the *Ta Hsüeh* is concerned with education, with social and political matters and emphasizes the methods and procedures by which the goal of a perfect society is to be attained, the *Chung Yung* is philosophical, dealing primarily with human nature and the Way of Heaven. To quote W. T. Chan, 'the *Great Learning* is generally rational in tone, but the *Doctrine of the Mean* is religious and mystical'.[16] Yet it is essentially 'a Confucian document, and as such it has never deviated from its central interest in practical affairs'.

The *Chung Yung* is, philosophically speaking, a very considerable development on any of the ideas attributed to Confucius in the *Analects*, and actually deals with topics about which Confucius was reluctant to speak.[17] Nevertheless, the *Chung Yung* is a competent philosophical development of one of the most central beliefs of Confucius, namely that the Way of Man (*Jên Tao*) is intimately related to and dependent on the Way of Heaven (*T'ien Tao*), and that man owes his moral nature to Heaven. In this Confucian doctrine that our moral nature has its roots in the decree (*ming*) of Heaven there is the germinal idea that man and Nature form a unity and that the same fundamental laws underlie both. Yet it remains true that whereas in the *Analects* the characters *chung yung* denote 'moderation', in this work *chung* denotes what is central and generally refers to human nature, whereas *yung* implies what is 'universal and harmonious'. By linking together these two concepts the author argues that the equilibrium and harmony which are characteristic of the Way of Heaven are at the same time the basis and motivating power of human nature as constituted by Heaven. Thus man, in the highest expression of his personality, is linked to that which transcends time and space, substance and motion, and is part of a universal process which is unceasing and eternal.

The *Chung Yung* shows signs of composite authorship.[18] The first part, in which the Confucian theme of moderation is taken up and developed may well be the work of Tzǔ-ssǔ, the grandson of Confucius to whom the work has traditionally been attributed. But there are indications that his original work was expanded later and used in teaching the sons of rulers, for there is a long discussion of the duties, responsibilities and relationships of those who hold political power.[19] The latter part of the book is by a highly religious and philosophical scholar in the Confucian tradition who belonged to a time not earlier than that of the first emperor Chin Shih-Huang-ti (221–209 B.C.). His great concern was the centrality of 'sincerity' (*ch'êng*) or 'being real in oneself' as the quality which, above all others, unites men and Heaven and has power to transform things and bring them to completion.

One of the chief aims of Confucius had been to teach moderation in all things. The noble-minded man avoids going to extremes, and seeks moderation both as regards the expression of opinions and as regards the conduct of affairs. Mencius tells us that Confucius himself abstained from extremes,[20] and the *Analects* says, 'to go too far is as bad as not going far enough'.[21]

This idea of practising moderation is presented to us in the early chapters of the *Chung Yung*,[22] in which the author again and again invokes the authority of Confucius, and also cites the example of the legendary sage-emperor, Shun, who 'was a man of great wisdom who loved to question others and examine their Words, however ordinary. He disregarded what was evil and set forth what was good. Taking hold of the two extremes, and putting into effect the mean between them, he applied it in dealing with the people. This was how he became Shun (the sage-emperor).'[23]

Is not the attainment of the Mean very difficult in practice? It is the purpose of the author of the *Chung Yung* to show that it is in the ordinary relationships of human life, those between rulers and ministers, parents and children, brothers, friends, that one must constantly strive to attain the Mean. This is not easy, for even Confucius acknowledged his failure in this respect. But however difficult, it is the Way of the noble-minded man. The Way to attainment is not followed by separating oneself from one's fellow men, nor by disciplines and asceticisms in rigorous pursuit of some seemingly impossible ideal as some religions seem to suggest, but it is pursued in the common relationships and activities of ordinary life. 'Ordinary men and women, ignorant though they are, have some knowledge of it; and yet, in its perfection, even the sage finds that there is something he does not know.'[24] 'In practising the ordinary virtues, and in the exercise of care in ordinary conversation, when there is deficiency, the gentleman never fails to make further effort, and when there is excess, never dares to go to the limit. His words correspond to his actions, and his actions correspond to his words.'[25]

In the earlier part of the *Chung Yung*, attributed to Tzŭ-ssŭ, there is a passage which suggests that Confucius possessed a religious sensitivity contrasting sharply with the agnostic humanism which, according to many Chinese scholars, characterized him. It is, I believe, well to remember that the minds of great men are many-sided and complex and cannot be pigeon-holed under any particular 'ism'. Chapter 16 of the *Chung Yung* runs as follows: 'The Master said, "How irrepressible is the spiritual power of the *manes*! Look for them and they are not to be seen. Listen for them, and they are not to be heard. They are in things, and there is nothing without them. They stir all the people in the

Great Society to fast and purify themselves and wear their ritual robes, in order that they may sacrifice to them. They fill the air, as if above, as if on the left, as if on the right. As the *Odes* has it: *The coming of the spirits! Incalculable. And yet they cannot be disregarded.*'"[26] If this passage did indeed come from Tzŭ-ssŭ it provides strong testimony to the fact that there was a deeply religious side to Confucius's nature. E. R. Hughes, referring to certain Chinese scholars who doubted whether such a sympathetic appreciation of sacrificial religion was in Confucius's true vein, writes, 'For my own part I do not doubt. He fought certain features in the religion current in his day, and so warned his disciples against spirit-mongering. He believed it was better to keep away from that sort of thing. But where religion seemed to him part and parcel of high ethical endeavour, he was in no sense opposed or indifferent to it. Thus he criticized certain phases of filial-piety religion on the ground of its low ethical standard, but he had a deep reverence for Shun, the sage-king, who was famous for his exquisite filial piety.'[27]

In the first part of the *Chung Yung*, Tzŭ-ssŭ had made it clear that it was the conviction of Confucius that in the very centre of one's being could be established a harmony similar to that which pervaded the universe, and the establishment of that harmony, that 'singleness of purpose' or absolute sincerity was the Way for all good men to tread. The importance of this theme is taken up by the author of the second part of the book, who seeks to show that the Way of Heaven and the Way of the Sage are both characterized by an absolute 'sincerity' or 'singleness of purpose' which lie at the root of all that is great, noble and right, and which form the basis of the transforming and nourishing operations of heaven and earth. 'The Way of Heaven and Earth may be completely described in one sentence: they are without any doubleness and so they produce things in an unfathomable way.' 'Great is the Way of the Sage! Overflowing, it produces and nourishes all things and rises up to the light of heaven.' 'Only the perfect sage in the world has quickness of apprehension, intelligence, insight and wisdom, which enable him to rule all men; magnanimity, generosity, benignity and tenderness, which enable him to embrace all men; vigour, strength, firmness and resolution, which enable him to maintain a firm hold; orderliness, seriousness, adherence to the Mean, and correctness, which enable him to be reverent ... He appears and all the people respect him, speaks, and all the people believe him, acts and all the people are pleased with him. Consequently, his fame spreads ... he is a counterpart of Heaven.' 'Only those who are absolutely sincere can order and adjust the great relations of mankind, establish the great foundations of humanity, and know the transforming and nourishing operations of heaven and earth.'[28] This absolute sincerity by which a man is true to himself and loyal to others is the 'central harmony' stressed in the *Chung Yung*, and this has been the basis of Confucian philosophy and life down through the centuries.

Mencius

Of all the pre-Han interpreters of Confucius, Mencius is recognized as the greatest, second only to Confucius himself. Yet his influence only gradually asserted itself, for Hsün Chi'ng, who was growing to maturity when Mencius was an old man, exerted a greater influence on the Confucianism which emerged during the Han dynasty. Mencius (*c.* 390–305 B.C.), whose name in its Chinese form was Mêng K'o, was born a century after the death of Confucius and grew up to follow a similar pattern of life. He was a great student of history, and became familiar with the *Odes* and *Documents* which he liberally quotes in his own writings. He became a teacher with his own following of disciples, and an adviser of princes, though his idealistic and highly moral teachings concerning government seldom seem to have been acted upon. He aspired to hold high office and was given the rank and title of minister of state at the court of Ch'i but he does not seem to have played a significant role in the state councils, and remained throughout life an obscure teacher.

The *Works of Mencius*, of which many translations into English are available,[29] follows the pattern of the *Analects*, though many of the paragraphs are longer and the treatment fuller. But, as with the *Analects*, there is very little attempt at logical sequence or arrangement under the various topics discussed.

Mencius himself defined his mission in life as that of perpetuating the influence of Yü the Great,[30] the Duke of Chou and Confucius: 'I also wish to rectify men's hearts, and put an end to perverse doctrines; to oppose their one-sided actions and put away their licentious expressions, thus to carry on the work of these three sages.'[31] Just as Confucius conceived himself as having been given a unique mission to transmit the doctrine of the ancient sages and uphold the culture of King Wên, the founder of the Chou dynasty, so Mencius conceived his task to be the transmission of the teachings of Confucius in their purity. 'From Confucius down to the present day there have been more than one hundred years. Thus I am not yet far from the generation of that sage, and am extremely close to the place where he lived. Under these circumstances is there no one [to transmit his doctrines]? Yes, is there indeed no one?' 'Now what I desire to do is to study to be like Confucius!'[32]

Already in Mencius the process which led to the apotheosis of Confucius in the Han dynasty is in evidence. He regards Confucius as the greatest of all sages since the days of far antiquity. When asked if the two sages, Po-i and I-yin, could be ranked along with Confucius he replied, 'No, since there were living men until now, there never was [another] Confucius.'[33] He assumed that Confucius occupied the high position of minister of justice in the state of Lu, and that he voluntarily left that office because he was not accorded by the prince the respect that was his due, and because his advice was disregarded.[34] He believed that Confucius only took office when he was convinced that the practice of his principles was possible, and when he himself was properly received and supported. He affirmed that Confucius also held office under Duke Ling and Duke Hsiao of Wei.[35] He even argued that Confucius was not called from his humble station in life to be supreme ruler over the country, as were Shun and Yü the Great in ancient times, because Heaven could not set aside the legitimate heir to the throne since he had not, like the tyrants Chieh and Chou, rebelled against the majesty of Heaven and therefore must be deposed.[36] He was, however, in no doubt that the virtue of Confucius in the sight of Heaven equalled that of Shun and Yü. It was in the light of this doctrine of Mencius that Confucius became for later generations 'the king who was never crowned'. Mencius's estimate of Confucius was based on an extensive knowledge of his teachings. He quoted from the *Analects* on many occasions,[37] but also seems to have had at his disposal a collection of the sayings of Confucius which are not recorded in the *Analects*.[38]

In the time between the death of Confucius and the manhood of Mencius great developments had taken place. Confucianism was only one among several rival systems. Mencius was particularly concerned to demonstrate the superiority of Confucianism over the teachings of Mo-tzǔ, whose altruistic doctrine of universal love was thought by Mencius to be destructive of the special relationships of family life, and Yang Chu, whose self-regarding hedonism was deemed to be contrary to the loyalty owed to one's ruler. These doctrines, according to Mencius, were flooding the country and he saw in the teachings of Confucius an antidote to their poison.

Turning now to the development by Mencius of Confucius's teaching, we find that what Mencius conceived to be most central and important were the Confucian virtues of human-heartedness (*jên*) and justice (*i*). In working out the implications of human-heartedness and justice in their applications to political life and to family and social relations, Mencius went much further than his master Confucius, and developed a political philosophy which was to have a profound and permanent effect on government in China. Mencius was also far more concerned than was Confucius over questions dealing with human nature, and in particular the question as to what differentiates a human being from animals and makes him characteristically human. According to Mencius, there is fundamentally very little to distinguish men from animals. Like them, man is possessed of an animal nature with the senses of seeing, hearing and so on, but, unlike them, there has been bestowed upon him by Heaven an intelligence, a mind which can think and reason, and a capacity to know what is just and right and what is a fitting expression of one's humanity. It is this part of human nature which he calls 'great', and the wise and noble expend their utmost efforts to cultivate it. Inferior people, on the other hand, expend most of their efforts in cultivating those parts of their nature which they share with animals, and neglect the cultivation of what is peculiarly human.[39]

Mencius takes up the essential virtues which had been expounded by Confucius, especially the virtues of human-heartedness (*jên*), justice (*i*), propriety (*li*) and wisdom (*chih*), and shows how at least the early beginnings of, or 'tendencies' towards, these virtues are common to all men. Human nature is fundamentally good, having been bestowed by Heaven, but it needs individual effort, education, good government and the example of the great and good to bring these 'beginnings' to full fruition. Mencius insists that all men have within them the capacity to become a sage, like Yao or Shun. 'Human-heartedness is the [proper] quality of man's mind, and justice is man's [proper] path.'[40] Unfortunately, the majority of men neglect the path of justice and lose their human-heartedness and do not know how to regain it. Men, who are extremely sensitive to physical defects and will make every effort to overcome them, are not sensible to moral and mental defects. In all this Mencius goes far beyond Confucius, but nevertheless his exposition is simply an extension of the teachings of Confucius on the primacy of human-heartedness and justice. By means of numerous illustrations and examples Mencius revealed that he believed that what a man ought to be in himself is human-hearted, and that he ought to act towards others in all human relationships with justice. For the ruler who possesses these qualities the goal of true kingship is not impossible. That goal is the prosperity of his state, the perpetuation of his line and ultimately the allegiance of all men.

The political, social and economic implications of this fundamental teaching concerning human-heartedness and justice are brought out by Mencius, and in this also he goes far beyond Confucius. He seems to have been regarded by some of the rulers of his day as an impractical idealist whose moral teachings would prove to be impossible of application in a disturbed and warlike age. Confucius had pointed out that the aim of government should be to 'enrich and educate the people'.[42] For Mencius the basis of his political and social philosophy was that all government is established for the benefit of the people. They are Heaven's primary concern. Hence, the only legitimate ruler is he who governs by moral force (*tê*) which is engendered by human-heartedness and strict justice. People will be so delighted to live under a human-hearted ruler that they will all wish to co-operate with him in every way possible, so that the country will be immeasurably enriched.[42] Mencius pictures a utopian society as a result of benevolent government: 'An enlightened prince provides for his people's livelihood, ensuring that they have sufficient on the one hand to nurture their aged, and on the other to feed adequately their wives and children . . . There has never been a state where the elderly had silk to wear and meat to eat and the common people were neither starving nor cold and the king was other than a True King.'[43] A ruler who relies on military force is unfitted to rule.[44] Consequently, Mencius deprecates the rule of the tyrant (*pa*) and advances the doctrine that when the conduct of a ruler becomes vicious and evil Heaven sends down repeated warnings which are revealed in the discontent of the people and in economic disaster. If these warnings go unheeded by the ruler, then Heaven transfers its mandate to rule to another who has not only the right to rebel but the duty to do so in obedience to the promptings of Heaven. Mencius showed both his boldness and his independence in putting forth such a doctrine in an age when rulers exercised autocratic control and absolute power over the lives of their subjects. In his writings Mencius boldly criticized the extravagance of rulers, especially as it was paid for by exorbitant taxation, forced labour, land enclosure and an embittered and starving peasantry. His ideal government was that of the 'kingly way' which would ensure that all men would be able to 'nourish their living and bury their dead without dissatisfaction'. But mere material satisfactions are not enough. Mencius would have the ruler institute schools whereby the people could be given teaching in the basic human relationships.

Like Confucius, Mencius was a great student of history and found his ideal in the 'way of the former kings'. He idealized the reign of King Wên who had lived seven hundred years before his time. He believed that the re-application of the agrarian and educational policies of ancient times would work out to the economic advantage of the country.[45]

Hsün Ch'ing (Hsün-tzǔ, c. 320–235 B.C.) [46]

Hsün-tzǔ lived in the stirring times which presaged the final collapse of the Chou dynasty and the establishment of a Chinese empire under Ch'in Shih Huang Ti. Disciples of his, and in particular Li Ssǔ, have been credited with much of the responsibility for the oppressive totalitarian regime of that emperor. A native of the state of Chao, Hsün-tzǔ became a leading Confucian scholar, but it was not till he had reached the age of fifty that he went to Ch'i where he was able to spread his teachings. He had the high honour of presenting the wine offering at the Great Sacrifice three times. He left Ch'i because of being slandered and finally settled in a comparatively lowly position as magistrate of Lan-ling in Ch'u (in present-day South Shantung). There he died in 235 B.C.[47] His writings, probably more influential than any other early interpreter of Confucianism in moulding the Confucian orthodoxy, were finally collected and published some two hundred years after his death by imperial command. They comprise thirty-two books, edited by Liu Hsiang (80–9 B.C.).

Attaining maturity soon after Mencius died, Hsün-tzŭ became the most prominent advocate of the Confucian tradition and its ardent defender. Like Mencius, he was an orthodox follower of Confucius but whereas Mencius placed his main emphasis on human-heartedness (jên) and justice (i), Hsün-tzŭ emphasized external authority and exalted li, or the rules of proper conduct, as the basis of morality. Whereas Mencius believed in the fundamental goodness of human nature and sought human perfection through the nurture, training and development of the 'shoots of goodness' which were in all men, Hsün-tzŭ believed that human nature, being originally evil, tends naturally towards vice, and therefore needs external restraints if social life is to be possible. Hsün-tzŭ therefore emphasized the need for rules of conduct and standards of action, and these he found pre-eminently in the li which had been devised by the sages of old and which were upheld and exemplified by an authoritarian ruler.

Undoubtedly in Confucius there is to be found a great respect for authority, and a recognition that each individual has his appropriate place in a political and social hierarchy. He accepted that civilized life is governed by an elaborate system of rights and privileges and sustained by customary rules, rites and ceremonies. Confucius, as we have seen, placed li very high among the virtues. But Hsün-tzŭ took this aspect of his teaching and made it the basis of his ethical and political system. More than any other early Confucian, he exalted the principle of authority: to quote Professor Dubs, 'He gave a philosophical foundation to the authoritarianism which has been one of the fundamental characteristics of Confucianism throughout the ages.'[48] He found in li the basis of morality and the standard of action both for the individual and for government.

More of a philosopher than Mencius and with a more logical mind, Hsün-tzŭ wrote connected compositions on a great variety of subjects, including government, education, psychology, philosophy and on the practical problems of administration. He wrote with cogency, closeness of reasoning and great analytical power. He produced a coherent analysis of human nature and of human society. To quote Professor Dubs again, 'He gave a stable and consistent foundation and expression to the Confucian philosophy, developing its logical implications, defending it and founding it firmly on an analysis of human nature and of history.'[49] Consequently Hsün-tzŭ's interpretation of Confucianism had a very great influence during the Han dynasty and some of his work was incorporated in the *Li Chi* and in the writings of Ssŭ-ma Ch'ien.

Like Confucius before him, Hsün-tzŭ was a practical philosopher. He aimed at the political goal of an ideal state and everything else was subservient to this ideal. Consequently, the problem of morality, as Hsün-tzŭ saw it, was that of the adjustment of the individual to others within a complex society, and the guiding element in such social adjustment was *li*. The *li* were therefore an external authority imposed upon all, and the basis of Hsün-tzŭ's ethics is that the well-being of the individual and of society as a whole rests on the acceptance by the individual and by society of that external authority.

If *li*, then, is the basis of all morality, how did *li* originate in the first place? When Hsün-tzŭ addressed himself to this problem he was unable to make use of a solution which is common to most religious systems – that the rules of morality are divinely revealed, imposed on men or given to men through divine inspiration or some supernatural agency. According to Hsün-tzŭ, Heaven is purely naturalistic; it is unvarying law or Nature. 'Heaven has a constant regularity of activity ... Respond to it with good government, and success will result. Respond to it with misgovernment, and calamity will result ... To make complete without acting, and to obtain without seeking: that is what is meant by the activities of Heaven ... Heaven has its seasons. Earth has its material resources, man has his government. That is what is meant when it is said that man is able to form a trinity with Heaven and Earth.'[50] W. T. Chan makes the comment that 'the influence of supernatural forces over man is completely ruled out by Hsün-tzǔ. What he calls spirit is but cosmic change and evolution. To him, in religious sacrifice, whether there are really spiritual beings to receive them or not does not matter. The important thing is one's attitude, especially sincerity, in the performance. These sacrifices are "ornaments" or refined manifestations of an inner attitude.'[51] 'Instead of regarding Heaven as great and admiring it, why not foster it as a thing and regulate it? Instead of obeying Heaven and singing praises to it, why not control the Mandate of Heaven and use it?'[52] Hsün-tzǔ criticizes the people's superstitious beliefs in spirits, omens, divination, and so on. Such things as eclipses, wind and rain at unseasonable times, strange occurrences of nature, are due to the natural evolutions of *yin* and *yang* and should not be feared as omens. For happiness and human well-being are fundamentally based on human effort. 'When stars fall or trees make a [strange] noise, all people in the state are afraid and ask, Why? I reply: there is no need to ask why. These are changes of heaven and earth, the transformation of *yin* and *yang*, and rare occurrences. It is all right to marvel at them, but wrong to fear them.' 'When people pray for rain, it rains. Why? I say: there is no need to ask why. It is the same as when it rains when no one prays for rain. When people try to save the sun or moon from being eclipsed, or when they pray for rain in a drought, or when they decide an important affair only after divination, they do so not because they believe they will get what they are after, but to use them as ornament to government measures. Hence the ruler intends them to be an ornament, but the common people believe they are supernatural.'[53] Hsün-tzǔ believed that man must depend solely on human efforts to achieve a good life and must place no reliance on supernatural agencies. To that end man's efforts must be directed to the cultivation of virtue and to the promotion of good government.

Hsün-tzǔ, however, was faced with the problem of finding a philosophical basis for an external moral authority without provoking any doctrine of divine inspiration. He did this by developing a purely humanistic philosophy of history. He believed that man is congenitally evil, but at the same time he possesses intelligence and a capacity for knowledge. Being a social animal, and dominated by his emotions and self-interest, he soon found that the only way to avoid self-destruction was to recognize and apply certain standards of behaviour. These standards acted as a restraint on man's natural tendencies, but were absolutely necessary if man was to have any kind of decent life. Certain men developed their intelligence and their capacity for knowledge far more than others, and were therefore exalted and recognized as rulers. These rulers had to be men whose wisdom and correctness of judgement could be relied on. So it was that sages ruled in ancient times, and all men gave obedience to them. It was they who gradually built up a great corpus of rules, ceremonials and rites by which alone society could function. Thus, the external authority on which Hsün-tzǔ bases all morality is the authority of the sage-king, the wise man who has learned the art of government. The *li* are the rules of proper conduct established by the sages of old and so they become the foundation of all civilization and culture.

Hsün-tzǔ had no belief in democracy. For him, as indeed for Confucius before him, the ruler was absolute, but he needed to be a sage-king. Once remove the authority of the sovereign and the whole society would disintegrate into chaos. 'Without a sovereign to keep his subjects in order . . . the whole of society is injured and unbridled desire is born.'[54] 'Men's nature is evil, and the fact is that because of this sage-kings in the past saw men as reprobates and wholly out of true . . . and therefore set up the authority of an over-ruling sovereign to be a blessing to men; set forth ritual (*li*) and justice (*i*) in order to effect the transformation of men; made a beginning with the rectifying influence of laws in order to exercise control over men; enhanced the severity of punishments in order to restrain men.' 'Remove the authority of the sovereign and the transforming effects of ritual (*li*) and justice (*i*), and watch how men will treat each other. The strong would rob and maltreat the weak, the many would oppress and shout down the few. In no time there would be universal anarchy, everybody destroying everybody else.'[55] So, according to Hsün-tzǔ, kingship was necessary, but the ruler must be a sage in order to govern properly; otherwise, government would be tyrannical. Kingship should be by the most worthy and hence should not be hereditary. In this he agreed with Mencius. But the king must have absolute power, because human nature, being evil, could not be allowed freedom. Equality in wealth and rank would only lead to quarrelling, followed by anarchy and penury, and so there should be degrees and inequalities of station. But it was the duty of a ruler to advance the worthy and competent in the service of the state without depending on seniority.[56]

In exalting *li* to be the greatest of all virtues and, indeed, the sum of all virtues, and in including under it all the observances of morality, whilst at the same time giving to it a purely rational foundation, Hsün-tzǔ was, perhaps more than any other early Confucianist, responsible for the humanistic and agnostic development within Confucianism. Yet even he had to come to terms with the fact that a great part of their *li* was directly concerned with religious rites and ceremonies, such as the funeral, mourning and sacrificial rites. The very term *li* is itself made up of elements betokening 'worship' and 'sacrificial vessels', and this Hsün-tzǔ well knew, but he argued that such rites and ceremonies were necessary, not because they gave any satisfaction to the spirits of the deceased (which were, in fact, non-existent) or to any super-human beings functioning in a spiritual realm, but because such rites and ceremonies gave a poetical interpretation to the emotions of thankfulness, grief and sorrow, thus beautifying human existence. Rites are the beautiful expression of emotions. Sacrifice consists of beautiful actions which give expression and relief to human emotions. The early kings established ceremonies for the purpose of honouring the honoured and loving the beloved to the utmost. 'Hence I say: sacrifice is because of the emotions produced by memories, ideas, thoughts and longings; it is the extreme of loyalty, faithfulness, love and reverence; it is the greatest thing of the rites [*li*] and of beautiful actions ... Hence the bells, drums, pipes, stone chimes, lyres, lutes, reeds and organs ... are that whereby the superior man adapts himself to the situation in beautifully expressing his joy. Mourning garments, a rush staff, living in a hovel, eating rice gruel, using firewood for a chair and clods for a pillow – this is the way the superior man has of adapting himself to the situation in beautifully expressing his sorrow and distress.'[57]

For Hsün-tzǔ the purpose of *li* is to educate and nourish human nature, and in doing so the distinction between superior and inferior which forms the basis of human society is recognized. Like Confucius he does not accept the doctrine of human equality. Society is organized on the basis of social inequality. The *li*, by emphasizing political and social inequalities and the duties implicit in the relationships of ruler and ruled, father and son, husband and wife, form the basis of government both within the family and within the state. The *li* also form the basis of education, providing the standard to which every individual should train himself.

Hsün-tzǔ had a great faith, as indeed had most Confucians, in the power of example and education, and in self-cultivation. He differs little from Confucius and Mencius in his belief that in virtue there is power to rise to the highest position, and that the lessons of history taught that virtue is necessarily rewarded and vice punished. In spite of his rationalism, he conceived of *li* as a metaphysical principle, and identified it with *tao*. '*Li* is that whereby Heaven and Earth unite, whereby the sun and moon are bright, whereby the four seasons are ordered, whereby the stars move in their courses, whereby rivers flow, whereby all things prosper, whereby love and hatred are tempered, whereby joy and anger keep their proper place . . . Is not *li* the greatest of all principles? When it is established grandly, it becomes the centre of all, and the whole world will not be able to subtract from or add to it . . . The rules of proper conduct [*li*] are the utmost of human morality [*tao*] . . . They who follow *li* and are satisfied with it are gentlemen who have a direction to their life . . . He who is able to think deeply and to be firm and adds to that a love of *li* is a sage. For as Heaven is the utmost in height, and earth is the utmost in depth, the compass points are the utmost in breadth, so the sage is the utmost in *tao*. Hence the student who resolutely studies *li* becomes a sage.'[58]

Hsün-tzǔ was undoubtedly among the greatest of the early interpreters of Confucius, yet though he exerted a great influence upon Confucianism in the Han dynasty, he was in large measure neglected after that until the nineteenth century. It was then that he began to have a special attraction for the modern Chinese because, in the words of W. T. Chan, 'of his naturalism, his realism, his emphasis on logic, his belief in progress, his stress on law, and his sound criticism of the various philosophical schools'.[59]

The Hsiao Ching or Classic of Filial Piety

In the *Analects* there are recorded many sayings of Confucius on filial piety. In its earlier usage it seems to have meant piety towards the spirits of the dead ancestors, but in the *Analects*, although this meaning is frequent, it also means the attitude of obedience and reverence towards living parents.[60] This duty to one's parents is linked to an attitude of respect towards one's elder brothers. 'Surely proper behaviour towards parents and elder brothers is the trunk of goodness?'[61] 'While they are alive serve them according to the rules of proper conduct [*li*]. When they die, bury them according to *li*, and sacrifice to them according to *li*.'[62] In stressing filial piety and brotherly affection, Confucius was emphasizing that the closest of human relationships are those within the family, and in those close and intimate relationships the highest qualities of personality may find their development. But Confucius was not responsible for exalting the virtue of filial piety above all other virtues. After his time, during the fourth century B.C., Confucians regarded *hsiao* as extremely important in the sense of care for, duty towards and obedience to living parents. By the time the *Hsiao Ching* was written this was supreme among all the virtues.

The *Hsiao Ching*, as we possess it in its present form, was the work of a Han dynasty pietist who drastically revised a much earlier work, a work which was already being quoted by the middle of the third century B.C. According to J. Legge, the *Hsiao Ching* can be traced back to within less than a century after the death of Confucius, and purports to record conversations between Confucius and his disciple, Tsêng-tzŭ.[63] On the other hand, Fung Yu-lan writes that the doctrine that filial piety is the source of all virtues must have arisen comparatively late.[64] It may, in all probability, be ascribed to the school of Tsêng-tzŭ, but its date and authorship remain unknown. Confucians came to regard the family as the incubator of morality. The *Chung Yung* emphasized the filial piety of the ancient sages,[65] 'Consider Shun, a man of superb filial piety', whilst Mencius wrote, 'There has never been a man possessing human-heartedness who neglected his parents.'[66] It may be that some Confucians saw in the disintegration of so many ancient and noble families during the Warring States period the main reason for growing instability and social anarchy, and so they insisted on the primary importance of family life.

The *Hsiao Ching* is a book of eighteen short chapters. Its influence has been out of all proportion to its size. It had great vogue during the Han dynasty, and was later a favourite composition of many of the greatest of China's rulers. It is a thoroughly Confucian book in the way it quotes the examples of ancient kings and sages, regarding them as the ones who preeminently exercised the virtue of filial piety and encouraged their people in the practice of it. According to the *Hsiao Ching* they showed filial piety in their attitude to Heaven, and in their government of the people. The book sets forth as the ideal government one in which the ruler is everywhere regarded as the parent of his people, who form a huge family. On his side he exercises benevolence and justice towards all his subjects, while they, for their part, render obedience and dutiful service according to their ability. This concept of government has had an enormous influence in Chinese history and has proved to be a stabilizing and unifying force.

We have seen in this chapter how several of the formative ideas of Confucius found expression and amplification in the writings of his followers during the closing centuries of the Chou dynasty. All this time Confucianism was only one of several systems of political and ethical thought which were contending for the allegiance of intelligent and educated people. Mohists, Hedonists, Taoists, Legalists, Agronomists, the Yin-Yang school, were all setting forth their different panaceas for social ills which were obvious to all. The developments and amplifications of Confucius's teaching resulted, on the one hand, from the practical need to find a solution to social and political problems, and on the other from the need to combat the criticisms of non-Confucian schools, and prove the superiority of Confucius above all other philosophers. In the continuing debate between the various schools of thought, Confucianism was greatly enriched, but also contaminated, so that the Confucianism which finally emerged in the Han dynasty was something very different from that of Confucius himself.

At the time of Confucius a process was only in its early beginnings which was to lead to the break-up of the so-called feudalistic system established by the early Chou kings, and the founding of a vast empire, centrally controlled, and administered by an army of trained officials who formed a scholarly élite. Confucius looked back to a society with a graded hierarchy, in which heredity determined one's station in life, and in which every person had his stated duties and obligations to fulfil. At the top of this graded structure was the king, the Son of Heaven, holding Heaven's mandate to rule. He governed by the power of his moral personality (*tê*), and all the relationships of life were governed by the Rules of Proper Conduct (*li*) and not by codified law. Confucius believed that peace and prosperity would result from a return to such an idealized system. But such a return to the past was impossible. As D. Bodde points out, 'Government of this kind, being based upon personal contact between ruler and subject, and upon the influence of *li*, is one ideally fitted for a small state having a stable homogeneous culture and a fixed population . . . Government in a state of this kind is a paternalistic one, similar in many ways to that existing within the family clan, which, since earliest times, has been the basis of Chinese society.'[67] Already in the time of Confucius, under the pressure of vast economic and social changes, there was growing up in the minds of leading statesmen the concept of a code of law applicable to all. By the middle of the third century B.C., Han Fei Tzŭ was encouraging the ruler of the state of Ch'in to establish the authority of law over all his subjects, suppressing by force all ideas which did not accord with it. 'The establishment of laws and orders is done so as to do away with private standards. When laws and orders are practised, private ways of conduct will disappear. Private standards are what throw the laws into confusion . . . What gives good government is law; what brings disorder is private standards. When law has been established, no one is permitted to have any private standards.'[68] The strict and universal application of law, with harsh penalties for those who disobeyed, was the instrument used by the Legalists to strengthen the power and prestige of the ruler and to bring all into subjection to his will. It resulted in the absolutism of the ruler of Ch'in, who conquered all the other states and finally unified China under one head in 221 B.C., taking the title Shih-Huang-ti. His government was only possible through the use of brute force, and it is to the credit of many Confucians of his day that they fearlessly attacked this idea of autocratic, totalitarian and punitive government, and by doing so brought upon themselves a fierce persecution.

When the short-lived Ch'in dynasty was overthrown and the Han dynasty established it was found that, in administering and controlling a vast empire, many of the ideas and innovations of Ch'in had to be retained. On the other hand, the need for a large body of trained and educated men to carry on the day-to-day government of the empire led the way for the triumph of Confucianism. The emphasis which Confucianism had always placed on education, on human-heartedness and justice, on loyalty and good faith, and on long-established and customary rules of behaviour was eminently suited to meet the needs of a new era. The Confucian scholars made themselves indispensable. The way to state employment was through the Confucian examination system, and the Confucian disciplines became the basis of education. Now it was that, under the ruler, Confucians came to occupy the most powerful positions in the empire, and, as so often happens in history, men who not long before had been denigrated and persecuted, became the persecutors of those who deviated from an established Confucian orthodoxy.

Part 2

A Confucian Civilization

5. The Triumph of Confucianism in the Han Dynasty

IN the last chapter it was pointed out that during the Warring States period (400–221 B.C.), when the great Chou dynasty was in its death-throes, many other ideologies were competing with Confucianism for the allegiance of men's minds. Probably the first and greatest rivals of the Confucians were the Mohists, followers of Mo-tzŭ (*c.* 479–438 B.C.). Over a considerable period of time his teachings had a widespread appeal, so that Mencius lamented that his teachings and adherents filled the kingdom.[1]

Mo-tzŭ had not only preached an altruistic love for all, without discrimination, but had based his teachings on love and righteousness in a belief that Heaven (*T'ien*) is an omnipotent spiritual power which exercises a will towards benevolence and righteousness. The Mohists also emphasized the spirit-fraught nature of the universe, and encouraged the worship of the spirits. At least among the general populace the religious beliefs and practices of the Mohists had a far greater appeal than the agnosticism of the Confucians. Besides this influence exerted by the Mohists, the practitioners of the ancient magico-religious system, exorcists and shaman-diviners, had a widespread appeal, an appeal by no means confined to the illiterate peasantry, but often attracting support from court circles.[2] Later on, in the Han dynasty, when Confucianism became dominant and Mohism practically disappeared as an organized system, Confucianism came to terms with and in some measure absorbed into itself religious and even superstitious beliefs and practices which were endemic among the general populace.

Throughout the fourth and third centuries B.C., interest was growing in questions relating to the origin and nature of the universe, the nature of man and his place in the scheme of things. Beliefs of an earlier age had envisaged a universe controlled by spiritual powers whose will and pleasure could be discovered by means of the arts of divination, and whose actions could be influenced by lavish sacrifices and by prayer. No doubt most of the common people still clung to these ancient beliefs, but from the time of Confucius onwards, thinkers in general had come to accept belief in a rational, well-ordered and dynamic universe controlled, not by some anthropomorphic deity, but by the natural and inevitable operation of elemental forces. Scholars could find in the teaching of Confucius no concern at all with philosophical and cosmological speculations which were now, more and more, occupying the minds of intelligent men, but the *Tao Tê Ching*, the writings of Chuang-tzǔ, the *Yin-Yang* and Five Elements theories and the Philosophy of Change, which were all developing at this time, were not only providing satisfying and stimulating answers, but were also being recognized by Confucians as a fitting philosophical basis for their own system. A process of syncretism was in evidence. Generations of Confucian scholars were growing up who, whilst acknowledging their supreme debt to Confucius, were taking over and making their own the ideas of thinkers who had been strong opponents of Confucianism.

In particular, Confucians came to accept the theory that the universe was one of perpetual change and unremitting activity. It had come into being and was eternally sustained by the interaction, within a primaeval unity (*T'ai I*) of two opposite and complementary cosmic forces, the *Yin* and the *Yang*. All the myriad phenomena of nature were seen to be primarily the result of the interplay of *Yin* and *Yang*. Man himself, being an integral part of nature, was also the result of the interplay of these cosmic forces. They constituted by their interaction and harmony the life-force within him. The same forces working in human history take the form of cycles which issue in the development of society, morality and civilization. These have their slow maturing, and then their period of decline, and their final demise, at which point another cycle begins its course. As Fung Yu-lan writes, 'The arts of divination practised in antiquity, those of astrology, the almanac, and the Five Elements, all laid emphasis on the relationship believed to exist between "the Way of Heaven" and human affairs. This form of thinking was further developed by the *Yin-Yang* school ... which had a tendency to coalesce with a section of the Confucian school.'[3]

Another school which was rapidly growing in influence during the fourth and third centuries B.C. was what is known as the Legalist School (*Fa Chia*).[4] The teachings of this school were in almost every respect abhorrent to the Confucians. Their ruthless application led to the rise to absolute power of the First Emperor (Ch'in Shih Huang-ti), the unification of China, the destruction of a feudalistic form of society, and the proscription of Confucian literature. The Legalist movement had received great impetus from the teachings of Shang Yang,[5] prime minister of Ch'in (*d.* 338 B.C.) who had little use for the Confucian ideas on the cultivation of virtue, the nurture of individual personality, the need for harmony in social relationships, and the duty of a ruler to put first the interests of the people. In place of the Confucian emphasis on moral principles and moral persuasion, the Legalists advocated one law for all, which the ruler should vigorously apply. The interests of the state must completely override the interests of the individual, and in order to build up a strong state the energies of the people must be directed towards primary production and the building up of a large and efficient army. Unfortunately, as the interests of the state came to be identified with the arbitrary will of the ruler, the inevitable result was tyranny. If the wealth and security of a state could only be guaranteed by emphasizing the importance of agriculture and the army and drafting into these employments practically the whole of the population, a rigorous control had to be exercised. People could not be allowed to decide for themselves; their employment and way of life had to be directed from above, and all opposition to politics which the ruler deemed to be for the good of the state had to be ruthlessly suppressed. Social gradings, with higher and lower ranks, were recognized as inevitable in a society in which talents and ability varied enormously, but Legalism proclaimed that all must be subjected to the law, and the laws set forth in such clear and simple form that they could be really understood, so that those who broke them would have no excuse.

The doctrines of the Legalists ruthlessly applied over a number of years in the state of Ch'in made that state so powerful that its ruler was able to achieve victory over all the other states and bring about the unification of China. With the unification a new political system came into being to replace the feudalistic kind of society which had existed for hundreds of years. There was a centralization of authority which made possible the enactment of many laws which were of undoubted benefit to the people. The peasants were no longer attached to the land as virtual chattels of their masters, but were themselves given the right to own, buy and sell land. Efforts were made to standardize the currency and weights and measures. Communications were vastly improved and travel facilitated by making the gauge of all the wheels of carts throughout the empire equal.[6] A reform which was to prove of great importance for Han dynasty Confucianism was the standardization and simplification of the script, and the more common use of a style of writing known as the *Li* or clerk script.[7] In the words of Bodde, what Li Ssŭ, the minister of Ch'in Shih Huang-ti, did was to 'simplify the cumbrous seal forms current before his time, standardize variant forms into one coherent system, and make this system universal throughout China'.[8]

In spite of these reforms, which were to have a great effect on the development of Confucianism throughout the Han dynasty, the oppression of the people under the short-lived Ch'in dynasty, the brutal disregard for human life and human dignity, and the harsh penal laws of what amounted to a police-state, led to such a revulsion among the Chinese that with the fall of Ch'in the Legalist school was discredited and rejected. Nevertheless, it remains true that Legalism made important contributions to the Confucianism which finally emerged in the Han dynasty. Many measures advocated during the Ch'in dynasty (221–206 B.C.) helped to make possible the dominance of Confucianism in the Han dynasty over all other ideologies. This is particularly true in three respects.

First, when Liu Pang rose to power as the first emperor of the Han dynasty, although he did at first re-establish fiefs for loyal dependants and his own relatives, he followed the Ch'in precedent of dividing the empire into provinces and districts which were controlled by governors and magistrates who were appointed by and directly responsible to the central government. 'The new feudalism, or rather the façade of feudalism under which the Han Emperor concealed the hard fact of autocracy, was very different from the old. The new kings ruled over small and diminished territories. Their states formed enclaves in the midst of provinces governed by imperial officers in the Ch'in manner. They were frequently displaced, either to be given a new kingdom in some other part of the empire, or to be degraded altogether.'[9] Subsequently the break-up of the feudal estates by the simple expedient of compelling the princes to bequeath their estates to be divided among all their children, making no special provision for the eldest son, further assisted in what was in effect a stupendous social revolution.[10] Whilst the power of the feudal princes was thus diminished, the influence of a government bureaucracy increased steadily. To administer effectively a vast empire of thirteen provinces, divided into prefectures and districts, demanded the services of a huge army of educated and trained officials. The scholars enlisted for this purpose belonged in the main to that body of Confucian scholars who had formerly regarded the feudalistic system as sacrosanct. Thus Confucianism came into its own because it and it alone could supply an educated scholarly élite to administer the affairs of a rapidly expanding empire, growing wealthy by increased trade and production, and with extensive urban development.

Secondly, the demands of the state organization revealed the need for a great development in education. The Confucians, with their special emphasis on education, were peculiarly fitted to meet this need. The Ch'in dynasty, though it had proscribed and attempted to destroy the ancient texts, made possible this growing emphasis on education by on the one hand unifying the written script and on the other hand making easy communications to all parts of the empire through a system of radial roads which went out from the capital. When the proscription of ancient literature was removed, scholars had in a standardized form of script a magnificent tool at their disposal, whilst the system of communications made possible a wider dissemination of learning and the building up of a country-wide Confucian system of education and examination.

Thirdly, with the destruction of feudalism and the decline of most of the great aristocratic families of the past, the almost exclusive Confucian emphasis on the ancestor cult gave place to a state cult in which the emphasis was upon the worship of high gods and nature gods with special emphasis on those gods who were deemed to be concerned with the principal agents of national productivity, namely the gods of soil and grain (*Shê chi*). Werner Eichhorn writes: 'The state religion of the Ch'in empire centred round the gods who influenced the yield of the harvests. A large number of star-gods came to be venerated. The official deities were collectively referred to as "the Eight gods". Among them were The Lord of Heaven, a Lord of Earth, Lords of *Yin* and *Yang*, and gods of moon, sun and the seasons. There were spirits of important mountains and rivers.'[11] We find that the Confucianism of the former Han dynasty, in its organization of the state cult, came to lay great emphasis on these high gods and nature gods who were believed to have a profound influence on human affairs. The practical organization and orientation of the state was intimately connected with the idea that a close correspondence exists between man and Nature, the microcosm man reflecting in almost absurd detail the organization and functioning of the macrocosm Nature. In consequence of this, those Confucian texts, such as the *Book of Changes* (*I Ching*) and commentaries, which especially emphasized this conception of the universe as a dynamic whole in which there is not only correspondence but an actual unity between man and Nature, came to be highly prized and assiduously studied.

The triumph of Confucianism came only gradually. Lui Pang, who became the first Han emperor, known later under the dynastic title of Kao Tsu, had risen to his exalted position from the ranks of the common people. He was a peasant who in his youth was idle and arrogant, but whose talent for leadership led him to become first a petty official and then a bandit chief,[12] 'a man of little education and obscure origin'.[13] He had little understanding of the importance of intellectual activities. Even as a military strategist his talents were limited, but he was a good judge of character and a shrewd and able politician. When he came to the throne he felt he must reward those who had assisted him and also elevate cadet members of his own family, and so he created a number of new fiefdoms. This new aristocracy was very carefully controlled by the emperor. At the least breath of suspicion, members of the royal family or supporters who had been given fiefs were degraded or put to death. In any case the new fiefs were simply enclaves within the larger administrative districts, which were governed by officers appointed by and responsible to the emperor. Lui Pang was astute enough to surround the throne with able advisers, and to give the impression that he was indeed acting on their advice. In this way the Confucian principle was established which has been the basis of government right up to modern times: that is, that the emperor chose able ministers to govern on his behalf, exercising a strict supervision over them, but in normal times interfering in government as little as possible. In this way success could be attributed to the emperor, whilst failures could be reckoned as due to the evil advice of incompetent ministers. Some of the best counsellors and closest advisers of Lui Pang were Confucian scholars, who had a strong influence upon him, though he never seems to have lost the peasant's crude contempt for the mere pedant. Professor Dubs [14] claims that 'the accession of Kao Tsu marks the victory of the Confucian conception that the imperial authority is limited, should be exercised for the benefit of the people, and should be founded on justice, over the legalistic conception of arbitrary and absolute sovereignty.' Kao Tsu wished to be a popular monarch and he found that it was political wisdom to do all within his power to placate the Confucian scholars who had received such harsh treatment under the preceding dynasty.

Many factors contributed to the growing influence of Confucianism during the early decades of the Han dynasty. In Ch'in times a decree had been promulgated and enforced which proscribed and ordered the destruction of most of the literature from the Chou era. It had had considerable effect, graphically symbolized in the 'Burning of the Books' [15] (213 B.C.) and remembered with horror and loathing by orthodox Confucians ever since. Though this proscription was not repealed until after the death of Kao Tsu in the year 191 B.C., it had not been effective for some years before that. When, under the Han emperors, Confucians were offered all kinds of important posts, and rewards were offered for the recovery of lost classical writings, a great revival of scholarly activity was the result. Confucian scholars set up a canon of sacred writings, selecting for that purpose what purported to be the most ancient and reliable works, the Six Disciplines which they believed had formed the basis of the teaching of Confucius himself. These Six Disciplines, which consisted of the *Odes*, the *History*, the *Ritual*, the *Music*, the *Book of Changes* and the *Spring and Autumn Annals*, had been recognized by Confucian scholars even before the Han dynasty as the basis for a liberal Confucian education. They now became the subjects of ardent study and research.

Apart from the *Classic of Music* which was either lost or incorporated as Chapter 17 in the *Book of Rites* (*Li Chi*), the writings on which the Six Disciplines were based were expanded and edited to form the Five Confucian Classics. To these five were later added two books on ritual, the *Chou Li* and the *I Li*, whilst three different commentaries on the *Spring and Autumn Annals* (*Ch'un Chi'u*), those called *Ku Liang*, *Kung Yang* and *Tso*, were accepted, and still later were added the *Classic of Filial Piety*, the *Analects of Confucius*, the *Works of Mencius* and the *Erh Ya* dictionary: in all thirteen classical works which remained a definitive Confucian Canon throughout the course of the Han dynasty.

It was the Confucians more than anyone else who were the custodians of the ancient literature and who were also the experts in the ritual. They were able to instruct and guide the emperor in all matters of the elaborate court ritual. They were called upon to be tutors of princes, and thus were able to wield an enormous influence in shaping the minds of future rulers. Above all, with their hatred of Legalism, of which they had had practical experience during the Ch'in régime, they tended in the main to stand for a mild and benevolent rule which exercised a paternalistic control over the common people. The reign of Wên Ti (179–156 B.C.) reveals the way in which Confucianism was not only influencing the personal conduct of the ruler, but was also pervading all aspects of political and social life. Professor Dubs writes, 'Emperor Wên accepted whole-heartedly the Confucian doctrine that the ruler exists for the welfare of his subjects, and put that doctrine into practice. He reduced the taxes, and lightened the burdens of the people, economizing in his personal expenses and avoiding any grand displays ... He asked the people for criticism of his rule (in his case the request was sincerely meant) and he sought for capable commoners to assist in the administration.'[16] Professor Creel cites many of the excellent measures taken by Wên Ti.[17] These included famine relief at government expense, pensions for the aged, manumission of slaves and the abolition of punishment by mutilation. He writes 'Such an emperor seems too good to be true, but there is ample evidence that the picture is genuine. He undoubtedly made life more tolerable for the people than it had been (or was in the future to be) for some time. China became prosperous and populous.' Here, in Wên Ti, was perhaps the first example of a monarch ruling a vast empire on Confucian principles. Later in this book we shall look in more detail at the reign of a monarch of an alien race, the Manchu emperor, K'ang Hsi, who throughout a long and illustrious reign sought to model his personal life and his government on those Confucian principles which were formulated during the Han dynasty, some eighteen centuries before his time.

Of all the Former Han emperors, Han Wu-ti (140–87 B.C.) was undoubtedly the greatest, and it was during his long reign that Confucianism was finally accepted as the state orthodoxy, a Confucianism, however, which because of its absorption of ideas derived from many other schools, in particular the Philosophy of Change and the *Yin-Yang* ideology, was radically different from the Confucianism of the *Analects*. Han Wu-ti came to the throne as a boy of fifteen, and soon proved to be a strong and even ruthless leader who established a control almost as despotic and authoritarian as that of Ch'in Shih Huang-ti. He realized, however, that the methods of Shih Huang-ti were so abhorrent to the majority of those whom he needed to administer the country that in his own interests he must refrain from rousing the discontent and hatred that had brought the Ch'in dynasty to ruin. At the beginning of his reign Wu's principal ministers were Confucians and under their influence he dismissed certain Legalists from office.

Tung Chung-shu and the New Text School

Among some hundred scholars who were recommended to the emperor for high office and who were examined by him was Tung Chung-shu (*c.* 179–*c.* 104 B.C.) who became the most prominent and influential Confucian of that period and whose chief work *Luxuriant Gems of the Spring and Autumn Annals* (*Ch'un Ch'iu Fan Lu*)[18] helped to establish in a dominant position the ideology of what has been called the New Text School of Confucianism, which acquired unrivalled prestige in the Former Han dynasty. Though Tung was an ardent Confucianist, especially devoted to a study and interpretation of the *Ch'un Ch'iu*, which he believed to have been composed by Confucius himself, he was greatly under the influence of the *Yin-Yang* and Five Elements schools and sought to bring about a synthesis between these teachings and Confucianism. He was particularly concerned to develop the idea of the close correspondence between nature and man. He taught that there is a constant mutual interaction, so that the actions of men are reflected in nature and vice versa. This is particularly true of the ruler who, because he has been entrusted by Heaven with the heavy responsibility of ruling over men, must needs model himself on Heaven and seek to love and benefit men as Heaven does. But this close correlation of human affairs and natural events is seen by these Han dynasty Confucians to bear on all aspects of human life. Disharmonies and abnormalities in political and social life are reflected in abnormalities in the natural world, since all unrighteous conduct by human beings produces a mechanical response in the *Yin-Yang* ethers,[19] resulting in abnormalities.

Two theories arose in an attempt to explain the link between the course of human history and the laws of nature. The first was that every period or dynasty lies under the influence of one of the Five Elements, materially represented by wood, fire, water, metal and earth, which succeeded each other in an inevitable but orderly sequence. The second theory attempted to explain history in terms of the three sequences of blackness, whiteness and redness. Actually, this doctrine of the inter-relationship between human life and nature was carried to absurd lengths by the Han dynasty Confucians of the New Text School. They worked out a pseudo-science of numerology, a system of detailed correspondences, and a view of history in which history moves in cycles which are controlled by the interplay of *Yin* and *Yang* and the orderly rise to dominance of each of the Five Elements.[20]

In his ideas concerning human nature, Tung Chung-shu tried to find a mean between the teachings of Mencius and those of Hsün-tzǔ. He argued that human nature is not wholly good. For that reason the institution of kingship is necessary and the emphasis on education and training. Human nature has the beginnings of goodness which need to be developed through education. Confucius, he argued, did not say that human nature is good, but only that it is capable of achieving goodness. Feelings, which are part of nature, are evil.

As a true Confucian, Tung exalted love and righteousness together with wisdom as the essential virtues. He also stressed that three bonds held society together and were essential for its healthy existence, the bonds between ruler and subject, father and son, husband and wife. The ruler, the father and the husband he regarded as corresponding to the *yang* element and therefore the dominant and active principle within the relationship. The subject, the son and the wife correspond to the *yin* element, which is the passive and submissive principle.

Tung Chung-shu was largely responsible for the movement which began to exalt Confucius as the unique sage, the 'uncrowned king', and finally as a super-human being worthy of divine honours. Through his study of the *Ch'un Ch'iu*, which he regarded as the most important of the Confucian Classics, Tung came to credit Confucius with super-human wisdom. He believed that Confucius used this work to make moral judgements on men and history, and to set down his own political ideas. For reasons of polity these had been veiled in obscurity, and could only be correctly interpreted and understood by the initiated. Furthermore, Tung believed that before he died Confucius had received from Heaven marks of its approval and its mandate to establish the basis of an ideal rule in place of the decadent Chou dynasty. In this way Tung Chung-shu and the Confucians of his day exalted Confucius to be 'uncrowned king'.

The theories of Tung Chung-shu and the New Text School continued to be influential throughout the Former Han dynasty, but came more and more to be challenged by more rationalistic thinkers. They were in large measure the subject of debate at a great meeting of Confucian scholars which was held at the capital in the year A.D. 79 at a place called White Tiger Hall (*Po Hu T'ung*). The discussions were recorded and published.[21] From them we can gather an impression of the tremendous appeal which the Five Elements Theory, the *Yin-Yang* Philosophy, the idea of sequences in history and the close relationship of man and the physical universe had upon the Confucianism which existed about the middle of the Han dynasty.[22]

It was at Tung Chung-shu's suggestion that the Emperor Wu proclaimed Confucianism as the recognized state cult in the year 136 B.C. Other teachings were allowed to exist but did not have the benefit of official recognition and encouragement. A university, which was set up in the capital city of Ch'ang-an, and the numerous schools which sprang up throughout the empire, laid their main emphasis on the Confucian Classics. Confucianism was acquiring a new authority with its appeal to ancient precedents, its strong moral emphasis, and its close alliance with an elaborate state cult. Scholars who indulged themselves in the study of works other than those recognized as Confucian Classics were excluded from official preferment. By this means it was thought that Confucianism would maintain its unrivalled position, and at the same time be kept pure from heterodox ideas. Actually, as Professor Creel has pointed out, quite the reverse was true. 'In effect it was to cause a great many students, whose real interest lay elsewhere, to become professional Confucians and interpret Confucianism in the light of their basic Taoist, Legalist or other philosophies.'[23]

Emperor Wu was astute enough to realize the enormous popular appeal of religious rites and ceremonies, their emotional and aesthetic appeal, their value in demonstrating the unity of the empire, and their effect in surrounding his own person, as the supreme moral and religious figure in the state, with an aura of semi-divine majesty and magnificence. He gave imperial patronage to widespread and popular cults, especially the worship of T'ai I, the Supreme Unity, who was supposed to reside at the Pole Star and was exalted supreme over five Celestial Emperors.[24] In addition, after elaborate and costly preparations, on three separate occasions during his reign he made a magnificent pilgrimage to the sacred mountain of T'ai Shan (in modern Shantung) with a huge retinue of court officials and princes. There he engaged in special sacrifices to Heaven and Earth, known as *Fêng* and *Shan*, the former sacrifice performed in solitary grandeur at the top of the mountain, and the latter sacrifice performed near the foot of the mountain. In this way the Emperor Wu sought for divine approval for himself and for his rule, and at the same time impressed upon the general populace visual evidence of his own exalted majesty.

All men knew that the Han emperors had sprung from lowly origin, and could therefore boast no long line of illustrious ancestors remembered and honoured in the ancestor cult. It was during this period that the religious emphasis shifted from the ancestor cult to the development of an elaborate state cult for the worship of Heaven and a hierarchy of gods and spirits who functioned in the universe around. With the destruction of the ancestral temples of most of the aristocratic families, and the freeing from serfdom of the bulk of the peasant population, the popular and universally recognized gods of the soil and grain came to be accepted as the principal objects of worship among the populace at large. The elaborate rituals and ceremonial of the state cult, designed as they were to enhance the prestige of the throne, formed an integral part of Confucianism from this time onwards. Confucian scholars turned to the *Odes* and the *Documents* in their Classical writings in order to prove that the Han emperors were only reviving again an ancient Chinese worship of August Heaven, personified as Shang Ti, the supreme ancestor of all, the ruler of the universe, who had delegated control on earth to his own appointee, the emperor, son of Heaven. They read into the far distant past, the times of the legendary or semi-legendary kings Yao and Shun, of T'ang and Wên and Wu, the kind of situation with which they were familiar, that is, a vast and unified empire centrally controlled by an emperor who had at his beck and call an army of loyal ministers and officials. Furthermore, from their studies of the rituals of the Chou dynasty they were able to elaborate a magnificent state ritual for the performance of which they made themselves indispensable. Thus, the Confucians of the Han dynasty, as regards the religious aspects of Confucianism, were able to achieve three important objectives. First, they enhanced the prestige of the ruler, giving him a distinct and unique religious status, and exalting him as high-priest of the state cult. At the same time, by fostering the cult of August Heaven (*Hao T'ien*) as the supreme power of the universe they limited the absolute power of the monarchy. They took up the older Confucian doctrine that the ruler derived his mandate and his authority to rule from Heaven, and even the emperor could not do as he liked. Secondly, they claimed that Heaven's will could be known and interpreted by those scholars who had made themselves proficient in interpreting the strange phenomena of nature, the movements of the stars, and the evolutions of the *yin* and *yang*. In addition, since Heaven's will was reflected in the murmurings of the people, the Confucian ministers of the crown had a duty to bring the disaffections of the people and their criticisms to the notice of the emperor. In these ways the Confucian scholars became indispensable, not only for the conduct of the state ceremonies but also for advising the emperor and warning him whenever his conduct seemed likely to bring down the displeasure of Heaven. Fitzgerald describes this Confucian theology of Heaven, developed under the Former Han dynasty in the following terms: 'Heaven, the presiding deity, rewarded virtue with auspicious signs, prosperous seasons, and peace. The wrath of Heaven, excited by evil conduct on the part of the ruler, was manifested by warnings and catastrophies. Such were eclipses of the sun, floods, drought, earthquakes, and plagues of locusts. The culminating punishment of a ruler's ill-conduct was the withdrawal of the "mandate of Heaven" and the fall of his dynasty to make way for another family. Thus deity stood in a peculiar relation to the Emperor, who alone had the right to perform sacrifices to Heaven. It was his virtue which was rewarded by prosperity, his vices which were punished by calamities.' [25]

Great strides were made during the Former Han dynasty both in education and in setting up an examination system. The basis of the educational curriculum became and remained the Confucian Classics. The professors in the central university which was set up in the capital city of Ch'ang-an were selected from the best scholars in the land, and most of them were regarded as authorities on at least one of the Classics. Entrance into this university was strict and competitive. Schools had been established all over China, and scholars who wished to qualify for the university had to be at least eighteen years of age, of good appearance and sound character, intelligent and eager to learn, and they had to bear the recommendation of the local magistrate. In the reign of Wu-ti the number of students in the central university was never more than fifty, but by the end of the Former Han dynasty it had reached to over three thousand. Besides their teaching duties the professors were also advisers to the government. [26] This emphasis on a Confucian education continued into the Later Han dynasty, and, with modifications, down to modern times. The Emperor Kuang Wu (reigned A.D. 25–58) was himself a Confucian scholar and surrounded himself with Confucian scholars, many of whom enjoyed great prestige as men of personal integrity and courage, guardians of the public conscience. Kuang Wu's successor, Ming Ti (reigned A.D. 58–75) sometimes 'took the role of a professor and lectured on Confucian subtleties among scholarly academicians'.[27] Thus, Confucian learning was encouraged and patronized by government and was by no means confined to the capital. The central university continued to expand so that, at one time in the first century A.D. there were 30 professors, 360 instructors and no less than 10,800 students.[28] The time came in the Later Han dynasty when the need for scholarly officials in the government made it imperative to establish the rule that local magistrates should make yearly recommendations of the most talented young men living within their jurisdiction. The position of Confucianism thus became unassailable so long as the basis of educational training was the Confucian Classics, the teachers in the main men who had been nurtured from childhood in the Confucian tradition, and the examination system which opened the way to official position was itself controlled by Confucian scholars. Through subsequent centuries, until the firm establishment of the neo-Confucian system in the eleventh and twelfth centuries, the rival ideologies of Taoism and Buddhism were to make great headway even among the literati, but even when the bulk of the population of China had gone over to Buddhism, or when the early T'ang dynasty emperors favoured Taoism, the pervasive influence of Confucius remained.

We have already referred to the unique status accorded to Confucius by Tung Chung-shu and the New Text School. Before many years had passed the increasing respect for Confucius, as his teachings were accepted as state orthodoxy, led to his being deified and worshipped, though, apart from the ancestral worship of Confucius at Ch'ü-fu by members of his own family, that worship has been confined in the main to members of the scholar class only. The compilation of the *Book of Rites* (*Li Chi*) as a result of the researches of Tai Tê and his nephew Tai Shêng, who published two recensions about the beginning of the Christian era, gave a great impetus to the custom of honouring the great men of the past by making official and public sacrifices to them. According to the *Li Chi*, 'sacrifices should be offered to him who had given (good) laws to the people; to him who had laboured to the death in discharge of his duties; to him who had strengthened the state by his laborious toil; to him who had boldly and successfully met great calamities; to him who had warded off great evils'.[29] The chief motive for such sacrifices seems to have been gratitude for benefits received. By A.D. 1, the practice began of conferring posthumous honorary titles on Confucius by imperial authority. Han P'ing Ti gave him the title 'Duke Ni, all complete and illustrious'.[30] The first mention of an officially recognized cult of Confucius was in A.D. 57. Before that time worship of Confucius had been confined to the former state of Lu, but a decree of Han Ming Ti (A.D. 59) established a regular cult of Confucius in the schools and thus took his worship beyond the confines of the K'ung family. Confucius, no longer just a model for scholars, became their patron saint.[31] In A.D. 72 the Emperor Ming Ti himself, during a tour of the provinces, went to Ch'ü-fu where a temple had been erected in honour of Confucius, and there sacrificed. So it was that, at the insistence of the scholars, the cult of Confucius was deliberately adopted by the state, and came to occupy a place in the state religion alongside the cult of Heaven, Earth and a host of nature deities, and the worship of the royal ancestors.[32]

It was inevitable that there should arise within Confucianism a reaction to the New Text School, with its strange and distorted interpretations of Confucian texts, notably the *I Ching* and the *Ch'un Ch'iu*. Its strong tendencies towards syncretism, the proliferation of apocryphal and prognostic texts, and the acceptance of a view of nature and of history built up from fantastic ideas culled from Taoist, *Yin-Yang* and Five Elements theories, all led to a reaction. How that reaction came about is not known for certain.[33] A rival Confucian school arose and became prominent during the first century B.C., claiming to base its teachings upon Confucian texts which had been written in the ancient script which had been in current use before the 'Burning of the Books' in 213 B.C. It became known as the 'Old Learning' or the 'Old Text School', and claimed that these texts of the Confucian Classics had been brought to light as a result of the discoveries of Prince Hsien of Ho-chien and Prince Kung of Lu during the reign of Han Wu-ti in the second century B.C. Several notable scholars had thereupon made recensions of these ancient writings, which were considered to be a more trustworthy guide to Confucianism than the texts favoured by their rivals. Many modern Chinese scholars have discounted these writings of the Old Text School as forgeries executed by a scholar called Liu Hsin (c. 45 B.C.–A.D. 23), who with his father, Liu Hsiang (79–8 B.C.) 'had been entrusted by the government with the compilation of a detailed catalogue of all the literature extant in their day'.[34] However that may be, the Old Text School rejected the extravagant doctrines of their rivals, together with the *Yin-Yang* ideology, the whole mass of apocryphal and prognostic literature, and the idea that Confucius should be elevated and worshipped as a supernatural being.

Archaeological evidence from Han dynasty tombs seems to suggest an almost universal belief in some form of survival after death. The tombs were furnished with cult objects designed to assist the spirits of the deceased in the next world. 'The bas-reliefs (carved on the tombs) were intended solely for the dead, for they were placed with their carved surfaces facing inwards, a position which made it impossible to see the carvings as long as the tomb remained undisturbed. The bas-reliefs were therefore intended for the pleasure of the dead man's ghost, not merely to commemorate his achievements.'[35] One may take it that this belief in some form of survival represents the general attitude of the time, but there were many Confucian scholars who repudiated it, and that agnostic attitude concerning the existence of spirits and a future life, evinced by so much of the Confucian writing, became, as we shall see later (pp. 142–3), one of the main differences between the Confucians and the Taoists and Buddhists in China. The influence of Hsün-tzǔ on Han dynasty Confucianism was very great indeed,[36] and a more rationalistic strain of Confucianism which derived from Hsün-tzǔ always existed alongside the Confucianism which derived from the *Chung Yung* and Mencius. The rationalism of Hsün-tzǔ is particularly evident in certain passages of the *Li Chi*, in which it is argued that the doctrine of personal immortality is unacceptable to the intellect and impossible of proof. Our intellect tells us that as birth is the beginning of a human life as we know it, so death is the end. Nevertheless, our emotional nature entertains a hope that the dead, whom we have loved and cherished whilst they were living on earth, do not eternally perish. To satisfy that emotional nature the sages of old devised the mourning and sacrificial rites. But their value is purely subjective. They are designed to give a beautiful and poetical expression to the emotions of grief and loss, fear, affection and tenderness. They are of no value to the dead, and in no way can they serve their interests, because the dead only exist in the imagination of the living. The rites do, however, give great satisfaction to the mourners. They provide a fitting outlet for the emotions, and express the feelings of love, reverence and gratitude. There were, no doubt, a few with the cynical attitude expressed so forcefully in the *Lieh-tzŭ* book, where it says, 'It does not matter how we take leave of the dead . . . Once I am dead, what concern is it of mine? It is the same to me whether you burn me, or sink me in a river, bury me or leave me in the open, throw me in a ditch wrapped in grass or put me in a stone coffin dressed in a dragon-emblazoned jacket and embroidered skirt.'[37] Such an attitude does not represent the view held by the majority of Han dynasty Confucians. Their ideas on ritual are seen in the *Li Chi* more than any other book. In that work, though it is prepared to accept that those to whom sacrifice is made have neither substance nor shadow, and the sacrifices are performed only 'as if' the deceased drank the libation from his goblet, yet it insists that 'of all methods for the good ordering of men there is none more urgent than the use of ceremonies . . . and there is none of them more important than sacrifices'.[38] It is the political, social and ethical benefits of the rites of mourning and sacrifice which are stressed in the *Li Chi*: 'In sacrificing there is a recognition of what belongs to ten relationships. There are seen in it a method of serving spiritual beings; the righteousness between ruler and subject; the relation between father and son; the degrees of the noble and the mean; the distance gradually increasing between relatives; the bestowal of rank and reward; the separate duties of husband and wife; impartiality in government affairs; the order to be observed between young and old; and the boundaries of high and low.'[39]

The more rationalistic attitude of the Old Text School is reflected in the writings of Yang Hsiung (53 B.C.–A.D. 18) and Wang Ch'ung (A.D. 27–97). Both these men were greatly influenced by Taoist as well as Confucian writings, and both of them rejected the magical techniques, the superstitious beliefs and the popular ideas concerning immortality which were extremely prevalent in their day. Wang Ch'ung especially revealed a spirit of critical and sceptical scientific inquiry, and made devastating attacks on the numerology, the pseudo-science of prognostication, and the ideas concerning immortality which were current among the exponents of the New Text School. 'People say that the dead become spirits, are conscious and can hurt people . . . Yet man is a creature like other creatures. These creatures do not become spirits when they die. Why, then, should men alone become spirits when they die? . . . Man is brought into existence by means of vital forces, and when he dies these forces are extinguished . . . Before his birth he forms part of the primal ethers, and upon his death he reverts to these primal ethers . . . Before birth, man has no consciousness, and after death he reverts to this original condition of unconsciousness . . . Human death is like the extinction of a fire. When a fire is extinguished, its light does not shine any more; and when a man dies, his intellect does not comprehend any more.'[40]

Before the end of the Han dynasty the position of Confucius as 'the greatest sage', towering above Lao-tzŭ and Chuang tzŭ and all the other ancient worthies, was generally recognized, and Confucianism had established itself as a system ideally suited to the administration of a great empire. But already movements were afoot to challenge this supremacy of Confucianism. In the first place, the great Han empire was rapidly disintegrating under the impact of external pressures and internal dissensions. Throughout the next four hundred years China was to experience a long, dark period of disunity. The land would be divided into north and south, and the north, which had been the cradle of the Confucian civilization, would be ruled over by non-Chinese dynasties. In the second place, amidst the chaos and confusion of war, the hopeless miseries of an oppressed population were to find relief through the organization of a para-military Taoist church with strong religious and emotional appeal. In the third place, Buddhism was entering China, and gradually spreading its influence, and bringing a challenge to Confucianism by offering an answer to those problems of human life and destiny for which, as yet, Confucianism had no satisfactory solution.

6. Confucianism and its Rivals: Taoism and Buddhism

WHEN the greatest of Han dynasty monarchs occupied the throne, holding the reins of government with strong hands, and when all power and authority was centralized in a capable ruler, conditions proved ideal for Confucianism. Confucian scholars alone were able to provide that wealth of talent needed for the efficient running of a vast governmental administration. Confucian historians found no difficulty in citing historical precedents from ancient times to buttress the authoritarianism of an absolute ruler. The rites and ceremonies of a national religious cult, which were deemed by the Confucians to have been established by sage-kings of high antiquity, were not only presumed to assure a universal harmony between the spiritual and the human, between Heaven, Nature and man, but endowed the emperor's person with a numinous quality as he performed high-priestly functions on behalf of 'all under Heaven'. Granted that Han dynasty Confucianism was an amalgam of many diverse beliefs and many schools of thought, this tended towards a religious toleration which accorded to every man a right to his own personal beliefs. The Confucians could even view with a cynical and indulgent eye the gross superstitions and magical practices to which scholars were not altogether immune and which attracted the patronage of emperors. Han dynasty Confucianism flourished so long as it was able to recruit and maintain an educated élite, well-versed in Confucian learning, and disciplined by constant study of the Classics and by the Confucian code of behaviour.

There was little in Confucianism to appeal to the multitudes of ordinary men and women whom destiny had appointed to a low station in life. Its main function was to produce a well-ordered framework in which men and women could live out their lives; a state wisely and justly administered in which all people were given opportunity to nourish their living, give decent burial to their dead, and at the end pass into oblivion, mourned only by the closest relatives. Han dynasty Confucianism could set before men an ideal of human perfection and a blueprint for a perfect society, but it had very little religious appeal to individuals striving to find a way of rising above the sea of sorrow, suffering and sin in which so many felt themselves to be engulfed. For the multitudes of ordinary men and women it had no message of hope and comfort either for this world or for an existence beyond the grave. That is why, from the Han dynasty onwards, religious Taoism became the indigenous faith of the Chinese people, and Buddhism, imported from India and Central Asia, spread like wildfire, offering to the masses the hope of salvation, and to the educated a highly philosophical and well thought-out challenge to the Confucian interpretation of reality.

According to Confucian doctrine the better a state was administered the fewer the governmental duties that devolved upon the supreme ruler. In a perfect state he would reign but would have no need to rule. All rule and administration would be done in his name by worthy and highly competent ministers. The Confucian theory, which exalted the emperor so that he was regarded as 'Son of Heaven' and supreme ruler of 'all Heaven' led inevitably to the isolation of the emperor's sacred person from the people over whom he reigned. Their eyes were unfitted to behold him. Even the most exalted minister of state must stand humbly and with downcast eyes before the steps leading to the throne, when he wished to present memorials for the emperor's approval, recommend new candidates for office, bring forward the petitions of his subjects or ask that the emperor's seal might be placed on laws or enactments which had previously been drawn up. Unfortunately the isolation of the emperor, so that he became virtually cut off from all that went on in the world outside his palaces and gardens, was a direct cause of the rapid decline of Confucianism. Isolated in his palace, encouraged to live a life of idleness and luxury, surrounded by intriguing wives and concubines ever alert to advance the interests of their own families and served by vicious eunuchs whose only object was personal gain; flattered, coaxed, persuaded, the mind of even the most well-disposed emperor could be turned against his loyal ministers and counsellors outside. History records how, during the course of the second century A.D., the emperors of China came increasingly under the baleful influence of court favourites and eunuchs, until there was no longer any hope of saving the dynasty from collapse and ruin. By the reign of Han Huan Ti (A.D. 146–167) eunuchs 'established in the centre of the governmental machine soon obtained complete control of the civil service which they filled with their relatives and creatures. Promotions and appointments depended upon eunuch goodwill, and their favour was only purchased with gold. Honours, rewards, titles and power were bestowed upon those whom the eunuchs praised to the Emperor, whilst imprisonment and the torture-chamber were the fate of upright officials who tried to stem the tide of corruption.'[1] Confucian scholars, enraged and disgusted by the hold of the eunuchs upon the emperor and by the decline of public and private morality, sought to curtail their power. They founded a college devoted to the spread of Confucian teaching, which became the centre of an association to oppose the eunuchs. After a fleeting success at the time of Han Huan Ti's death (A.D. 167) the association was proscribed and leading Confucian scholars condemned and executed. With the government and even the provincial and district administrations controlled by eunuchs and their sycophants, the whole country was rapidly moving towards anarchy and ruin. The emperor was kept from all knowledge of the misery of the people, the widespread discontent and the mounting unrest in various parts of the empire. Towards the end of the second century A.D. several regions erupted in violent revolt.

In such conditions Confucianism had little to offer save exhortation and moral example. It remained for Taoist preachers and faith-healers to organize vast hordes of peasants into a dynamic semi-religious, semi-military movement, which gave release to pent-up emotions and the sense of frustration, grievance, injustice, and which assured men that they might join a mighty crusade to bring peace on earth. At the same time the leaders of the movement offered atonement for sins, healing for sickness and hope for a better future in this life and felicity beyond the grave. Towards the end of the second century A.D., religious Taoism was beginning to fill a vacuum which Confucianism could not hope to fill. Before long it was to make a strong appeal to scholars and intellectuals by the development of coteries to engage in 'Pure Conversations' (Ch'ing T'an) and to take up the study of 'Dark or Mysterious Learning' (*Hsüan Hsüeh*).

Meanwhile, as early as the beginning of the Christian era, Buddhism had entered into China along the main central Asian trade routes. For a while its influence remained comparatively small, confined mainly to a few foreign monks and merchants and their Chinese associates in some of the larger cities. But during the four centuries which followed the end of the Han dynasty, known as the Period of Disunity, Buddhism rapidly increased in strength, making a strong religious appeal to the masses, and attracting the intelligentsia with its profoundly philosophical treatises.

The Period of Disunity (A.D. 221–589)

After the fall of the Han dynasty there followed a hundred years of turmoil and bloodshed, an era of treachery and violence in which China was divided into three rival kingdoms, and war and famine stalked the land. The country was finally united for a brief period under the Chin dynasties, but so great had been the chaos and destruction in the previous decades that a national census taken in A.D. 280 showed a total population of only 13,863,000, one half of the population of A.D. 200.[2] Further civil war gave opportunity to Turkic[3] Hu tribes to descend upon China from the north. In A.D. 311 the capital city of Loyang fell to the invaders, and five years later all resistance in the north collapsed and the Chin emperor with his court, together with hosts of Confucian scholars, fled south of the Yangtzu River, to set up a new capital city at Nanking, and bring a measure of civilization to the more backward southern regions. For the next two hundred and fifty years China was divided into north and south. Non-Chinese dynasties ruled in the north, notably the Wei dynasty of Toba Tartars (A.D. 386–557). The rulers of this dynasty rapidly assimilated Chinese culture, intermarried with the Chinese, made the adoption of Chinese customs and language compulsory and sought to preserve the Confucian ideas and literature of Han times. Throughout the fourth and fifth centuries Buddhism rapidly expanded in the north of China until almost the whole of the population was converted, accepting Buddhist rites and ceremonies and contributing enormous sums of money for the building of monasteries and temples and for the support of Buddhist monks. In the capital city of Ch'ang-an a famous school of Buddhist missionaries and translators was set up to translate the voluminous Buddhist scriptures into literary Chinese. In spite of this paramount influence of Buddhism, many of the Wei dynasty emperors were greatly attracted to Taoism, which also became firmly established as a popular religion, adopting the practices of alchemy, astrology and medicine and offering the achievement of immortality by magical practices and the use of potent drugs. This rivalry between Taoism and Buddhism resulted in the comparative eclipse of Confucianism, and occasionally led to periods of persecution in which both religions suffered.

In the south of China several short-lived dynasties followed each other in rapid succession. Though many Confucian scholars had followed the court in flight from the barbarian invaders, few indeed amongst them retained the Confucian virtues. Cut off from their ancestral homes and the graves of their forefathers, and called upon to serve upstart princes who had little, if any, claim to the throne, the virtues of filial piety and loyalty to one's superior were neglected. The insecurity of life encouraged self-interest and licence rather than self-discipline and moral cultivation. Confucian learning was never discarded, but there was little encouragement to pursue a rigorous course of study in the Confucian Classics at a time when scholarship and virtue were at a discount and no one could be guaranteed his just deserts. The intellectuals turned rather to the study of Taoism with its philosophy of inaction, escape from the burdens of office, and retirement into a leisured way of life in the countryside.

The period of disunity, so unfavourable to Confucianism, which flourished best in times of comparative stability, peace and orderly government, was far more favourable to the development of Buddhism and Taoism. Both of them emphasized the emptiness of worldly ambitions and taught the advantages of withdrawal from the world. They offered men release from the sufferings and uncertainties of the transitory life, in the case of Taoism through the attainment of immortality, and in that of Buddhism through perfect enlightenment, such as the Buddha himself attained when he was on earth. In general, both in the north and south, it was Buddhism which made most headway among the peasants and also with the literati. Many of the latter joined the monastic communities which were springing up everywhere under the patronage of rulers, or they became close lay associates, joining lay orders and spending their time in the study of the Buddhist *sūtras*[4] under the guidance of Buddhist masters. They were attracted to the philosophy of the Mahāyāna, whose scriptures were being translated by teams of scribes under the guidance of distinguished Buddhist missionaries. Educated men found in the monasteries havens of peace from the turmoil and strife outside and in the *sūtras* a stimulus for the mind and a message of hope and salvation which the Confucian Classics could not offer.

Those who rejected the appeal of the foreign religion found in the study of the 'mysterious learning' of Taoism a way of satisfying their hunger for knowledge without having to exercise that knowledge in the dangerous field of government service. Scholars, whether Buddhist or Taoist, were prepared to give to Confucius an honoured place beside Lao-tzŭ and the Buddha. Various attempts were made to harmonize the three schools of thought and to promulgate the idea that they were simply different ways by which to reach the same ultimate goal.[5] It was during this period that the phrase *san chiao* arose to designate Confucianism, Taoism and Buddhism. The phrase has often been translated as 'the Three Religions', but more accurately refers to the 'three teachings' or the 'three systems of thought' which, intricately interwoven, came to be recognized as the ideological basis of Chinese culture.

In spite of the great popularity of Buddhism and Taoism, and the patronage given to them by the rulers, Confucianism was not altogether neglected, In A.D. 267 the Emperor Chin Wu-ti decreed that, both in the imperial academy and at the birthplace of Confucius, the sacrifice known as the *T'ai Lao*, in which an ox, a pig and a sheep were slaughtered, should be made to the sage at the four seasons of the year.[6] Again, it is recorded that in A.D. 319 the same sacrifice was offered to Confucius and in A.D. 325 a descendant of Confucius was elevated to the rank of marquis.

Though there were few Confucian scholars of any great distinction throughout the whole period of disunity – and in the four hundred years from the fall of Han till the establishment of a united China under the Sui dynasty only three names are represented in the Confucian temple[7] – there were some scholars with the intellectual ability to bring forceful arguments against Buddhism, representing the rationalistic and agnostic attitude of Confucianism in face of the Buddhist assertion that the soul is indestructable. The most noteworthy among these Confucian scholars in the latter part of the fifth century was Fan Chên (c. A.D. 450–515), an official and the author of a famous essay called *Shên mieh lun* or 'The destruction of the soul'. In this work we see revealed the typical Confucian attitude. 'The Body is the substance of the soul, the soul is the functioning of the body ... The relationship of the soul to its substance is like that of sharpness to a knife, whilst the relationship of a body to its functioning is like that of a knife to its sharpness. The sharpness is not the same as the knife, and the knife is not the same as the sharpness. But there can be no knife if the sharpness is discarded and no sharpness if the knife is discarded. I have never heard of the sharpness surviving if the knife has been destroyed, so how can it be admitted that the soul can remain if the body is annihilated?'[8] Fan Chên also attacked the Buddhist doctrine of *karma* and the indestructibility of the soul by claiming that birth and death are all part of a natural and inevitable sequence. The Buddhists, on their part, were not slow to quote the *Classic of Filial Piety* (*Hsiao Ching*) which emphasizes the cult of ancestors. Was this worship, they asked, a mere mockery and empty show or had it real meaning? One does not sacrifice to a non-entity.

It was not until the beginning of the sixth century A.D. that there was sufficient stability in China for a revival of Confucian culture to take place, and with it a new interest in Confucius. The long reign of Liang Wu-ti (A.D. 502–550) probably represents the height of Buddhist influence in China, yet the emperor early in his reign took measures which helped to promote Confucianism. He became the patron of the Confucian literati, and was the first emperor to erect public temples to Confucius in which every year sacrifices were made in memory of the sage.[9] He sought out men who had been educated in the Confucian Classics and rebuilt Confucian establishments which had fallen into ruin. The short-lived northern Ch'i dynasty (A.D. 550–577) also laid great emphasis on education, and in the schools on the first day of the new moon a libation of wine was offered to Confucius, the students were made to do obeisance to him, and lectures on him were given. Sacrifices were offered to the sage twice a year, in spring and autumn.[10]

It seems probable that during the period of disunity, when Buddhism and Taoism were in the ascendant, both these religions had considerable influence in shaping the future pattern of Confucianism, especially as regards the cult of Confucius himself. Worship rendered to Lao-tzǔ and the Buddha in the numerous temples built to their honour provided a strong inducement to build similar temples in honour of Confucius, universally recognized as China's greatest sage. As the chief deity worshipped in Buddhist and Taoist temples always had other deified beings associated with him, so it was natural that, when sacrifice was made to Confucius, honours should also be paid to Yen Hui, his favourite disciple, and later on were added a long list of illustrious Confucians who had distinguished themselves by their learning and filial piety. Thus, the growth of a Confucian cult outside the confines of Confucius's own family received a great impetus during the period of disunity, when most of the emperors had strong leanings either to Buddhism or Taoism, but maintained a profound respect for Confucian learning. They saw no reason why they should not give patronage to Confucianism along similar lines to their patronage of Taoism and Buddhism.

One reason why Taoism and Buddhism flourished among the general populace was because of the important place they gave to legends and the supernatural. The Confucian Classics, on the other hand, are remarkably free from this kind of material. There are very few references in them to supernatural events in the life of Confucius. On the whole Confucian scholars tended to follow the advice of their Master not to discuss 'feats of prowess, prodigies and the supernatural'.[11] Mainly under Taoist influence, the period of disunity saw a large increase in the production of legends concerning supernatural events relating to the conception, birth, life and death of Confucius. Unfortunately, as Creel suggests,[12] late and fanciful stories about Confucius have had more influence upon the generally accepted picture of him than has the *Analects*.

Confucianism in the T'ang Dynasty

In A.D. 618 a rebel leader named Li Yüan, ably assisted by his vigorous and talented son, Li Shih-min, assumed the imperial title at Ch'ang-an, and called his dynasty T'ang. With the establishment of this dynasty there began one of the most glorious periods in Chinese history. Li Shih-min's prowess in war, his undoubted talents for administration and his by no means negligible gifts as a scholar all contributed to the promotion of an era of internal peace and prosperity which was to last for more than a century. The cross-fertilization of Confucian, Taoist and Buddhist scholarship was to produce works of literature and art which have been rarely, if ever, surpassed. Li Shih-min was only sixteen years old when the Sui dynasty collapsed, and for the next nine years the titular sovereignty was exercised by his father, Li Yüan. It was not until A.D. 627 that Li Shih-min ascended the throne; in later times he was better known under his imperial title T'ang T'ai Tsung. His reign lasted for only twenty-two years but during that time he established the administration on such a firm basis that it was only wrecked one hundred and thirty years later by the great rebellion of the Tartar general, An Lu-shan. T'ai Tsung modelled his administration on that of the Han dynasty, dividing the country into ten large provinces and controlling the empire from the capital city of Ch'ang-an. Even before he ascended the throne he had gathered round him a group of Confucian scholars as his supporters and once he was firmly established, he proceeded to enlarge the imperial academy in the capital and to open schools for the training of officials. No fewer than 3,260 scholars were enrolled in the imperial academy as residents and their education consisted of the study of the Confucian Classics and their commentaries.[13] So famous was this imperial academy that students came from foreign countries to attend it and a library of some 200,000 volumes was gathered together.

Though Taoism and Buddhism both flourished throughout most of the T'ang dynasty, and though the T'ang emperors were patrons of Taoism, the influence of Confucianism in the administration was paramount. It was officials trained in Confucian doctrines who formed the council which advised the emperor, who ran the six ministries[14] which controlled the affairs of state, and who transmitted orders to and received reports from the Confucian scholars who administered the prefectures and county seats.

Realizing the great influence of religion in the life of the nation and people, T'ang T'ai Tsung sought to bring religion under the control of the civil administration so as to serve the national interest. His own personal preference was for Taoism, and he gave exceptional honours to Lao-tzŭ, from whom he claimed descent. Nevertheless, he recognized the enormous strength and widespread influence of the Buddhist clergy, and so he patronized their monasteries and temples. The protective influence of both Taoist and Buddhist deities was sought on behalf of him and of the nation. Towards the end of his reign he seems to have become genuinely interested in Buddhism, largely through the influence of the pilgrim-monk and scholar, Hsüan-tsang.[15]

The emperor was determined to add a religious element to the ideal of education and make Confucianism much more than a secular, ethico-political system. If Taoism and Buddhism erected their temples all over the country, why should not Confucianism have its temples too? If Lao-tzŭ and the Buddha were worshipped as deities, then Confucius was more than the patron saint of scholars: he was the supreme deity of the civil administration of government, and as such must occupy an important place in the state religion. Consequently, in A.D. 630 T'ai Tsung issued a decree that all prefectural and county seats (*chou* and *hsien*) throughout the empire should establish a temple to Confucius. From now on, at stated times, the scholars in their capacity as government officials were ordered to offer appropriate sacrifices in the Confucian temples.[16] Another change took place in A.D. 647 when the emperor placed in the temples the tablets of twenty-two famous Confucian scholars of former times along with those of Confucius and Yen Hui, his favourite disciple. In this way a precedent was established and subsequently followed, by which the Confucian temples became national shrines in which men distinguished for their high principles and classical scholarship were honoured.[17]

It was during the T'ang dynasty that Confucianism became a religious cult, undoubtedly owing much to the influence of Buddhism. Though there were a few short periods when Buddhism was persecuted, it was, on the whole, an age of religious toleration. Contacts were made with foreign countries, and numerous foreigners came into the country, bringing with them their own religious ideas. The temples of Confucianism, Taoism and Buddhism were built upon very similar patterns, and though they had their own distinctive objects of worship, there was considerable mutual influence. We do not know what were the objects of worship in the Confucian temples before the year A.D. 720, but it is probable that images representing Confucius and Yen Hui had been introduced. In A.D. 720 the Emperor Hsüan Tsung, himself a devotee of Taoism and later on ardent patron of Buddhism, adopted the suggestion of one of his officials, Li Yüan-kuan, that there should be ten seated images in the main hall of Confucian temples, ranged on either side of the images of Confucius and Yen Hui, and that the seventy disciples of Confucius and the twenty-two distinguished Confucian scholars should have their pictures painted on the walls. Sixty-seven more names were added in A.D. 739, and it seems as though the Confucians were definitely trying to imitate the Buddhists, whose temples were filled with the images and pictures of Buddhas and *bodhisattvas*. From the year A.D. 720 until A.D. 1530 the objects of worship in Confucian temples were images. It was only in the latter year that the images were destroyed and their place taken by the spirit-tablets, which are now a familiar feature of the Confucian temples. During the whole of this period Confucius was regarded and treated as a divinity, represented in his temples by an image and surrounded by the images or pictures of his disciples. At certain appointed times in the year, in spring and autumn, sacrifices were made to him. Those offered in the central Confucian temple in the capital city were the most elaborate. They were presided over by the three highest dignitaries (*san kung*) who were advisers to the emperor. The *T'ai Lao* sacrifice, consisting of an ox, a pig and a sheep, was offered. Prayers were modelled on the sacrificial odes to be found in the *Classic of Poetry* (*Shih Ching*), and a ritual dance was performed to the accompaniment of solemn, grave and dignified music. This ritual dance and the music which accompanied it were believed to follow ancient precedent. In T'ang times Confucius was accorded the honour of six ranks of dancers, the maximum of eight ranks being reserved for the emperor alone.

While these developments in the cult of Confucius were taking place, both in court circles and among the educated gentry there was little interest shown in Confucian traditionalism. It was not possible to repudiate altogether the Confucian doctrines which formed the basis of the educational and the governmental system, and there were always scholars belonging to ancient and distinguished families who would never dream of forsaking the Confucian learning for the study of Buddhist *sūtras* or for excursions into Taoist mysticism. For the majority of Tʻang dynasty scholars, however, the period was one of extraordinary freedom for experiment with new philosophical ideas and varied forms of literary and artistic expression. Most of the Tʻang rulers were either fervent Taoists or became devoted to Buddhism. The century of peace which followed on the reign of Tʻang Tʻai Tsung extended through the latter half of the seventh century and the first half of the eighth. It was an age of unprecedented prosperity in which literature, drama, arts and crafts were encouraged and poets, painters, calligraphists and sculptors were honoured at court. Numerous foreign contacts brought into the country people with different ideas and new skills. Buddhism reached the peak of its popularity about the end of the eighth century, and no scholar could fail to be influenced, at least to some extent, by its philosophical ideas and its aesthetic and emotional appeal. Nevertheless, it was at the time of Buddhism's greatest triumph that a movement began to gain strength which opposed Buddhism and reasserted the importance of Confucianism. Led by the famous Confucian essayist, Han Yü (A.D. 768–824), his pupil Li Ao (*d.* 844) and the Confucian scholar, Liu Tsungyüan (A.D. 773–819) Buddhism was attacked both on theoretical and on practical grounds. On the one hand it was argued that Buddhism pandered to gross superstitions and deluded the minds of men by fanciful legends and false hopes. On the other it was argued that Buddhism was a social and economic disaster, draining off much of the country's wealth for the support of hordes of unproductive monks and nuns, striking at the roots of family life, and neglecting social duties for the contemplative life.

The new movement sought to revive Confucian classical learning. It claimed to be a school for the study of the *Tao*, but it taught that the true meaning of the *Tao* could best be understood by a thorough study of the Confucian Classics, and particularly by a study of *Mencius*, the *Chung Yung* and the *Ta Hsüeh*. The scholars sought to return to the ancient style of writing in which the Confucian Classics had been written. They regarded as decadent the style of writing which had developed in the centuries which followed the fall of the Former Han dynasty.

Han Yü possessed the moral courage which has always characterized the noblest Confucians, who risked the loss of position, rank and fortune and even life itself rather than condone the foolish or wicked actions of autocratic rulers. Han Yü wrote and presented to the throne a famous memorial protesting against Buddhism at a time when the emperor, besotted by Buddhist superstition, proposed to exhibit in the capital city of Ch'ang-an a celebrated relic, reputed to be a finger-bone of the Buddha himself. For his temerity Han Yü was banished from the court and was sent as magistrate to a backward and unhealthy district of Kuangtung in the southernmost part of the empire. It is said that he administered the district in such strict accord to Confucian principles that he won the esteem of all the inhabitants. He remained to the end of his life a zealous opponent of Taoist and Buddhist superstitions. He regarded the worship of relics, the prayers to the Buddha, and the teachings concerning heaven and hell as gross superstitions which deluded the populace. He believed that Buddhism and Taoism were both antisocial and too speculative. Yet he, and his pupil, Li Ao, even more, were influenced by the Buddhist concept of perfect enlightenment and the idea of attaining Buddhahood. Han Yü and those associated with him were the forerunners of that great movement which became known as Neo-Confucianism, a movement, as we shall see, which restored Confucianism to the position it had occupied under the Former Han Dynasty, and set it far above Taoism or Buddhism as the orthodoxy which was to dominate the intellectual life of China right up to modern times. W. T. Chan says of Han Yü that 'he stood out like a giant in the history of Confucianism from the second century to the tenth. He was of course one of the greatest literary masters China ever produced. So far as Chinese thought is concerned, his greatness and that of Li Ao lies in the fact that they saved Confucianism from its possible annihilation by Taoism and Buddhism, and that they defined the direction and nature of its resurgence.'[18] It was Han Yü especially who established what has ever since been accepted as the orthodox line for the transmission of the teaching of Confucius, through the *Chung Yung*, the *Ta Hsüeh* and *Mencius* rather than through Hsün-tzŭ, who had such an influential following in the Han dynasty. By the eighth century, when Han Yü and Li Ao flourished, the highly metaphysical speculations of the *Hua Yen* and *Ch'an* (Zen) schools of Chinese Buddhism were being avidly studied by scholars. No intelligent person could fail to be influenced by them. Yet Han Yü took up the this-worldly attitude of traditional Confucianism and emphasized the Confucian goals of the perfect sage and the ideal society. In his *Inquiry on the Way* (*Tao*) he criticizes the Taoists and Buddhists because they discard the relationships of ruler and minister, father and son, and so on, which form the basis of human societies, and he re-emphasizes the teaching of the *Ta Hsüeh* (*Great Learning*) that the good ordering of family and state and the establishment of world peace ultimately depend upon those men who have gained such an understanding of the nature of reality that their own purposes are marked by utter sincerity, leading them to unremitting effort towards the rectification of the mind and the cultivation of the self.

More than two centuries were to elapse after the death of Han Yü before the great Neo-Confucian revival was to take place in the course of the eleventh century.

7. The Revival of Confucianism in the Sung Dynasty

THE final extinction of the T'ang dynasty in A.D. 907 was followed by half a century of anarchy and chaos. Five ephemeral military dictatorships followed each other in quick succession. The period is known as that of the Five Dynasties, but they are hardly worthy of the name. In a period of fifty-three years some thirteen military adventurers, mainly of barbarian stock, assumed the title of emperor and ruled over the northern provinces of China. The provinces of the south and west lay outside their jurisdiction.[1] Times such as these were unfavourable to Confucianism. Incessant warfare devastated the country, impoverished the people and reduced many of the educated and propertied class to penury. There was one event, however, which was to have a powerful influence on the spread of Confucianism as soon as times became more propitious. That was the invention of wood-block printing, which came into use about A.D. 930 on the recommendation of a Confucian scholar called Fêng Tao. From the Han dynasty onwards the Confucian Classics had from time to time been incised on stone tablets, and from these stone tablets impressions were made on paper by means of inked rubbings. The use of wood-blocks in place of stone tablets made the production of books much easier, and by the year A.D. 953 the whole of the nine recognized Classics of the Confucian Canon had been printed. As R. Wilhelm wrote, 'The spread of block-printing dates from this time. The fruits of the invention reached maturity in the Sung dynasty, when printed books came into vogue, in which art notable achievements were recorded within the lifetime of the dynasty. Owing to the ease with which printed books could be circulated education was rendered largely accessible to the masses. It is thanks to the possibilities created by this invention that Confucianism has become a possession of the whole Chinese nation.'[2]

The founder of the Sung dynasty, the general Chao Kuang-yin, who came to the throne in A.D. 960 and is known by the reign title as Sung T'ai-tsu, soon showed himself to be a shrewd and able administrator. Realizing that the troubles which had beset the T'ang dynasty had been caused in large measure by the growing power of the war-lords to whom had been entrusted the expansion of the empire, T'ai-tsu determined to strengthen the central administration and make the military subservient to the civil authority. He persuaded the semi-independent war-lords, who had placed him on the throne, and whose continued exist-ence was a menace to the peace and unity of the empire, to relinquish their military commands, and in return he rewarded them by giving them large and rich estates. He accepted the Confucian principle that virtue in the ruler, good government and honest administration were the best means by which to foster the loyalty of the people and the prosperity of the realm. In spite of serious troubles which arose through the aggressive conduct of neighbouring states to the north, Sung T'ai-tsu inaugurated an era of unprecedented cultural advancement in which the arts and crafts, literature and philosophy were to flourish, and in which the Chinese people were to be taught to glory in their own rich native heritage. In his determination to strengthen the central governmental authority and to build up a first-class administration, T'ai-tsu sought out the Confucian literati and from their ranks recruited his ministers of state and other officials. In order to assure a regular supply of trained personnel he re-established and recognized the civil service examination system, a system which was to remain with little change until its abolition in 1905. As once more Confucian learning was respected and Confucian scholars began to take the highest offices in the land, there occurred a great expansion of cultural and intellectual activity. The T'ang dynasty examination system was followed but was greatly enlarged in scope. The imperial examination was held in the capital every other year, and after A.D. 1064, because of the hardship and expense to scholars who had to travel to the capital from distant parts of the empire, every three years. But whereas, under the T'ang, only a few dozen candidates were allowed to pass on each occasion, under the Sung the numbers of successful candidates amounted to several hundreds. Successful candidates received at once generous pecuniary compensation, whilst the one whose name was placed first on the list rode like a conqueror at the head of a magnificent parade through the main streets of the capital city, receiving the praise and adulation of thousands of onlookers. Messengers set off from the capital to ride to the homes of successful candidates to announce the glad tidings, and suddenly a family, however poor and insignificant before, became celebrated in a community as the family of a scholar. When the candidate himself returned home, flushed with his success, he was regarded with all the hero-worship of a successful Olympic medallist of modern times, and was admitted to the élite circle which formed the local gentry.[3] Education, as indeed in nearly all predominantly agrarian societies, remained the proud distinction of the few, and though, on the whole, the families of the wealthy literati had a great advantage in that they could afford to provide the very best tutors for their sons, it sometimes happened that the bright and intelligent son of a poor farmer would rise to occupy the high dignity of minister of state. A strict code of Confucian morality was imposed on the scholars, together with the moral obligation to use talents and ability in the service of community and nation. During the Sung and subsequent dynasties the Confucian scholars formed an élite, a highly privileged class who, in theory at least, were expected to conform, both in public and private life, to the high moral standards set forth in the teaching of Confucius. However far removed from the ideal individual scholars might be, the ideal did inspire generation after generation of dedicated scholars to serve the state with unstinting devotion, to put first the welfare of the people, and to be shining examples of integrity and uprightness within the communities to which they gave intellectual and moral leadership. Though they were expected to perform such religious duties as were customarily imposed by tradition, they and their families were free to follow the tenets and practices of Buddhism or Taoism.

As far as education and state administration were concerned, Confucianism continued to have an unassailable influence. The pre-eminence given to Confucian scholarship in the Sung dynasty meant that practically the only way for a man to gain political influence or to be recognized as a gentleman and a scholar in his own community was by way of a rigorous academic training in the Confucian Classics and subsequent success in the examinations. From this time onwards, though Buddhism and Taoism remained influential, especially among the general populace, and their monasteries were places to which even the most orthodox Confucian scholars might go for relaxation and retreat, public life, whether on a national scale or within the smaller administrative districts of prefecture and county-seat, was dominated by the Confucians. The control of practical politics by Confucian scholars meant that within Confucianism there arose diverse political parties. Whereas in T'ang times the higher Taoist and Buddhist clergy were powerful enough at times to exercise control over the emperor, and the weight of Confucian polemic was directed against these different ideologies, in the Sung dynasty Confucians had gained such an unrivalled position in the government administration that it was grave differences between rival groups of Confucians as to the policies best suited to the welfare of the state which led to acrimonious rivalry. The main differences arose between the more conservative and traditionalist on the one hand and a radical reforming party on the other. The difference between these two parties is best exemplified in the two men who for a time undertook the leadership of each party, the historian, Ssǔ-ma Kuang (A.D. 1019–86) on the one hand and Wang An-shih (A.D. 1021–86) on the other. Both were Confucian scholars of great eminence. Both were men of the highest integrity. Yet in their ideas as to what policies would serve the country best they could not have stood further apart. For some twenty years Wang An-shih had the enlightened support of the emperor Shên-tsung, and served him as prime minister. In that capacity he was deeply concerned on account of the economic and military weakness of the empire. He put through a number of far-reaching reforms by which he fostered a tighter governmental control over the lives and activities of the people. To do this he called for a reorganization of higher education, and a radical reappraisal of the examination system for the civil service. He insisted that, though the Confucian Classics should still be the basis of examination, the emphasis ought not to be placed on memorizing their contents, or on literary style, but rather on the practical application of Confucian ideas to current problems and situations. In all his reforms Wang An-shih was bitterly opposed by the conservatives, and when his patron and protector, Shên-tsung, died in A.D. 1085, the Conservative party came back into power and Wang's reforms were swept aside. Ssŭ-ma Kuang believed that government should interfere as little as possible in the financial and economic affairs of the people and in their private pursuits. The good Confucian ruler was one who gave a moral example to his people, and the chief role of government was an ethical one. Had Wang An-shih's reforming policies been adopted, Sung China might have been made strong enough to resist the aggression of its northern neighbours. As it was, the dynasty which became for ever famous for its cultural achievement, its poets, historians, artists and craftsmen, remained politically weak and militarily ineffective.

The Confucian control of education and the examination system was accompanied by a revival of interest in the cult of Confucius himself. For centuries Confucius had been the patron saint of scholars and of education. Under the Sung he became the patron deity of the civil government. In A.D. 960 the Emperor T'ai-tsu had the Confucian temple restored and the images of Confucius and his chief disciples repaired, whilst representations of the seventy-two disciples and the famous scholars of former times were painted on the walls. The emperor himself sacrificed to Confucius and Yen Hui. In A.D. 1055 the head of the Confucian clan was ennobled as duke, whilst in A.D. 1084 Mencius was given the posthumous title of duke and his image was placed beside that of Yen Hui. In A.D. 1074 an abortive attempt was made to give Confucius the title *ti*, a title which had long been associated in the Chinese mind with the idea of divinity. A decree was made that officials should dress themselves in their robes of state when making sacrifices to Confucius, thus signifying that they acted not simply in their capacity of Confucian scholars but as representing the civil government.[4]

In both religion and philosophy Buddhism was regarded as the chief rival of Confucianism. Though throughout the Sung dynasty it declined both as a moral and as an intellectual force, it continued to receive the patronage and support of emperors. Sung T'ai-tsu, whilst contributing so much to the revival of Confucianism, was by no means averse to Buddhism. After he had ascended the throne, on the anniversary of his birthday he ordered the ordination of eight thousand Buddhist monks. He frequently invited virtuous monks to his palace, conferring on them the honour of wearing a purple robe. He despatched a large mission to the west in search of Buddhist teachings, and established a translation bureau[5] under imperial patronage. He ordered the first printing of the Buddhist *Tripitaka*,[6] and was one of the few Chinese emperors who took the Buddhist layman's vows. Succeeding Sung emperors were favourable in their attitude towards Buddhism.[7] Large numbers of the scholar class, whilst acting as orthodox Confucians in their official capacity, were privately attracted to Buddhism. It had so much to offer them: its colourful rituals, its profound philosophy and its religious comfort and consolation. At that time Confucianism had nothing to match the aesthetic and religious appeal of Buddhism, whose temples and monasteries were places of architectural beauty, richly decorated with the gilded images of Buddhas and *bodhisattvas*, with vivid paintings of scenes from the life of Gautama, the glorious promise of life in Amitabha's western paradise, the fate of the unrepentant in hell. Its magnificent festivals and processions brought colour and pageantry to the drab lives of the people, whilst the monks moved among them preaching a message of hope to the sorrowful and the suffering. Confucianism had no firm philosophical basis on which to counter Buddhist theories as to the origin and nature of the universe, and the origin, nature and destiny of man. It was not enough simply to denigrate Buddhism as a foreign religion and therefore unsuited to the Chinese mentality; nor was it enough to point to the obvious shortcomings of Buddhism, its economic and social disadvantages and the moral laxity of many of the clergy. Confucianism needed two things if it was to triumph over Buddhism and Taoism and become the recognized state orthodoxy. In the first place, it needed a coherent and logically satisfying philosophy to counter that of Buddhism, and it had to present that philosophy as an extension and development of ideas already expressed, at least in germ, in the ancient Confucian Classics. That is, it had to endow that philosophy with the authority of Confucius himself. Secondly, it had to organize the cult of Confucius and with it the worship of ancestors and the nature-gods in such a way that its religious and aesthetic expression in rituals, symbols, pageants, music, art and architecture would prove more satisfying to the intelligentsia than that of

Buddhism or Taoism. In both these respects, from the Sung dynasty onwards, Confucianism developed in ways that Confucius himself could never have envisaged, and which might even have merited his condemnation.

We shall leave to Chapter 8 a discussion of the state cult of Confucianism which reached the peak of its magnificence in the days of the Emperor K'ang Hsi and his immediate successors. In the rest of this chapter we shall discuss the Neo-Confucian revival, which is always associated with the Sung dynasty and which re-established the pre-eminence of Confucianism as a way of life and provided it with metaphysics.

The Neo-Confucian Revival

As we saw in the last chapter, there were Confucian scholars in the T'ang dynasty who protested strongly against the growing influence of Buddhism and the introduction into China of foreign ideas and practices. They sought to inculcate the Confucian teaching concerning the cultivation of the self, the regulation of family, social responsibility, good government and universal peace. They protested not only against obvious abuses within the Buddhist *Sangha*,[8] but against the Buddhist emphasis on other-worldliness, the illusoriness of all phenomena and the doctrine of the Void (*Sunyatā*.)[9] They sought to return to China's own cultural heritage.

When, with the establishment of the Sung dynasty, there came about a revival of the influence of Confucianism in the state administration and in education, a growing need was felt to find in Confucianism answers to the intellectual problems that had been raised by Buddhism. The Chinese intelligentsia had come under the spell of the cosmology and the metaphysics associated with the great Buddhist *Mahāyāna sūtras* as expounded by learned Buddhist masters. These Buddhist masters repudiated the idea of a permanent self. They placed emphasis on transience, impermanence, continuing process. They taught that all phenomena are bound up in a nexus of relationships with everything else, and are only transient expressions of the universal One, the abiding Reality, which went under various names: the Buddha nature, the Void, Nirvāna. They held a cyclical rather than a linear view of time. In opposition to these Buddhist views the Confucian scholars insisted on the reality of the self and of the phenomenal universe. For them this experienced universe is the only reality. For the most part they rejected the idealistic philosophy of Buddhism and believed that 'material force' was an essential constituent of reality. When they turned to the Confucian Classics they found only in the *I Ching* the basis for philosophical theories with which to oppose the metaphysical speculations of the Buddhists. In their study of what they believed to be the teaching of Confucius they found certain fundamental teachings which they felt must be re-emphasized. These may be summed up under four headings: (a) human nature and the cosmic order; (b) the way to achieve human perfection and an ideal human society; (c) the principle of government by moral example; (d) the cardinal importance of education. What was needed, however, was to find philosophical justification for this Confucian way of life. What was the use in insisting on individual and social perfection in this world if, as the Buddhists taught, everything is transitory, impermanent and illusory and the only reality is to be found beyond this world in Nirvana? 'The effect of Buddhist metaphysics was to drive Chinese Confucians into thinking in universal terms.'[10]

Five names stand out in the history of Chinese philosophy as the great Neo-Confucianists of the eleventh century They were Chou Tun-i (1017–73), Shao Yung (1011–77), Chang Tsai (1020–77), Ch'êng Hao (1032–85) and Ch'êng I (1033–1107). These men were followed in the twelfth century by Lu Hsiang-shan (1139–93) and Chu Hsi (1130–1200) who has been universally recognized as the greatest of them all. Through the writings of these men Confucianism was provided with a metaphysics which proved to be on the whole more satisfying to the Chinese mind than the philosophies of either Buddhism or Taoism. In addition, the basic doctrines of Confucianism, and their ethical and social implications, were so firmly re-established as the norm for human behaviour that for the next seven hundred years Neo-Confucian interpretations of Confucius's teaching dominated Chinese thought, and extended their influence in Korea and Japan.

These Neo-Confucian philosophers all believed that they were simply adapting the basic teachings of the Confucian Classics to the needs of their own time. They believed that they were going back to the original teaching of Confucius and his disciples. They were, in fact, relying on a syncretistic philosophy which had emerged in the latter part of the Han dynasty, and in particular on the *I Ching* (*Book of Changes*), which, though regarded as an integral part of the Confucian Canon, was itself the result of a strange admixture of early divination texts with *Yin-Yang* and 'five elements' theories and Taoist cosmological speculations. When they turned to theories of human nature and a system of ethics they relied on *Mencius*, the *Chung Yung* and the *Ta Hsüeh*, and in doing so were probably much nearer to the actual teaching of Confucius than was Tung Chung-shu and the Confucian–Taoist syncretists of the Former Han dynasty.[11]

All movements in the realm of thought, however unique they may seem to be, rely in all kinds of ways on what has gone before. The Sung philosophy has been called Neo-Confucianism and yet it drew heavily on Buddhist and Taoist ideas. In a very real sense it was a synthesis. Confucian texts, which were themselves the result of the synthesis of many different post-Confucian philosophies of the Warring States and Han periods, were now re-studied in the light of the philosophical teachings of Buddhist and Taoist schools. The Neo-Confucian philosophers were unable to divest themselves of ideas represented by such terms as 'non-action'; 'returning to the root'; 'cosmic rhythm'; 'consciousness only'; 'the void'. Nearly all of them spent some considerable period of their lives in the study of Buddhism and Taoism.

It would prove tedious in a book of this nature to attempt even a superficial survey of the contributions to philosophical thought made by each of the leading Neo-Confucian scholars.[12] All we can do is to refer briefly to those ideas which seem to be of greatest significance in establishing Confucianism as the orthodox Chinese way of life. Two very short works, produced in the early stages, were to have a seminal influence on the development of Neo-Confucianism. They were the *Diagram of the Supreme Ultimate and its Explanations* by Chou Tun-i, and 'The Western Inscription' of Chang Tsai, a brief essay which was originally part of the seventeenth chapter of a longer work known as *Correct Discipline for Beginners*.[13]

Chou Tun-i, the first of the Neo-Confucian philosophers, has been called the peerless founder of Sung philosophy. His explanatory commentary on the *Diagram of the Supreme Ultimate* owed much to Taoist inspiration,[14] and yet was based on the *I Ching* (*Book of Changes*). It was a systematic attempt to explain the origin of all things in the universe, and it became the basis of almost all subsequent cosmological speculation in China. According to Chou Tun-i's theory, the Supreme Ultimate, which is real and not void, produces *yang* and *yin* through the alternations between movement and quiescence. Then, by the transformations of the *yang* and its union with *yin*, the five primary elements (*ch'i*) of water, fire, wood, metal and earth are produced. From these, through their various convolutions, all the phenomena of the universe come into being. Chou Tun-i does not attempt to explain why there is this alternation of rest and motion within the Supreme Ultimate. He just accepts that this is so, probably because he saw that all things in nature were subject to alternations of quiescence and movement.

In his explanations to the *Diagram of the Supreme Ultimate* Chou Tun-i uses two terms which became of key importance in Neo-Confucianism. There was *ch'i*, which may be translated as 'ether, material force, substance', and there was *li*, which is translated as 'principle'. By 'principle' he means an immaterial and metaphysical principle which underlies and yet transcends the physical universe. It is 'the principle of organization', the 'order and pattern in nature', the 'dynamic pattern' as embodied in all phenomena, in human relationships and in the highest human values. All phenomena ultimately derive from the Supreme Ultimate which, besides providing the matter or substance of every individual thing, also endows it with its constitutive principle. Principle is like the *Tao*, which transcends all things yet is inherent in all things. Without *Tao* they cannot exist. It is what gives them 'being'.

Undoubtedly influenced as he was by Taoist thought, as a true Confucian Chou Tun-i believed that in man the Principle of the Supreme Ultimate and also the material essence of the Five Elements were unmixed and supremely good and so he was the highest of all creatures. His nature, in its original state of quiescence is fundamentally good. Evil arises because human nature, in the stirrings of activity and in its relation to external things, loses its accord with the golden mean, and the result is that man's observable conduct might be either good or bad or a mixture of both. Man's aim should be a return to the original state of quiescence, which is represented by the golden mean. W. T. Chan claims that Chou Tun-i 'was the one who laid the foundation of Neo-Confucianism, and determined its direction. He provided the cosmology and ethics for later Confucianism.'[15]

Chang Tsai's teaching that all things are manifestations of the one principle of the universe led him to the concept that Heaven and Earth, human beings and all things in the universe are members one of another. We should regard Heaven and Earth as our parents, all people as our brothers and sisters, all things as our companions. Though all things have their own individual characteristics, and as such differ from each other, they are all equally of one substance with the principle of the universe. Nothing exists in absolute isolation from other things, but all form part of a continuous cycle of creation and dissolution. Accepting this kinship of all creation, the superior man knows that the one thing that encompasses and binds together the whole universe is the supreme Confucian virtue of love (*jên*). In the words of Mencius, 'The superior man ... loves all things.'[16] Chang Tsai criticized both the Buddhists and the Taoists, in that Buddhism sought the destruction of life as we know it and entrance into Nirvāna from which there is no return, whereas Taoism aimed at the infinite prolongation of life by clinging to the present form of existence. According to Chang Tsai, the sage should seek neither to destroy nor to prolong existence, but should conform himself to the will of Heaven, model himself on his parents, Heaven and Earth, and do nothing to violate or destroy humanity (*jên*). The sage nourishes his mind and his nature with untiring effort. He regards wealth, honour, blessing and benefits as life's enrichment, and poverty, humble station and sorrow as life's disciplines. So in life he follows and serves his parents, Heaven and Earth, and when death comes he will be at peace. In this way Chang Tsai summarizes the Neo-Confucian attitude to life and death, based on the philosophy that human life is but a manifestation which results from the evolution of the supreme principle of the universe to which all shall ultimately return.

According to Fung Yu-lan it was the Ch'êng brothers, Ch'êng Hao and Ch'êng I who established Neo-Confucianism as an organized school. They studied under Chou Tun-i and were friends of Shao Yung and related to Chang Tsai.[17] W. T. Chan says that the two brothers set the pattern for Neo-Confucianism and that, though utterly different in temperament, they agreed essentially in their philosophy, which was based on the concept of the Principle of Nature or Heavenly Principle (*T'ien Li*) which is 'self-evident, and self sufficient, extending everywhere and governing all things and cannot be augmented or diminished . . . All things exist because of it and can be understood through it. It is universal truth or natural law. It is the principle of order, the universal process of creation and production.'[18]

Ch'êng Hao is regarded as the forerunner of the idealistic school of Neo-Confucianism, later known as the School for the study of Mind (Hsin-hsüeh-chia). His younger brother, Ch'êng I, who placed great emphasis on the importance of extending knowledge by the investigation of things, developed a more rationalistic spirit, and was the forerunner of the Rationalist school or the School for the study of Principle (Li-hsüeh-chia). Both these brothers had a great influence on the political and philosophical thinking of their own time. Ch'êng I lived on for some twenty-two years after the death of his elder brother. In the highest Confucian tradition he felt free to criticize openly those in power, and in consequence aroused such bitter opposition that his teachings were prohibited till almost half a century after his death. By that time Chu Hsi had reached manhood and as a result of his teaching, based on the philosophy of Ch'êng I, what is known as the Ch'êng-Chu school of Neo-Confucianism rapidly developed.

Chu Hsi (*1130–1200*)

No one did more than Chu Hsi to re-establish Confucianism in China. By his prolific writings and his commentaries on the Confucian books he created a version of Confucianism which gained general acceptance after his death and continued to remain Confucian orthodoxy till the twentieth century. 'His most radical innovation was to select and group the *Analects*, the *Book of Mencius*, *The Great Learning* and the *Doctrine of the Mean*, as the Four Books. He wrote commentaries on them, interpreted them in new lights, and made them the foundation of his social and ethical philosophy.'[19]

Born into a literary family, he studied Buddhism and Taoism, finally rejecting them both in favour of Confucianism when he was about thirty. A brilliant student, he passed the government examinations when he was nineteen, and from that time onwards held a succession of official posts. His teachings were far from being universally accepted in his own lifetime, and it was not till several years after his death that he was posthumously ennobled as duke. His tablet was given a place of honour in the Confucian temples.

Chu Hsi had a marvellous gift of being able to synthesize into one coherent system the ideas of the Neo-Confucian scholars of the eleventh century. His metaphysics was based on the cosmology of Chou Tun-i and the numerology of Shao Yung, both in large measure derived from the *I Ching*. He took over Chang Tsai's theory of 'ether' or 'material force' (*Ch'i*). From the Ch'êng brothers he learned the distinction between 'what is above shapes' and 'what is within shapes', between 'principle' (*li*) and 'material force' (*ch'i*). Chu Hsi believed that the universe and every single thing within it, though they came into being as a result of the activity of 'material force' (*ch'i*), could not exist apart from the immaterial principle of their organization (*li*). All things in the universe, whether natural or man-made, exist because of archetypal principles which were there before the things themselves had any actual existence. Somewhat in the same way as the *idea* of a building or a machine is there before the actual construction – and though in no way an actual part of the structure, is yet absolutely essential, so that the structure succeeds in so far as it approximates to the idea – so everything in existence is dependent on 'principle'. There is 'principle' before there is 'material force', but only when there is 'material force' has 'principle' a place to rest. Neither existence nor non-existence may be attributed to it, for it is eternal, transcending the distinctions of existence and non-existence. All the individual principles of things are contained in the universal principle, and each individual thing contains in its entirety the principles of everything else. One is reminded of the Buddhist simile of Brahman's net, in which the innumerable jewels which hang from the intersections reflect the light which is endlessly reflected in every other jewel. No doubt Chu Hsi owed something to Buddhism, but he rejected the Buddhist emphasis on 'pure consciousness' or 'mind only' and over against their doctrine of the 'Void' he thinks of 'Reality' in positive terms as a transcendent principle, a Supreme Ultimate which in conjunction with 'material force' (*ch'i*) produces a dynamic universe.

Chu Hsi thought of human beings as being originally produced, like all other things in the universe, spontaneously through the natural evolutions of material force in which principle adheres. It is the principle (*li*) contained within material force to form a human individual which is known as his 'nature' (*hsing*). This nature is therefore wholly good. Nevertheless, as soon as it is actualized in the material form the result is loss of perfection owing to the limitations imposed by the latter. The nature, which is nothing but principle, is distinguished by Chu Hsi from consciousness or mind. Mind results from the union of principles with material force, and when activated produces feelings and desires. Thus, while nature is wholly good, the mind is not so. All men are endowed with the same principle, but they differ as to the nature of the material force with which they are also endowed. So they differ in intellect, in natural capacities, in the strength of feelings, emotions and desires. Chu Hsi likens human nature to a precious pearl lying in water. In the case of a sage the water is pure and clean and so the pearl shines in all its loveliness. With most men the water is turbid and muddy so that the pearl can hardly be seen or its quality perceived. Chu Hsi, whilst recognizing that the nature of men and of other creatures is essentially the same, so that animals have some things in common with man, believed that man was distinguished by having moral principle. He was born endowed with the 'Mean', the attribute of Heaven and Earth, and by following this he gives full expression to the four cardinal virtues of love (*jên*), righteousness (*i*), propriety (*li*) and wisdom (*chih*). 'For the nature to attain the Mean is as natural as for water to be cold and fire hot; but the Mean is disturbed because men becloud it by habits engendered by the material element.'[20] It is this recognition by Chu Hsi that in the constitutive principle or 'nature' of man there was a moral endowment which led him to his emphasis on moral cultivation and especially on what he recognizes as the supreme virtue of the mind, namely love (*jên*), by the operation of which it is possible to practise righteousness. It is selfish desire and excess of feelings which obscure the Principle of Nature or Heavenly Principle (*T'ien Li*) in man. This Heavenly Principle can be realized by those who follow the instruction found in *The Great Learning*. It is necessary to rectify the mind through the extension of knowledge by the investigation of things. As Fung Yu-lan has pointed out, 'When Chu speaks of the investigation of things, he really has in mind only a system of moral cultivation, and his aim is solely to reach an understanding of the workings of our own minds ... It is a mistake to regard Chu as here displaying a truly scientific spirit, or to consider him as seeking only for pure knowledge.'[21]

Like the other Neo-Confucians, Chu Hsi is basically concerned, as was Confucius himself, with ethical and political problems and their solution. Accepting that human nature is 'principle' and inherently good, the Confucian aim in life was to eliminate everything which stands in the way of uncovering the true nature, which being 'Heaven implanted' is perfectly sincere (*ch'êng*), containing within itself the virtues of love, righteousness, propriety and wisdom. The purpose of moral education is to cause 'illustrious virtue to shine forth'[22] because that is man's fundamental nature, unclouded and unbesmirched by undesirable movements of the mind towards external stimuli.

Just as for the individual the aim of education is to allow one's heaven-bestowed nature to shine forth, so the art of good government is to bring the state to approximate ever more closely to its own 'principle of organization' by which the welfare and peace of all the people is assured.

Contemporary with Chu Hsi was Lu Hsiang-shan (1139–93), the founder of the idealistic school of Neo-Confucianism known as Hsin-hsüeh or 'Teaching concerning the mind'. He was a strong opponent of Chu Hsi with whom, in the year 1175, he had a famous discussion, which was followed later by a long correspondence. As we have seen, Chu Hsi's philosophy tended to be dualistic in that he sharply distinguished 'principle' (*li*) from 'material force' (*ch'i*), and considered mind or consciousness to be a function of the human nature (*hsing*), which later he identified with principle. Lu Hsiang-shan, on the other hand, saw mind as identical with principle. 'The mind is one and principle is one. Perfect truth is reduced to a unity: the essential principle is never a duality. The mind and principle can never be separated into two.'[23] Mind is one and indissoluble, filling the whole universe: 'The universe is my mind, and my mind is the universe. Sages . . . shared this mind; they shared this principle.' 'There is only one mind. My mind, my friend's mind, the mind of the sages thousands of years ago, and the mind of sages thousands of years to come are all the same. The substance of mind is infinite. If one can completely develop his mind, he will become identified with Heaven. To acquire learning is to appreciate this fact.'[24]

Whereas for Chu Hsi the investigation of things means the investigation of principle in things, and the emphasis is placed on study and inquiry, for Lu Hsiang-shan the way of life to be advocated is to rid the mind of all selfishness, partiality and those physical desires by which it has become corrupted, and to study to bring it back to its original purity. According to him the purpose of Confucian education is to assist men to develop the inborn capacities of the mind, for 'moral principles inherent in the mind are endowed by Heaven, and cannot be wiped out. Those who are beclouded by material desires so as to pervert principles and violate righteousness, do so because they do not think, that is all.'[25] If men would think, they would recognize that there is a universal law, present in and apprehended by the mind, which provides a moral criterion for human conduct. Humanity (*jên*) and righteousness (*i*) are the original mind. Thus, Lu Hsiang-shan finds the basis for Confucian doctrine in the fact that there is a Way (*Tao*) for Heaven, a Way for Earth and a Way for Man. Man can only co-exist with Heaven and Earth in so far as he follows the Way for man, which is founded in beneficence and righteousness, and the result is seen in the Confucian urge to put the world in order. Lu contrasted the Confucian way of life with that taught by the Buddhists. He criticized the Buddhists because they failed to reach the goal of impartiality; their professed aim was to escape from this world of sorrow and suffering. Confucians, on the other hand, considered that the living of life in this world is our chief concern and well worthwhile if the result were the attainment of impartiality and the development of the capacity for reflective knowledge.

Lu's Idealistic school of Neo-Confucianism was to find its greatest protagonist some three centuries later in the famous

Ming dynasty philosopher, Wang Yang-ming (1472–1529). His fundamental doctrine was that all men possess an original mind whose unifying quality is 'love' (*jên*). This love is rooted in man's Heaven-born nature, but so often it is overlaid by selfish desire which results from the motions of the will. The original mind possesses an intuitive knowledge, which, however, has to be uncovered and developed. To bring intuitive knowledge into actual operation is the highest wisdom. 'The mind of man constitutes Heaven in all its profundity, within which there is nothing that is not included. Originally there was nothing but the single Heaven, but because of the barriers caused by selfish desires we have lost this original state of Heaven. If we now concentrate our thoughts on extending knowledge, so as to sweep away all barriers and obstructions, the original state will then be again restored, and we will become part of the profundity of Heaven.'[26]

A recurring theme of Wang's philosophy is the oneness of knowing and doing. There is no such thing as knowledge which cannot be carried into practice. Knowledge is the beginning of conduct and conduct is the completion of knowledge. But Wang's major concern is with ethical conduct. As with most Confucian philosophers, the task of achieving a good character is always uppermost in his mind. One preserves the innate goodness of the mind only at the price of eternal vigilance. Sincerity of the will is a prerequisite for the investigation of things.

In this brief account of the philosophy of the Neo-Confucians we have seen how Confucianism established itself against Taoism and Buddhism as the officially accepted doctrine and as the way of life for the scholar class. The Confucian Canon, now regarded as sacred and authoritative, as interpreted and reinterpreted by various Confucian schools which grew up from this time onwards, proved to be more conductive to the Chinese temperament than the recondite teachings of Mahāyāna metaphysics. Nearly all the Neo-Confucian philosophers were also men of affairs, and not recluses. They were for the best part of their adult lives immersed in politics, active in government administration, engaged in literary and artistic pursuits and in the study of history. Many of them suffered disgrace and punishment because of their sturdy independence, their criticism of abuse in high places and their intellectual and moral integrity.

The period in which the Sung emperors ruled, though politically disastrous, was one of the most productive in the whole of Chinese history for cultural achievements. Above all it was a period in which the contents rather than the literary form of the Confucian Classics were the subject of intense study, and because of this the idea was inculcated that to live and act in accordance with the precepts of Confucius was the highest and noblest achievement possible to man on this earth. If he accepted and followed as best he could the Confucian way of life, there would be no need to concern himself with what followed after death.

8. A Civilization moulded by Confucius

THE reassertion of Confucianism in the Sung dynasty and the revitalization of Confucian doctrine led to a general recognition of the superiority of the Confucian cultural heritage over a variety of foreign religions, especially Buddhism, which had spread their influence in China during the T'ang dynasty. From the Sung dynasty onwards, if we exclude the century of Mongol rule (1260–1368) when foreigners were used extensively in the government administration and Tibetan or Lama Buddhism was favoured by the Mongol emperors, the political influence of Buddhism and Taoism gradually declined and Confucianism dominated almost every aspect of the national life. The result was the emergence of a Confucian civilization which in times of imperial greatness brought about a state of peace and prosperity unequalled anywhere else in the world. The system also proved strong enough to weather those periods of imperial decadence and corruption which almost always led to a change of dynasty. Foreign visitors to China, from the time of Marco Polo onwards, again and again expressed their wonder and admiration, not only at the wealth and splendour of the teeming cities, but at the orderliness and industry of society, the regard for law of the common people, the peaceableness of the countryside, the display of mutual courtesy in human relationships, the obedience shown to parents and those in authority, and the consideration shown for the aged, the sick and the infirm. On all sides was evidence of the humanizing influence of the teachings of Confucius whose name was revered. Writing of the capital city of Hang-chou, where the last of the Sung emperors had made their court, Marco Polo refers to the 'dislike and distaste for strife or any sort of disagreement. They pursue their trades and handicrafts with great diligence and honesty. They love one another so devotebly that a whole district might seem, from the friendly and neighbourly spirit that rules among men and women, to be a single household.'[1] Elsewhere he speaks of the modesty of young men and women and their strict observance of decorum, of the industry of the people, the thriving commerce and industry resulting in great wealth, the lack of crime and the sense of order and justice. Marco Polo wrote of thirteenth-century China, but a similar picture is drawn for us some four centuries later by Friar Domingo Navarette who, travelling from Canton in 1659 for nine days with three soldiers, declared 'they could not have been civiler had they been good Christians. I was astonished at their courtesy, calmness and good behaviour.' He writes of China as 'the most glorious empire in all natural respects that the sun ever shines upon . . . great in all respects, rich, fruitful, abounding in plenty of all things and powerful.'[2] Undoubtedly there was, as in medieval Europe, much inequality, injustice and oppression and there were many evils to excite loathing and contempt. The Confucian bureaucracy never lacked its quota of hypocritical and self-seeking officials. Under weak and licentious rulers there was soon manifest on every hand a sad departure from the high standards of Confucian morality. But on the whole and over a remarkable period of time Confucianism worked well. It worked so long as in Chinese eyes their country was the central or Middle Kingdom of the world, their emperor the vice-regent or Son of Heaven on earth and their scholars, trained and educated in the classical Confucian tradition, allowed to run the administrative machinery of the whole country.

It was contrary to the spirit and temper of Confucianism to persecute anyone because of his personally-held religious beliefs and practices, so long as those beliefs and practices were not inimical to the interests of the state. Many Confucians were like the Sung dynasty scholar and poet, Su Tung-p'o (1036–1101) who seems always to have been torn between his Confucian sense of duty towards his fellow men and his desire to seek peace and personal salvation in Buddhist meditation or Taoist mysticism.[3] There were few Confucian homes which did not from time to time seek the ministrations of Buddhist or Taoist priests, especially at the time of death, when the funeral and mourning rites were largely performed by Buddhist monks, who were considered to be expert in the rituals and prayers by which the soul of the dead was conveyed into the Paradise of Amida Buddha.

Yet even though the ministrations of Buddhist and Taoist priests might be gratefully accepted, the strict Confucian family would meticulously follow the detailed rites of mourning as prescribed in the Confucian Classic known as the *Li Chi* or *Book of Rites*.[4] So long as education and the state examinations were controlled by Confucian scholars and the Confucian Classics remained the principal subject of study and examination, Confucianism remained in an impregnable position. However much an emperor might be personally inclined towards Buddhism or Taoism, the way to an official position was neither through the study of Buddhist *sūtras* nor the esoteric books of Taoism. There were few aspects of political or social life which could not be made to fit in with the teachings of Confucius or with the Classics which were generally attributed to him. The status and functions of the emperor, the class distinctions in society, the seclusion of women in the home, the cult of ancestors and national heroes, the educational system, the inculcation of morals, even such minor matters as dress, deportment and etiquette, were all laid down in the Confucian teaching and had the binding force of customary law.

It may seem strange that the Confucian scholars who had made themselves so indispensable to the efficient running of the state should have tolerated for so long an absolute monarchy, and made no serious attempt to curtail the emperor's powers. There were many times when Confucian statesmen were prepared to go to absurd lengths in their toleration of the misguided acts of self-indulgence and cruelty perpetrated by weak or vicious emperors. The history of China is full of instances in which the wrath of the ruler is directed against some loyal and honest Confucian official, so that he is stripped of all his honours and dignities, impoverished, banished, perhaps even deprived of life itself. His friends and colleagues, fully aware of his innocence, dare to do no more on his behalf than make 'gentle remonstrance' and that at the risk of their own demotion. What was written of the Ming emperor known as Wan Li (1573–1620), who came to the throne as a boy of nine and died at the early age of thirty-eight, is equally true of several emperors of China. 'During the last sixteen years he had seen no one but his concubines and eunuchs face to face. Formerly he had left the palace, but always with the strictest precautions as though travelling in enemy country, surrounded by thousands of soldiers, and hidden away in one of many litters – not even members of the court knew which ... The more the missionaries [Jesuit] heard about Wan Li, the more discouraged they became. The extraordinary honours and powers he enjoyed in so civilized a country had led them to expect an Augustus; instead he appeared to be a Nero, given to rapacity, anger and insatiable greed ... Laziness had turned him, at the age of thirty-eight, into a bloated monster whose voice could hardly be heard at ten feet. The only man in a city of eunuchs and women, emperor since the age of nine, he was nevertheless dominated by his favourites of the moment and by his own lusts. He issued the necessary rescripts but showed no interest in government; he cherished his harem, his porcelain and the cult of himself.'[5] And this was the man who, alone in all the land, was empowered to offer religious sacrifices to August Heaven.

How could a Confucian bureaucracy, schooled in Confucian morality, tolerate the absolute authority of rulers of this nature? Why did they not revolt against rulers who were for all practical purposes completely cut off from their people, served by hundreds and even thousands of vicious, self-seeking eunuchs, surrounded by concubines and numerous children, and subjected all the time to palace intrigues? As J. Levenson wrote, 'What could cause more revulsion in Confucianists with their code of ethical relationships, than the patricidal or fratricidal episodes that disfigure so many imperial family histories? Eunuchs, whom Confucianists scorned and often hated, and coupled with "monks" as "bad elements", were characteristic members of imperial retinues.'[6]

The Confucian administrators always had before them historical precedents to warn them of the fate that would inevitably befall any ministers of state who had the temerity to oppose the whims of misguided emperors. Such, for instance, was the vicious persecution of former high ministers of state when the young womanizing emperor, Chê Tsung (1086–1101) obtained absolute power on the death of his grandmother in 1093. The persecution extended to several ministers who had been outstanding in their loyal service and even to the family of the famous statesman-historian, Ssŭ-ma Kuang, who had died in 1086. 'The properties of Szema Kuang's family were confiscated, all official honours and emoluments were taken away from his children, the tomb structures built by the government in his honour were demolished and the inscription erected by the Empress Dowager was ground off.' [7] One of the glories of Confucianism has been the host of honest and incorruptible scholars who were prepared to die, if necessary, for their principles. One of its weaknesses has been that it all too often left to Taoist secret societies the task of inspiring those revolts which led to the overthrow of corrupt and evil rulers. Confucianism appealed to reason, to good sense and good manners, to a peaceable solution of problems. When all that failed, the good Confucian official sought permission to retire from office that he might spend the remainder of his life in the scholarly pursuits of the rural gentry. There are times in history when it seems that passionate hatred and burning fanaticism are the only weapons against evil in high places. These are qualities which have never been inculcated by Confucianism.

Is it not true that in the teaching of Confucius himself we can find one of the main causes of the failure to move towards a more democratic form of government and a more equitable society? So long as Confucian ideology was dominant in the state, only one loyalty took precedence over loyalty to the throne, and that was loyalty to one's own conscience and principles. When these two loyalties conflicted a minister of state was usually given permission to resign or was banished to some remote magistracy. Sometimes, however, his temerity resulted in a sentence of death upon himself and his immediate family. Confucius had stressed the virtues of filial piety and loyalty. He also insisted on the need for a strict grading in social relationships. Whilst teaching that those who rule, whether in family or in state, should exercise the virtues of benevolence and kindness, he never seems to have questioned their right to absolute authority. If a son believed his father to be wrong in the pursuit of a course of action which would inevitably lead to suffering and disaster, he could do no more than 'gently remonstrate'. A high minister of state had the right and, indeed, the duty to make his views known to the throne if he believed the ruler to be pursuing a harmful or dangerous course, but so long as he remained in office he must be completely loyal in carrying out his lord's commands. Confucius was strongly opposed to any attempt to usurp the honours, dignities and functions of one's overlord, even though that overlord might be weak or tyrannical. He was bitter in his condemnation of the head of the Chi family when he usurped the power of the Duke of Lu.[8] With his eye ever on the sage-kings of old, Confucius believed in autocracy, the absolute authority of the one who had patently received the mandate of Heaven. When, in the Han dynasty, Confucianism was adapted to the needs of empire, Confucian doctrine, whilst refusing to consider the emperor as divine, nevertheless so surrounded the emperor's person with an aura of majesty and sanctity as the 'Son of Heaven', that, from that time onwards and right through to the twentieth century the focus of social and national stability was thought to reside in the emperor's person and functions.

Until the shattering influences from the West and the forced recognition that China was only one among many great nations, each with its own distinctive and independent form of government, the Chinese people were quite content to accept a Confucian philosophy of the universe as modified by Taoism and Buddhism, and as worked out by the great Neo-Confucian thinkers of the Sung dynasty. According to their theory, built upon the teaching of the Confucian Classics and on Han dynasty precedents, Heaven controlled the destinies of men whilst Earth was the great sustainer and nourisher. Both these powers worked through innumerable spiritual agencies, which pervaded the natural world, and constantly impinged upon human affairs. Just as the emperor, supreme on earth, needed the services of a host of ministers, officials, soldiers, servants so that the power and influence of his 'virtue' might pervade the whole of his vast domain, so Heaven functioned through a host of spiritual beings. Since Heaven, Earth and Man formed a trinity, and the emperor owed his appointment to Heaven itself, the highest function of the emperor was to ensure that all human affairs should be kept in perfect harmony with the Will of Heaven, and that the nourishing and fructifying powers of earth should find their maximum effectiveness for the benefit of mankind. This meant that the rites and ceremonies which were designed to ensure the mutual cooperation of the human, natural and spiritual worlds so as to produce universal harmony were considered to be the most important function of government. Of all the six important ministers set up to assist the emperor, that of the *Li Pu*, or Board of Rites, was most important.

As in ancient times, right up to the founding of the Republic, the Confucian state was grounded in religion, or rather in the meticulous performance of an elaborate state cult. This state cult demanded for its observance a monarchical form of government. As the eldest male heir had the duty to offer sacrifices to the ancestral spirits of the family, so the emperor, as the appointed son of Heaven, could alone offer the appropriate sacrifices to Heaven and Earth.

It is interesting that from the Sung dynasty onwards, the tendency among Confucian scholars was to be agnostic, humanistic and rationalistic. Those who were religiously or mystically inclined found satisfaction in Buddhism or Taoism. Very few Confucians could, indeed, be said to accept a thorough-going belief in theism, and most of them scorned the polytheism and superstitions of popular religion in China, and yet there were equally few who were able to maintain a thoroughly agnostic and rationalistic attitude. Of course there were some scholars who argued that the sacrificial rites had a merely secular function, being a useful means to inculcate moral values and to regulate social conduct. In the same way they argued that the ancestral cult was designed to emphasize family loyalty, encourage filial piety and maintain the solidarity of the kinship group. Most Confucians, however, believed that the sacrifices were made to spiritual beings that had a real existence outside the imagination of the sacrificer, and that the souls of their beloved parents lived on after death. They were prepared to go to great expense to see that regular sacrifices to ancestor spirits were maintained. Though monotheism was practically confined to the minority groups of Islam and Christianity, the Confucians, on the whole, believed that human happiness and harmony are dependent upon the social and political order being adjusted to conform to a moral cosmic order of which man is a part. It was always a Confucian belief that attempts should be made to fathom and unravel the secrets of the course of events which Heaven had predetermined. In that way calamity might be avoided and man's welfare assured. Few Confucians could be found who did not believe in divination, astrology, the theories of *Yin-Yang* and the Five

Elements. As C. K. Yang wrote, 'The belief in Heaven and fate, the condoning of divination, the close alliance with the theory of Yin-Yang and the Five Elements, the emphasis on sacrifice and ancestor worship as a basic means of social control, and the lack of a thorough agnostic and rationalistic attitude towards spiritual matters – all these represented major aspects of Confucian doctrine. These religious factors were important for the functioning of Confucianism as the guiding doctrine in a society in which gods and spirits were thought to lurk in every corner.'[9]

As there was very little fundamental change in Confucian doctrine and practice from the Sung dynasty until the end of the monarchy, we shall now look at Confucian civilization when it reached the apex of its strength and influence in the days of one of the greatest of all the emperors who ruled over China, K'ang Hsi (1662–1722). At the focal point of this Confucian civilization, when K'ang Hsi came to the throne in 1661, was the city of Peking, which for more than two centuries had been the capital of the Chinese empire. The Mongol emperor, Kublai, had made Peking his capital so as to exercise control over his vast Asian dominions from a convenient centre. The city which he built, together with its extensive palace, greatly impressed Marco Polo in the thirteenth century,[10] but was downgraded and turned into a mere prefectural city in the early decades (A.D. 1368–1409) of the Ming dynasty. The first Ming emperor transferred the capital to Nanking, which was certainly more central and far more suitable than the northern capital for the control of the more populous south. It was not till A.D. 1409 that the vigorous and forceful Ming emperor, Yung Lo, once more made Peking the seat of his government and set about building a city of unrivalled splendour. Fourteen miles of protective walls, towering to a height of forty feet, surrounded the palaces, temples, halls and parks which still excite the wonder and admiration of all who visit the city. The plan of Yung Lo's city and the architecture of its building followed ancient Chinese precedents, revealing an essential conservatism and traditionalism. It is now no longer possible to envisage what Ch'ang-an, Loyang and other ancient capital cities looked like in the days of their imperial greatness, but undoubtedly, by the time of Yung Lo, the general architectural pattern of palaces and temples had become standardized. A typically Chinese style of architecture had emerged which, though not distinctively Confucian, yet witnessed to the Confucian sense of harmony and balance. The grace of the buildings harmoniously grouped in spacious courtyards and sited amidst carefully landscaped parks and gardens was greatly enhanced by the use of coloured porcelain tiles in the roof construction of palaces and temples, adding greatly to their aesthetic appeal, and making a pleasing contrast to the balustrades and stairways of glistening white marble and the bright vermilion of the supporting columns. Though the Manchus (A.D. 1644–1911) added very little to the original city design of Yung Lo, and in the period of Manchu decadence allowed temples and palaces to fall into appalling disrepair, in the days of imperial greatness under K'ang Hsi and his successors, Yung Chêng and Ch'ien Lung, a period of some one hundred and thirty-four years, Peking could justly be regarded as the capital city of the Middle Kingdom. To this centre flowed not only the rich and varied products of a vast empire: less civilized nations from near and far sent their tribute-bearing missions to acknowledge the cultural supremacy of a Confucian civilization, ruled over by the acknowledged 'Son of Heaven'. From this centre, in accordance with Confucian doctrine, the 'illustrious virtue' of the emperor flowed out into all parts, carrying with it a beneficent influence. At the most holy spot in the capital city the emperor, following ancient precedent, entreated Heaven and all the spiritual host to signify approval of his dutiful service by bestowing rich blessings upon people and land.

K'ang Hsi, a Confucian Monarch

K'ang Hsi came to the throne as a boy of eight and reigned for sixty years. Under his father a series of measures had been adopted which were aimed at winning the support of Confucian scholars for the new régime. Chinese were encouraged to accept posts in the administration alongside their Manchu conquerors. The imperial university, known as the Kuo-tsŭ-chien, was restored and at the same time several colleges were founded in Peking for the education of Manchu bannermen.[11] The boy emperor was assisted by a capable regency for some years and placed under the guidance of able and worthy tutors who gave him a thorough grounding in Confucian scholarship. From his early years he developed a studious disposition and a real love of learning, qualities which remained with him throughout life. Whilst still in his teens he dismissed his regents and began to exercise direct rule. He purged the palace of some four thousand eunuchs and established himself as a humane and enlightened ruler. It was no small achievement for him to win over many of the most celebrated Confucian scholars who had served under the Ming dynasty. In the *Records of the Hanlin Academy*, an academy composed of the most distinguished and learned Confucians of the age, it is stated that 'The Emperor K'ang Hsi, in the ninth year of his reign, said to the officers of the Board of Rites, "If one would learn the art of government, he must explore the classic learning of the ancients. Whenever we can find a day of leisure from the affairs of state, we spend it in the study of the classics."' [12] Again, in the twenty-third year 'his majesty was on a journey when, the boat mooring for the night, he continued reading until the third watch. His clerk, a member of the Hanlin Academy, had to beg his majesty to allow himself a little more time for repose; whereupon his majesty gave a detailed account of his habits of study.' [13] K'ang Hsi continued his interest in Confucian studies all his life, became an excellent calligraphist, and was famous for his encouragement of literature and learning. In the forty-third year of his reign he said to the members of the Hanlin Academy, 'From early years I have been fond of the ink-stone; [14] every day writing a thousand characters and copying with care the chirography [handwriting] of the famous scribes of antiquity. This practice I have kept up for more than thirty years, because it was the bent of my nature.' [15] When he had reigned for fifty years he said to the high chancellors, 'As for me, I have now reigned fifty years and have spent all my leisure hours in diligent study; and whenever the draft of a discourse was sent in, I never failed to read it over. If, by chance, a word or sentence appeared doubtful, I always discussed it with my literary aids.' [16] Here was an emperor whom Confucius could have respected and admired, and one whom he would have delighted to serve. He would have gloried in the evident signs of prosperity in the empire, the emphasis on using learned and worthy men in the administration, the encouragement of education, and the meticulous observance of those religious rituals by which the blessing of the unseen world was invoked. But it is doubtful if he would have recognized that his own teachings, given to a handful of disciples two thousand years before, had become the mainspring of this vast and complicated political and social organization. Fortunately, there were always some who recognized this fact, and were prepared, in consequence, to exalt Confucius to the place of highest honour in the national pantheon as the 'greatest Sage under Heaven'.

K'ang Hsi was an emperor who proved to be 'a generous patron of education and academic activities, an outstanding scholar in his own right ... He strove to become a Confucian model monarch and set a moral example to his subjects.'[17] He had all the instincts of a scholar and besides his knowledge of the Classics and traditional literature, he studied astronomy, mathematics, geography and music. He was even open-minded enough to accept tuition from Jesuit scholars from the West. We are informed that in the closing decade of the seventeenth century Father Gerbillon and Father Bouvet 'went every day to the palace, spent two hours in the morning and two in the evening with the emperor' teaching him science and mathematics, and he was so pleased with their tuition that he assigned to the French fathers a house in the palace enclosure, and presented them with a large plot of ground in the capital for the building of their church.[18] The thoroughly Confucian attitude of K'ang Hsi secured for him the support of the majority of the scholar class in spite of the fact that he was an alien ruler. This support of a trained and loyal body of civil administrators proved of inestimable value, especially during and after the disastrous rebellion of Wu San-kuei. The Manchus were not more than two per cent of the population, and it seemed for a time that the dynasty was in danger of collapse, but the boy-emperor won the support of the most stable and esteemed element in the country, the cultured and well-educated Confucian scholars. He became one of the greatest patrons of learning that China has ever seen, not so much because he stimulated the production of original and creative work, as by the emphasis he placed on gathering together into an accessible form the accumulated wisdom of the past. 'He found leisure to initiate and carry out, with the aid of the leading scholars of the day, several of the greatest literary enterprises the world has ever seen.'[19] Among these were the

K'ang Hsi Tzŭ Tien, the great standard dictionary of the Chinese language; the *P'ie Wên Yün Fu*, a huge concordance of literature in forty-four large volumes; and the *T'u Shu Chi Ch'êng*, a profusely illustrated encyclopedia in sixteen hundred and twenty-eight volumes of about two hundred pages each. At the age of sixteen he published under his own name a group of sixteen maxims which summarized the moral conduct which a Confucian emperor expected of his subjects. These maxims became known as the *Sacred Edict*, and were ordered to be read aloud on the first and fifteenth day of each month to the assembled teachers and pupils in all schools. Later, as elaborated by the emperor Yung Chêng, this summary of Confucian morality had a great influence in moulding Chinese opinion. The *Sacred Edict*, accepted throughout China as a standard for orthodox behaviour, well illustrates the Confucian principle that government should rely, not so much on force or on strict legal proceedings to ensure peace and prosperity, as on moral example and moral persuasion. So ingrained is this idea among the Chinese that even under a Communist régime, which repudiates Confucianism as feudalistic and reactionary, it is moral example and moral persuasion which are most commonly used to maintain social harmony and conformity with government. An examination of the *Sacred Edict* reveals a strong emphasis on filial piety, brotherly love, mutual respect, orthodox thinking and loyalty to the throne. Education and good husbandry are considered to be the two main essentials for a well run and prosperous Confucian state.

K'ang Hsi had a great regard for the rationalist school of Confucianism as it had been developed by Chu Hsi. This Sung dynasty scholar was regarded by the emperor as the greatest philosopher since Confucius and Mencius. In 1712, by the emperor's order, the spirit-tablet of Chu Hsi was placed among the tablets of the ten most distinguished Confucians which were ranged along the east and west walls in the main hall of the Confucian temples. The *Four Books*, which had been selected by Chu Hsi to form the basis of a Confucian education, became, with Chu Hsi's commentaries, the standard works which all students, who wished to pass the first examination leading to the civil service, needed to master. Chu Hsi's emphasis on ethics, on self-discipline and the building of one's own moral character, his teaching that through the use of reason one could control human desires and his belief that academic learning should find practical application in service to the state, were all in line with K'ang Hsi's own thinking.

So it was that Confucianism, which had been slowly maturing throughout many centuries, came to its highest expression in the reign of K'ang Hsi and his immediate successors, Yung Chêng and Ch'ien Lung. As medieval Europe thought of itself as a Christian civilization, so that the influence of the Christian church penetrated into almost every aspect of social and individual life, so the vast empire of China throughout the seventeenth and eighteenth centuries was so thoroughly Confucian that the ordering of the great religious rituals, the administration of government, the system of education, the morals of the people, the relationships of social and family life, were all based on what men considered to be the teachings of the Confucian Classics. The Chinese felt secure in the proud belief that they had inherited a way of life which, if sincerely followed, was as perfect as human society could attain. Whatever faults or imperfections there might be were due to aberrations from the Confucian norm and could be corrected by the application of reason.

The State Cult

As a Confucian monarch K'ang Hsi, and indeed all other rulers of China from time immemorial, had the sacred duty of regularly performing certain religious functions on behalf of the country and the people. These duties were onerous, and they could not be correctly performed without the assistance of a host of Confucian scholars who had had a thorough training in the knowledge of ancient rituals. In each religious function the emperor was expected to follow a particular pattern which tradition laid down. The kind of sacrifices to be offered, the ritual garments to be worn, the music to be played, the ordering of the service, the number of genuflections to be made, all the elaborate details of an intricate ritual were laid down in the Confucian *Book of Rites*.

The sacrifices of the state religion[20] were divided into Great, Medium and Small and were placed in charge of the Board of

Rites (*Li Pu*), considered to be the most important of the six departments of state. Any deviation from the traditional pattern as laid down in the Confucian books of ritual would impair the effectiveness of the sacrifices. The emperor himself did not need to officiate at the Small Sacrifices, some thirty in number, which were made to a variety of minor gods. Though in all the numerous sacrifices of the state religion the emperor was considered to be the sole celebrant, he could delegate his duties in all but the greatest and most important sacrifices, and, indeed, throughout the whole empire temples of the state religion were set up in provincial, prefectural and county seats, and the magistrates officiated in their capacity of appointees of the emperor.

Among the gods and spirits to whom Medium Sacrifices were made were the sun and moon and the planet Jupiter, the spirits of rulers and wise men of former dynasties, the sky gods who controlled the thunder, clouds, winds and rain, and the earth gods of mountains, rivers and seas. A very important sacrifice was to the patron god of agriculture, Shên Nung. Though a Medium Sacrifice, it was offered by the emperor at the temple of agriculture situated in the south-west [21] part of the city. Here, at the beginning of the agricultural year, the emperor in person ploughed six furrows in the sacred field, the rest of the field being ploughed by his attendants in order of precedence. This ritual was matched by that performed by the empress at an altar dedicated to the patroness of silk-worms. Among the Medium Sacrifices was that offered to Confucius in the temples dedicated to his honour throughout the land. It was not till 1906, when the Manchu dynasty was approaching its end, that the sacrifice to Confucius was elevated to be a Great Sacrifice at which the emperor should personally officiate.

For the Great Sacrifices the emperor was expected to attend in person, and perform the rituals assigned to him in all the panoply of imperial dignity. These sacrifices were four in number: those to Heaven, Earth, the Dynastic Ancestors and the Gods of Soil and Grain. These were sacrifices which had been performed in remote antiquity, long before the time of Confucius, and which had been continued ever since. They had long since become an integral part of the Confucian system. At the time of K'ang Hsi the magnificent temples and altars which had been built by Yung Lo were still kept in decent order and repair, and at certain appointed times during the year elaborate and colourful ceremonies were conducted there, ceremonies to which the public were never admitted, but only those princes and officials who had some function to perform. Thus, the performance of the religious rites was done on behalf of the people, but not by the people. No wonder that they turned to Buddhism and Taoism to find an outlet for their own religious expression.

The great religious ceremonies performed by the emperor on behalf of the whole empire and its people were simply an elaboration of those ceremonies which from ancient times had been used on grand occasions when all the male members of a particular clan gathered together to worship their ancestors. It was customary at this clan worship to offer to the spirits of the departed incense, candles, paper money, food and drink, together with the raw carcasses of a sheep and a pig and sometimes also an ox. A dish of blood and hair from the sheep and pig was poured out as a libation on the ground. All the sacrificial offerings were presented by the head of the clan with suitable ritual prostrations. Afterwards, each male present, according to seniority, performed his ritual prostrations. The rite was followed by participation in a clan feast. In the state religion, whether the worship was rendered to Heaven or Earth, the gods of Land and Grain, the Imperial Ancestors, or in later times by the emperor himself to Confucius, the general pattern of sacrificial procedure was much the same. It was always meticulously prepared, and was always performed under the guidance of a Master of Ceremonies, whose duty was to call out in turn each ritual act to be performed. Each particular ceremony varied as to the symbols used, the quantity and variety of the sacrifices offered, the hymns sung and the music performed, the number of prostrations and libations, the forms of address used in the prayers, the cut and colour of the ceremonial robes. The most elaborate ceremony of all was that performed at the Altar of Heaven, when under the superintendence of high officials many varieties of meats, grains, vegetables, fruits, cakes, were presented on dishes of a prescribed form and colour, when precious jades and silks were offered and whole bullocks were roasted, whilst libations of fermented liquors were poured out.

The emphasis throughout was upon gratitude and thankfulness, and a common sharing by men and spirits of the bounties bestowed by Heaven and Earth.

The Great Sacrifice to the Imperial Ancestors

Situated immediately to the south-east of the main entrance to the forbidden city were the palatial and dignified buildings known as T'ai Miao or Great Temple. It was here that the emperor, accompanied by the princes of the royal house, offered reverent worship and sacrifice before the shrines in which the spirit-tablets of the imperial ancestors had been set up. It was here that the monarch reported the successes and failures of his reign, and humbly acknowledged his unworthiness before the spirits of his ancestors. It was essentially a family ceremony to which no outsiders were admitted, a simple but deeply reverent ceremony for which the celebrants had prepared themselves by abstinence and fasting. It took place at the end of the year and at the beginning of the four seasons. In the same way every family in the land, as far as their means allowed, worshipped the spirits of their deceased ancestors, and in doing so re-emphasized the fundamental Confucian doctrine of filial piety.

The Great Sacrifice to the Gods of Soil and Grain

Another important religious function of the emperor was to sacrifice to the gods of soil and grain at the *Shê-chi-t'an*, an altar and group of buildings situated opposite to the *T'ai Miao* to the south-west of the palace entrance. In the ancient, and primitive nature worship of the Chinese, long before the time of Confucius, the spirits which controlled the productive powers of the soil and the seed had been universally recognized and worshipped. The feudalistic and agrarian society of the time of Confucius had recognized that only the lord of a territory could exercise the right to sacrifice to the gods of that territory, just as only a family could sacrifice to its ancestors. The *Shê-chi-t'an* or 'altar to the soil and grain' had become the primary symbol of territorial possession. Whenever a feudal vassal received a fiefdom from his lord, he built such an altar and incorporated into it a handful of soil given to him by his lord. If, for any reason, a vassal was deprived of his fiefdom, then the *Shê-chi-t'an* of his territory was covered over as a sign that his authority had ceased. So it came about that the worship conducted in the spring and autumn at the great national altar to the gods of the Soil and Grain, who exercised a spiritual control over the productive resources of the whole empire, could only be performed by the emperor in person. It was the symbol of his right to rule. Any attempt to usurp this function was tantamount to rebellion.

The Great Sacrifice at the Altar of Earth

This ceremony took place at the summer solstice at the Altar of Earth. The altar was square, not round like the Altar of Heaven, for in ancient times earth was thought to be a square, over which the round canopy of Heaven rested on mighty pillars. As Heaven represented the *yang* forces, so Earth represented the *yin* and, since the *yang* influences were thought to be strongest in the south and the *yin* influences strongest in the north, the altar was built in a park-like enclosure in the northern part of the city. Here, the emperor worshipped Earth, the consort of Heaven, the great nourisher and provider. Though the various prescriptions for the acts of worship at the Altar of Earth differed from those at the Altar of Heaven, and there were considerable differences in the symbolism, the main pattern of worship was similar.

The Great Sacrifice at the Altar of Heaven

We have left to the last our consideration of the worship of Heaven by the emperor, because this was undoubtedly the supreme expression of the Confucian state religion. A detailed account of the Altar of Heaven and the sacrifices and ceremonies which were annually performed there would take up far more space than can be given in a book of this nature, but a brief description of this highest and most complete ritual of the state religion will emphasize the fact that central to the Confucian civilization at the time of its greatest glory was a ritual performance of deep and abiding significance which, though owing nothing at all directly to Confucius, was a ceremony substantially the same as that developed by Han dynasty Confucians and one that could not have been performed without the aid of Confucian scholar-officials. However far removed this elaborate ceremony was from anything that Confucius knew, or from the practices of his day, this concept of a supreme link between humanity and Heaven resulted from the adaptation of ancient and traditionally held beliefs to the more sophisticated and ceremonial needs of empire.

The sacrifice to Heaven was recognized as the complete and perfect sacrifice in so far as it was the unique prerogative of the Son of Heaven to worship the Supreme Deity and act as high-priest on behalf of all his people. The ceremony consisted of nine separate acts, that is, three times three, which, according to Chinese ideas, was the Heavenly number. For the performance of this ceremony the resources of Chinese genius were brought into service. Every single item which contributed to this supreme act of worship had to be thought out with scrupulous care and in meticulous detail. The landscaping of the parkland, the siting, plan and architecture of the buildings, the preparation of the sacrifices and libations, the composition of the prayers, the traditional Confucian music and miming, the embroidered patterns on the ceremonial garments, the ordering and timing of the intricate ceremonial, all conspired to make this sacrifice, performed in darkness before the sunrise and in the almost arctic cold of the winter solstice, one of the most awe-inspiring acts of worship ever performed by man. Yet, apart from those who were privileged to take some part in the ceremony, none of the ordinary populace was admitted. Even the route between the palace and the sacred enclosure of the Temple of Heaven was cleared of all passers-by, whilst doors and windows were closed and side-lanes sealed off in case anyone or anything should intrude upon the imperial procession.

The place popularly known as the Temple of Heaven is situated about three miles south of the imperial palace in some seven hundred acres of parkland. Even in the days of the Republic, when it had ceased to function and was rapidly falling into disrepair, it was a most impressive sight, with the white marble of altars, stairways, balustrades and arches; the magnificent blue porcelain-tiled triple roofs of the temple to the auspicious New Year; the dull red of the surrounding walls and the dark green of the cypress avenues; the whole plan was remarkable for the symmetry and harmony of its arrangement. 'Without exaggeration one might say that no other sanctuary on earth has a more profound and grandiose conception, or more adequately expresses the instinctive desire of humanity to show reverence for a Power above and beyond its puny self.' [22]

The main altar, the most important of all Chinese religious structures, and open to the sky, stands in the centre of a square court which is surrounded by dull red walls, pierced by four marble archways. It is a beautiful marble structure in three terraces which are ascended from the four compass points by marble stairways each with twenty-seven steps. Each circular terrace is surrounded by an ornamented marble balustrade. The lowest terrace is 210 feet in diameter, the middle one is 150 feet and the topmost 90 feet. It was on this topmost terrace that the supreme acts of worship were performed. The platform is laid with marble stones, cut so as to fit in concentric circles round a central stone which is a perfect circle. Each circle of stones is in multiples of nine up to the outermost circle of eighty-one stones. Thus, the emperor, kneeling upon the central stone, and surrounded by the circles of the terraces and their embracing walls, and then by the circle of the horizon, seemed to himself and to his court to be in the centre of the universe. Turning to the north, and in the attitude of a subject, he acknowledged in prayer and by his humble position that he was inferior to Heaven and to Heaven alone. [23]

To the west of this altar is a building known as the Hall of Abstinence, *Chai Kung*, where the emperor prepared himself by fasting and vigil for the ceremony. To the north is a building in which the spirit-tablets of Shang Ti and of the imperial ancestors were kept. Beyond this was another series of three white marble terraces, on the topmost of which was erected a most beautiful circular temple towering to a height of ninety-nine feet and with a triple blue porcelain-tiled roof. In K'ang Hsi's day this triple roof had tiles of blue, yellow and green, but they were changed to blue by the Emperor Ch'ien Lung. The three heavy roofs were supported by huge lacquered wooden pillars, and the panelled ceilings and cross-bars were brilliantly painted. The doors and windows of the temple were carved with delicate tracery. Away to the south-east of the Altar of Heaven, at a distance of an arrow's flight, was the large green-tiled furnace for the whole burnt offering. Bullocks of one colour all over and without blemish were placed upon an iron grating and the fire kindled underneath. In eight open-work braziers nearby were burnt the rolls of silk and the prayers written on silk which were a part of the offering.

It was to this Temple of Heaven that the emperor proceeded on the twenty-first of December each year, accompanied by his personal attendants, princes, courtiers and great officers of state. Through the silent streets and out through the Ching Yang gate of the city, only opened for the emperor's use, the great procession wended its way. On arrival, the emperor visited first the tablets of Shang Ti and the ancestor spirits, and afterwards inspected the altar, where everything had been meticulously prepared in readiness for the early morning sacrifice. Having inspected the offerings he proceeded to the Hall of Abstinence, where he spent the night in fasting and vigil. One hour and forty-five minutes before sunrise, having performed his ablutions, he proceeded to the tent where he put on his ceremonial robes, whilst the tablets of Shang Ti and the ancestors were being reverently transferred to the topmost terrace of the altar, being placed so that the tablet of Shang Ti was on the north side, facing south, with the ancestor tablets ranged on the east and west. When every attendant was in the place assigned to him, the braziers and lanterns burning, the musicians below with their ancient instruments ready, 'at sunrise, under the dome of the blue sky, with nothing to symbolize God except the limitless dome of heaven and the far-reaching horizon, he knelt in prayer to offer sacrifices of joy and praise for all the blessings of the past year.'[24]

The service opened with a peal of music, and throughout the ceremony, except when the special prayers were being offered, the service was accompanied by the music of the orchestra, the posturing of the dancers, the roll of drums or the tinkling of bells, which signified the beginning and end of every part of the ceremony. The Son of Heaven mounted to the topmost terrace of the altar, accompanied by two masters of ceremonies, one who directed all the proceedings, whilst the other called aloud the next gesture the sovereign was to make. The first ceremony, performed to the strains of a hymn, was for the emperor to meet the spirits of Shang Ti and the former emperors, now thought of as inhabiting the spirit-tablets. Then he proceeded to offer jade and silks and the first offering of the bullock. This was followed by the first libation, accompanied by a dance of eight groups of dancers with halberds and shields, the 'dance of military leadership'. Then the emperor prostrated himself on the central stone, whilst prayers previously prepared with great care by some distinguished Confucian scholar-official were read by an officer. After a second offering of the bullock and a second libation, the emperor received from an official some of the wine and meat sacrificed and partook of them. Then, when the spirits had been courteously sent off, and the emperor had watched the burning of the rest of the offerings, the official in charge announced the ending of the ceremonies.

We cannot do better than conclude this short account of this most central of the imperial ceremonies of the state religion than by quoting the words of a great sinologist, James Legge. 'All semblances of an uncertain polytheism were swept away from the imperial worship soon after the middle of our fourteenth century, immediately on the rise of the Ming dynasty ... We may not be able to feel much sympathy with the way in which the solstitial services are conducted. We may deplore, as we do deplore, the superstitious worship of a multitude of spirits, terrestrial and celestial, that finds a place in them; but this abuse does not obscure the monotheism. Those spirits are not Gods, and are not called by the divine name. I do not think that, in the truly Confucian worship of the empire, that name, the name Ti, is applied to any spirit but Him whose right it is.'[25] Referring to the sacrifices made at the Altar of Heaven, Legge goes on to write, 'These offerings are oblations, and not sacrifices in our common acceptance of that term. There is not, and never was, any idea of propitiation or expiation in them. They are the tributes of duty and gratitude, accompanied with petitions and thanksgivings. They do not express a sense of guilt, but a feeling of dependence.'[26]

It might reasonably be argued that the religious rites and ceremonies performed by the emperor or his delegates in the state cult had little connection, if any, with the teachings of Confucius. Most of these ceremonies, as we have seen, can be traced back to ancient prototypes which were an integral part of the religious life of the Chinese people long before the time of Confucius. Nevertheless, it was Confucian scholars who had so directed the development of the state cult that it had become a magnificent expression in ritual form of a typically Confucian philosophy of life. There was no room in the state religion for spontaneous religious fervour or for uncontrolled religious emotion, nor any place for the feats of asceticism or self-mortification that have been a part of other world religions. Every ritual act had to be carefully planned beforehand so that it should be as perfect an expression as possible of what was considered to be fitting, proper, decorous and right. Every participant took up his own appointed station and performed his functions in accordance with time-honoured custom, which had established those degrees of relationship and official status which could not be over-stepped. Even the emperor himself, in the performance of each minutest ritual, had to be guided by Confucian scholars who were held to be most conversant with the Rites. There was always a pervasive sense of harmony and unity which linked together into one whole the spiritual, the natural and the human spheres, and it was a desire to maintain and uphold that harmony which led to the development of the symbolism dominating every aspect of the complicated ritual. Above all, there was a humble yet dignified attitude of reverence for a transcendental spiritual Power, and the assured belief that if man on his part faithfully carried out the role assigned to him, Heaven and Earth on their part would respond with the utmost beneficence.

The Worship of Confucius

Though the worship offered to Confucius was not in the same category as that offered to Heaven on the Altar of Heaven, it was greatly encouraged throughout the Manchu period. The Emperor Chien Lung personally offered regular sacrifices to Confucius until old age forced him to discontinue the practice.

There are three aspects to the cult of Confucius. First, from the time of his death, sacrifices were made to him by his own descendants at the family home at Ch'ü-fu in Shantung province. Secondly, Confucius became the patron saint of the scholar class and of all institutions of learning. Thirdly, Confucius gradually gained a place in the state religion, and was offered sacrifices and honoured as a deity because he was recognized as the most illustrious of China's sages.

It was not until the Han dynasty and some four hundred years after the death of Confucius that the cult of Confucius began to develop on a national scale. Before that time it is possible and, indeed, probable that Confucius was honoured by sacrifices only in the state of Lu. The historian Ssŭ-ma Ch'ien, writing about 100 B.C., gives the following account, which should, however, be accepted with great caution, as the process for the glorification and even the deification of Confucius was already well under way. 'Together with the disciples and men of Lu, houses were built near the grave [of Confucius] until there were more than a hundred, and the place was called the village of K'ung. Lu transmitted from generation to generation the custom of sacrificing to Confucius at fixed times during the year. Scholars performed the rites of the District Banquet and the Archery Bout at the tomb of Confucius. The building, which had formerly been used by the disciples during their mourning, was made into a memorial temple by following generations, in which were kept the clothes, the ceremonial hat, and lute of Confucius, besides his chariot and his writings. This was continued during more than two hundred years until the beginning of the Han. When the emperor Kao visited Lu, he offered the sacrifice of the three victims [ox, sheep and pig]. When the lords and officials arrived [in Lu] they first visited [the tomb of Confucius] before taking up their duties.'[27] Though this quotation from Ssŭ-ma Ch'ien would indicate that there was, in pre-Han times, a growing recognition of the greatness of Confucius so that pilgrimages are already being made to his grave, Shryock came to the conclusion that 'there is no satisfactory evidence for a cult of Confucius before the beginning of the Han period, apart from his inclusion in the ancestral worship of the K'ung family'.[28]

From the Han dynasty onwards, however, the fame of Confucius grew as successive emperors made liberal contributions to the Confucian temple at Ch'ü-fu, awarded posthumous honours to Confucius and ennobled his descendants. The building of Confucian temples in prefectural and county cities was encouraged. In A.D. I, for instance, the Emperor P'ing Ti repaired the temple at Ch'ü-fu, and conferred the title of duke on Confucius, at the same time giving the title of marquis to his descendants.[29] From this time onwards the temple at Ch'ü-fu, though still considered to be the ancestral property of the K'ung family, was regarded as a national institution to which imperial visits were occasionally made and sacrifices offered by emperors to Confucius. The first definite date when it is known that there was a regular cult of Confucius outside the K'ung family was in A.D. 59, when Ming Ti ordered sacrifices to him and to the Duke of Chou in the schools.[30] What had been an ethico-political school of thought was transformed into a religion. He who had been previously revered as a great man was now elevated to be worshipped as a god. It was the Confucian scholar-officials who deliberately encouraged the absorption of a cult of Confucius into the state religion, although, throughout Chinese history, there were always Confucian scholars who resisted this tendency to deify the Master. It was at those times when the power and prestige of the scholar class was most in evidence that the greatest pressures were exerted to emphasize the importance of the worship of Confucius as part of the state cult. During the reigns of the great Manchu emperors, K'ang Hsi, Yung Chêng and Ch'ien Lung, when Confucianism attained its maximum influence in the state, attempts were made on more than one occasion to enhance still further the honour paid to the spirit of Confucius. Huge sums were spent on the reconstruction of the temples of Ch'ü-fu and in Peking. In 1747 a petition to the emperor requested that, 'in order to show the proper respect to Confucius, the ceremony and music appropriate to the emperor should be used at the sacrifices', and in 1767 a petition requested that the birthday of Confucius should be added to the state sacrifices.[31] Both these petitions were refused on the grounds that Confucius himself disliked elaborate ceremonies and it would not be justifiable to worship him with ceremonies which he himself would have disapproved; and that the date of his birthday, being unrecorded in the Classics, was not definitely known. It was in this same period that Confucianism emerged as the principal buttress of tradition and reaction against the forces which made for progress and change. A system which was proving itself to be superbly efficient in providing a constant stream of the most talented and scholarly men for the administration of a vast empire was likely to be vigorously upheld by those who benefited most from the system.

On the first day at school the young scholar learned to pay homage to Confucius. From then onwards, right up through the hierarchy until, perhaps, he attained the supreme dignity of being a member of the Hanlin Academy, Confucius was never absent from his thoughts, as the one whose virtue was as great as Heaven and Earth, and as the one whose incomparable teachings had moulded the civilization of China.

The great temple of Confucius in Peking, second only in magnificence to the one at Ch'ü-fu, was first built on its present site at the time of the Mongol emperor, Kublai. It was begun in A.D. 1273 but was not finished till the year A.D. 1306. It is a magnificent building, located in the north-east corner of the Tartar city. In a large rectangular courtyard, surrounded by ancillary buildings and planted with ancient cypress trees, the imposing main hall of the temple stands elevated on a marble terrace. It contains no objects of veneration apart from the simple tablets of wood inscribed with the name of the Sage and those of his most illustrious disciples. Various emperors have from time to time erected gilded tablets in honour of Confucius. Since its completion, the building has been restored or rebuilt many times. There each year, on certain fixed days in the second and eighth months[32] of the lunar year, an elaborate and reverent service took place in honour of Confucius. It began at about 3 a.m. When all the preparations had been completed and everything was ready, the commencement of the ceremony was signalized by the striking of a great bell. This was followed by a long and complicated ritual in which the chief celebrants were guided and directed in all they did by a master of ceremonies. 'It would be hard to imagine a more solemn and beautiful ritual, or one set in more impressive surroundings'[33] to the accompaniment of solemn music and the burning of incense, with genuflections and prayers, the sacrifices and libations were respectfully presented, the animal victims, the grain and fruit, the oil and wine, the jade and silk. As Confucius loved music, and his spirit was supposed to delight in harmonies, one of the features of the semi-annual worship of Confucius was the groups of musicians dressed in ancient costumes of the Ming dynasty playing on instruments of great antiquity the hymns in praise of Confucius, and accompanying the various ritual actions of the celebrants with appropriate orchestral music, the chanting of specially composed poetry by the choir, and the posturing of rows of dancers, each holding a feathery wand.[34] A similar service, but with a less elaborate ritual, was conducted by local magistrates in every city.

Whilst the Confucian temple in Peking, being situated in the capital city of China, was easily accessible to the court and to the most distinguished Confucian scholars and officials, and consequently became the most important centre of the Confucian cult, it was the magnificent temple at Ch'ü-fu, and the cemeteries which lie about a mile beyond the north gate of the city, which brought to the pilgrim visitors a most vivid sense of the great debt that Chinese culture and civilization owe to Confucius. There lived the lineal descendants of the Master. In the early days of the Republic the only hereditary title still held in China was that of a little boy, still under the tutelage of his uncle, Duke K'ung of the seventy-fourth generation, stretching back in a direct line some twenty-four centuries. This lad was entrusted with the duty of guarding the tomb of his ancestor and of sacrificing to his memory.[35] The present temple, with its courtyards and halls planned on a magnificent scale in the T'ang dynasty, has been constantly repaired and embellished by successive emperors. Here, as at many other cult centres throughout the world, men have sought to embellish and glorify the reputation of a great man by means of relics and legends. The pilgrim visitor is conducted by an attendant through the courtyards where he is shown the 'Apricot Pavilion' in which the Master taught, the 'Dew Well' from which he drank, the stump of a tree which he planted with his own hands, the ink-box that he used. Here are scores of monuments recording tributes from the high and mighty to the Sage; the hall containing his portrait, the famous set of slates depicting his travels and the imposing spirit-tablet.[36] Yet, though in this sacred place the tradition and the influence of the Master are perennially kept alive, it is, perhaps in the educational system of pre-revolutionary China that the strength of Confucianism has been most evident.

A Confucian Education

The magnificent rituals of the state religion would probably have developed had Confucius never lived. If there had been no official Confucian scholar class to direct and control the state religion in all its ramifications, it is reasonable to suppose that a specialized priesthood would have developed, as in other countries, or the trained priests of Taoism or Buddhism might have taken control. As for the worship offered to Confucius himself, apart from that rendered by his own descendants in the ancestral temple belonging to the family, Confucius would have been the first to criticize it as being contrary to the teachings of the ancient sages. He would have been horrified to see the temples built everywhere in his honour, filled, as they were, with the flattering and laudatory inscriptions presented by emperors and scholar-officials. But with the educational system at its best Confucius would have been pleased, feeling that here, at any rate, his own primary concern was being met. He would have noted with deep satisfaction the emphasis placed on moral rectitude and learning. He would have delighted in the opportunities offered to the promising children of poor parents, and commended a system which, in theory at least, opened up the highest positions in the land to those who had proved their worth in open competition. He would, however, have disapproved of the way in which the educational system gradually became hidebound in conservatism, caring more for facility in language and correct literary expression than for independent and original thought, giving far more weight to the ability to memorize and quote ancient texts than to the practical application of learning to the current needs of society.

Unfortunately, even in the days of imperial greatness under K'ang Hsi and his illustrious successors, the educational system which produced the men to make that greatness possible became so firmly entrenched in conservatism and traditionalism that it stultified genuine initiative and made any attempts at innovation almost impossible. Those in power felt that a system which had proved its value over many centuries should be perpetuated intact. Any scholar who became receptive to ideas which might be thought to undermine the Confucian orthodoxy was a danger to the state. From the humblest village school right up to the *Kuo-tzŭ-chien* (or Imperial College) in the capital and the Hanlin Academy, composed of the most distinguished Confucian scholars in the land, the emphasis of the whole system was on maintaining the *status quo*. It was the Confucian educational system, more than anything else, which produced the peculiar character of the Chinese. The Chinese regarded the scholar as being at the apex of the social structure. They had a most profound reverence for learning. It was the aim of almost every village to possess a primary school, and on his first day at school every boy first made his obeisance to the picture of Confucius and then to his teacher. From then onwards he was disciplined to give respect and obedience to all his elders and superiors in a hierarchy of scholarship, and to consider the ancient Confucian Classics as the fountainhead of all wisdom. These became the focus of his studies. He learned to memorize them till he could recite them by heart. He was taught the traditionally accepted interpretations of their meaning. He spent interminable hours in copying models of calligraphy, model essays, model poems, until at last he became proficient in composing the traditionally acceptable eight-legged essays [37] on themes taken from the Classics. Under the Manchu dynasty the main emphasis of education was literary, in the belief that a classical education best fitted one for the service of the state.

Whilst education in Confucian China was left to private enterprise, public charity, the encouragement of enlightened magistrates and the liberality of wealthy gentry, it was geared to an examination system which always remained under the tight control of the civil administration. However educated a man might become, unless he managed to be successful in passing the required examinations at various levels he could not hope to enjoy the rich fruits of scholarship in service of the state. This examination system which had developed during the T'ang and the Sung dynasty was, ideally, a method of discovering and choosing out the most intelligent and gifted men for the service of the state. It was based on the ancient Confucian maxim '*chü hsien chin nêng*', which means 'promote the worthy and employ the capable'. A series of gruelling examinations, in which only the very best in each grade were allowed to pass, was considered to provide the best test of ability and worth.

There were three main grades into which the scholars of the empire were divided: those of *hsiu ts'ai* (budding talent); *chü jên* (promoted scholar); and *chin shih* (ready for office). Only the *chin shih* were eligible for the vacancies in the government administration as they occurred. It took years of arduous study and many preliminary tests before a candidate was prepared to compete in the first and lowest public examination for the degree of *hsiu ts'ai*, an examination under the supervision of a literary chancellor sent down from Peking to the local prefecture. There, isolated in a narrow cell, the student would produce a poem and one or two essays on assigned themes, knowing full well that not more than about one per cent of the candidates who had entered would be allowed to pass. Once he had successfully passed this first hurdle, the student was now recognized as a scholar. He was now allowed certain privileges, exempted from liability to corporal punishment, and considered to be too much of a gentleman to engage in any form of manual labour. It was from the ranks of the *hsiu ts'ai* that most of the village school-masters were recruited, and they were available also for many types of literary activity, but, in the main, they were wretchedly paid in spite of their proud position in the local communities. They were expected to continue their studies, and to try for the second examination which was held at the provincial city once every three years. Out of about ten thousand candidates drawn from all over the province perhaps a hundred or so would succeed in obtaining the second degree of *chü jên*. These men, though they still received no office, were acclaimed and acknowledged as notable scholars, and were allowed to place a pair of high flag-staves in front of their gate and a tablet over their door to proclaim to all passers-by their honoured position. In the spring of the following year these scholars went to Peking in order to compete for the next degree of *chin shih* which would prove a passport to office. In this competition with scholars from all over the empire, the chances of success were a little better, as some two to three hundred would be chosen. Finally, the successful candidates were obliged to go to the palace to be tested on themes specially assigned by the emperor himself, who presided over the examination in person. About twenty, whose scholarship and calligraphy were thought to be most excellent, would become probationers in the Hanlin Academy, that most exalted imperial institution whose members were considered to be the highest in literary rank. One candidate would be chosen by the emperor as *chuang yüan* or 'model scholar of the empire'. He would be, like an Olympic gold-medallist, loaded with honour, adulation and the glittering prizes of success.

Though this series of competitive examinations was designed to weed out all but the very best, and did in fact produce for the service of the state a body of men who, on the whole, were possessed of ability and intellectual acumen, the system was open to criticism in several respects. Under a strong administration and guarded by uncorrupt officials, the system worked reasonably well, but as soon as a dynasty began that inevitable process of moral decline which characterized all the dynasties of China, the examination system became riddled with bribery and corruption through the peddling of essays, the purchase of degrees, the bribery of officials and underlings, whilst nepotism and favouritism became rampant. Even under K'ang Hsi, the highest offices in the land were most unevenly distributed. The Manchus were given the same number of ministerial posts as the Chinese in a dual system of control, though they formed only two per cent of the population. The much more populous and intellectually vigorous southern half of China received a smaller share of the administrative posts than the north. In a society in which the scholar-official was raised high above the ordinary run of men and given power and wealth and honours all but those who possessed the highest probity soon succumbed to the vices of arrogance and self-seeking. 'Those stately officials for whom the people make way with such awestruck deference, as they pass down the street with embroidered robes and imposing retinue, are not possessors of hereditary rank, neither do they owe their elevation to the favour of their sovereign, nor yet to the suffrages of their fellow-subjects. They are self-elected, and the people regard them with the deeper respect because they know that they have earned their position by intellectual effort.'[38]

This system, which placed the administration of the country in the hands of the most educated men, who had reached their high position in competitive examinations, had the advantage of being a counter-poise to the power of an absolute ruler. It was more equitable and on the whole worked better than a system which gave all the great offices of state to a hereditary nobility who farmed out the more minor offices to their own favourites. Every three years a stream of new men, rising from the ranks of the people and understanding the people's needs, was being drafted into the governing class. Granted that the rich and powerful families, which already had an illustrious line of scholars on their ancestral role, were at a great advantage, it was nevertheless true that men of great intellectual stature sometimes rose to high position from the homes of the humble and poor. It was a mighty achievement so to exalt learning that the energies of the ablest and most intelligent section of the community were directed, not towards achieving fame on a battlefield, but in the quiet and persistent study of the Confucian Classics. One drawback to the system was the tendency to a hidebound conservatism which resisted all innovation. On the whole the governing class was opposed to any new ideas which, if put into practice, might possibly have the effect of depriving them of their exalted position or curtailing their enormous privileges. In addition, there developed a tendency among scholars to display obsequiousness towards superiors and contempt for inferiors.

At the apex of the whole educational structure stood the Hanlin Academy (literally forest of pencils) which had been founded by a T'ang emperor in the eighth century as a society of scholars to give him literary assistance. Membership of the academy came to be regarded as the highest literary attainment open to a scholar. The membership of the Hanlin Academy was probably about five hundred. Twice a year, in the second and eighth months, those who were free to do so gathered at what became known as Classics Feasts, at which the Confucian Classics were expounded by illustrious scholars. Members of the academy were called upon to perform many functions. It was they who compiled and edited the massive encyclopedic works such as the *Yung Lo Ta Tien*, the *T'u Shu Chi Ch'eng*, the famous *K'ang Hsi Dictionary*, and the *Dynastic Histories*. Few of them produced literary works of great originality. They composed the prayers to be read at the great religious ceremonies, prepared the honorary titles, patents of nobility, inscriptions on state seals and the posthumous titles of deceased emperors. Certain of the highest dignitaries attended on the emperor at court or when he travelled. From the Hanlin Academy were chosen the super-intendents of education, the government examiners and the imperial censors. Some were appointed to high civil and military posts in the government or became provincial treasurers and judges.[39]

The powerful influence of the Confucian educational system on the life of the Chinese is attested by the fact that it persisted practically without any fundamental change for some fourteen centuries, and even continued long after its usefulness had been undermined by the clamorous demands of industry, science and technology in the modern world. Entering the quiet precincts of the Confucian temple in Peking, the modern student cannot help being awed by the sight of long corridors in which stand one hundred and eighty-two stone columns inscribed with the thirteen Confucian Classics which gained recognition over two thousand years ago. Again, in front of the temple stand three hundred and twenty columns which contain the names of those who achieved the chief literary honour, some sixty thousand scholars who received their investiture in the *Kuo-tzŭ-chien* during the past six centuries.[40]

9. Confucius and the Modern World

THROUGHOUT the seventeenth and eighteenth centuries the rulers of China were confident that theirs was the greatest civilization in the world, both in the extent and political influence of the Chinese empire, and in the measure of her cultural attainments. To the Confucian intelligentsia, China had reached a level of civilized living that could hardly be improved upon. This was attributed to the Confucian philosophy of life. There was much room for differences of interpretation within the Confucian system: between, for instance, the rationalism of Chu Hsi's school and the idealism of Wang Yang-ming; but very little interest was shown by the Confucian hierarchy in any religion or philosophy save in so far as it might challenge the unique place given to Confucius as the main architect of Chinese civilization. Education, almost confined to the Confucian Classics, and competitive examinations based on a conventional interpretation of Confucian philosophy, produced a type of mind which was so convinced that the Confucian way of life could not be bettered that it became resistant to change, and closed to all idea of progress. This extreme conservatism in outlook was shared by the whole official hierarchy, Chinese and Manchu alike. The consequence was that, throughout the whole of the nineteenth century, when the Manchu dynasty was in rapid decline and China was faced with entirely new kinds of situation, the Confucian scholar-officials remained confident that the Confucian system of thought and of government could weather any storm of opposition, and come out victorious. China's history through two millennia had convinced them that, though from time to time dynasties disintegrated in confusion and chaos, out of the ruins new dynasties arose to reassert and continue, perhaps in modified form, the age-old Confucian tradition.

It was during the nineteenth century that the full impact of the modern world upon China began to be felt. Forced to accept increasing contact with the representatives of European and American government and trade interests, Chinese officialdom slowly began to realize that these Westerners, who were detested and despised as 'barbarians', were equally contemptuous of the Chinese government, which they regarded as medieval and obsolete, an anachronism totally unsuited to the conditions imposed by a modern scientific and technological outlook. 'It took over fifty years of failure, humiliation and defeat before China could see herself clearly in the new world context. The Opium War, the Arrow War, the Taiping Rebellion and the Boxer Rebellion rocked Imperial China, but did not deliver the *coup-de-grâce*. The Chinese response to these attacks from without and revolts from within was various attempts at reform, none of which reached down to the roots of the problem.'[1]

For the first time for hundreds of years the Chinese were being forced to admit into their country the representatives of foreign nations who refused to consider themselves as tribute-bearing missions from inferior states, happy to bask in the civilizing influences of a Confucian world-order and eager to be transformed into truly civilized beings by the irradiating 'virtue' of Confucius. These invaders from the West were actually insisting that China was only one nation among many others, and one that was so weak and backward that it stood in need of drastic reform in almost every aspect of its social and political life. Instead of being the 'middle kingdom', the centre and source of world culture, it needed a radical modernization before it was to be admitted as an equal in the family of nations.

To many of the more progressive among the leading Confucian officials, the weakness and backwardness of China were all too apparent. By the 1860s the dynasty was on the verge of collapse. It had suffered two major foreign invasions, and had seen the capital city, Peking, captured by foreign troops. It had experienced the devastation of the Taiping Rebellion. The country was impoverished, the state coffers empty and drastic reforms were needed. The Confucian officials still clung tenaciously to the idea that, whatever reforms were conceded, the ancient Confucian order must still continue to exist unimpaired.

They resented change, and resisted it as far as they were able, but they were intelligent men who saw that change was inevitable. Many of them hoped that the corrupt Manchu dynasty would be swept away, and that they would be able to put in its place a government headed by some form of constitutional monarchy which, whilst welcoming all the benefits of modern science and technology, would maintain the time-honoured moral and spiritual values of Confucianism.

By the end of the nineteenth century all the leaders of Chinese thought recognized the necessity for change. As W. T. Chan wrote, 'In the last decades of the nineteenth century the call for reform was getting louder and louder in China. The influence of Western science and Christianity was increasingly felt. Interest in Buddhism was being revived.'[2] The humiliating defeat by a modernized Japan in the Sino-Japanese War of 1894-5, was soon followed by the crass folly of a reactionary government in harnessing the fanaticism of the Boxer rebels[3] to the task of driving out the hated foreigners once and for all. The inevitable reprisals forced even the most diehard conservatives to recognize that China could no longer hope to retain even a vestige of a proud isolationism. The more forward-looking intellectuals became eager to assimilate those aspects of occidental culture which had fostered political and economic strength and material greatness. The problem which faced the Confucian intelligentsia at the beginning of the twentieth century was how to assimilate the flood of new ideas inevitably flowing in from the West, and at the same time conserve the Confucian morality and a traditionally Chinese way of life. How could Confucianism be preserved and its influence over the Chinese people be maintained in face of a reviving Buddhism, an evangelizing Christianity and also the insidious appeal of scientific materialism and Western forms of democracy?

In the closing decades of the Manchu dynasty there were few thinkers who envisaged the complete overthrow of the monarchical system which had lasted for more than two thousand years, and with it the destruction of the Confucian bureaucracy. Drastic reform was seen to be necessary, but it was conceived of as reform within the system and not the utter collapse of the system. The leaders of Confucian thought were bent on preserving what they felt to be distinctively and uniquely Chinese, namely, the Confucian tradition, which through the centuries had produced a distinctive Chinese civilization, and which represented to them the soul or essence of China. One of the outstanding Confucians, who had a great following, was the statesman-philosopher, K'ang Yu-wei (1858–1927). Believing that the strength of Great Britain, which at that time was the leading foreign power with which China had to deal, was derived from its political system and its religion, K'ang Yu-wei advocated that the monarchy in China should be reformed so as to become a constitutional monarchy, and that, at the same time, Confucianism should be accepted as the national religion of China, and Confucian doctrines prevail in government and in society. He considered Confucius to be not only a great teacher, but a reformer, whose radical ideas were destined eventually to bring humanity to a final stage of universal harmony within a unitary civilization. He attributed to Confucius the idea of three stages of human development: a period of chaotic strife in which egoism, individualism, nationalism and capitalism brought disunity to the world; a period when nations learned to co-operate under socialism and internationalism; and, finally, a period of Great Unity in a single world civilization. As a young man, K'ang Yu-wei took an active part in the reform movement, and in 1898, as chief adviser to the young Emperor, Kuang-Hsü, he was largely responsible for the issuing of the famous twenty-seven edicts which were meant to initiate sweeping reforms of the political, educational, economic and military institutions of the empire. Defeated in his object by the swift action of the Empress Dowager and her extremely conservative advisers, K'ang barely escaped with his life, and lived in exile till the early days of the Republic. During those years of exile, K'ang became more and more a fervent disciple of Confucius. He taught that the central Confucian virtue of *jên* (humanity, love, goodness) was pervasive, like the ether, so that, as it became accepted and practised, it would bring about the unity of mankind and lead to the abolition of all the distinctions and inequalities of race, class and sex. K'ang's greatest work was his Utopia, known as the *Ta T'ung Shu* (*Book of the Great Concord*), which he wrote at the age of twenty-seven. In this work K'ang tries to show the relevance of Confucius to the modern scene by linking Confucian ideas to those derived from Christianity and Buddhism, and with current Western concepts of internationalism and world peace. 'The whole work', writes Derk Bodde, 'is remarkable as a mixture of Chinese and Western Utopian thinking. It combined idealism, radicalism, and keen prophetic insight, with a curious naïve confidence in technological progress as the key to human happiness, which in this respect makes it quite un-Chinese and typical of Western nineteenth-century optimism.'[4]

K'ang Yu-wei was one of the leading Confucian scholars who sought to turn Confucianism into an organized state religion. These scholars were realistic enough to accept the fact that the Confucian 'way of life', which in former times had been regarded as having a universal validity for 'all under Heaven', was neither acceptable by nor applicable to other nations. They had their own religious systems which were believed by them to possess universal truth. When these scholars examined Western nations they found that their national life and thought were permeated by the ethical and spiritual teachings of Christianity; Arab countries were dominated by Islam; India was predominately moulded by the tenets of Hinduism. In the same way China could only hope to safeguard and preserve what was essentially and peculiarly Chinese by establishing Confucianism as a state religion. China's nearest neighbour, Japan, in her process of modernization, had deliberately adopted Shinto as the national faith of Japan, and it seemed that by doing so she was preserving the essential 'soul' of Japan against the inroads of alien ideologies. 'The Chinese people was urged to practise its own religion, Confucianism, on the ground that non-Chinese peoples, if well advised, were practising theirs ... Christians had their cathedrals; then let Confucianists build a cathedral and start out, not on the road to Rome, but nevertheless on the road to a holy city – Ch'ü-fu, in Shantung, the birthplace of Confucius, which ought to be a pilgrimage place like Mecca or Jerusalem.'[5]

When, in 1905, the centuries-old examination system was abolished, the appeal was made to revere the Confucian Classics so as to preserve the national essence. The following year an edict was issued in the name of the Emperor Kuang Hsü, announcing that sacrifices to Confucius would henceforth be reckoned among the Great Sacrifices at which the emperor himself was expected to officiate personally. Thus, the worship offered to Confucius was placed on a level with that offered to Heaven and Earth. It is possible that if, as K'ang Yu-wei hoped, a constitutional form of monarchy could have been established in place of the effete and alien Manchu dynasty, the state cult of Confucius would have persisted to this day with the rituals for the worship of Heaven and Earth. They were, however, all swept away in the early days of the Republic which was inaugurated in 1911. A valiant attempt was made to establish Confucianism as the national religion of the Republic, but it was doomed to failure from the start. Not only were Buddhists and Christians strongly opposed to the compulsion towards conformity inherent in any national religion, but most leading Confucians themselves were antagonistic to all that was implied in making Confucianism into an organized religious system. There was a strong desire on the part of many of them to conserve the Confucian morality, which in the past had brought great strength to China and supported her political system. On the other hand, they were totally opposed to the attempts being made by the more conservative politicians, headed by Yüan Shih-k'ai, to carry on the traditional rituals and sacrifices in honour of Confucius. Yüan Shih-k'ai decided that, as President of the Republic, he himself should sacrifice at the ancient spring and autumn sacrifices in the Confucian temple at Peking, whilst the leading government official in each provincial city should similarly officiate in the local Confucian temple. He issued a decree declaring that 'the doctrine of Confucius and the classic literature are without equal among mankind. The offering of incense and sacrifice is historic, and it is appropriate for the Republic to follow the old customs.'[6] A further edict stated that the teachings of Confucius were appropriate to the changed conditions under the Republic. It was true that Confucius had emphasized the duties of a subject to his ruler, but those duties had been exaggerated under the monarchy. Confucius had also taught the principle of universal brotherhood, a doctrine which should now be emphasized under the Republic. Confucius was also eulogized as the greatest sage, and the privileges which had been formerly conferred upon his descendants were confirmed. But the movement to make Confucius into the god of a state religion lacked spiritual vitality. Confucianism was being used as a tool of politicians, and when Yüan Shih-k'ai was discredited and the Nationalist movement gained strength, the weight of intellectual opinion in China favoured the view that all religions are the product of man's social and political immaturity, anachronisms in a modern world, incompatible with an age of science, reason and objectivity. Attempts were made to resuscitate the Confucian ethical system to form the moral basis of the Chinese social order.

The younger among the intellectuals and leaders of the revolutionary movement which created the Republic in 1911 had little or no interest in Confucianism. Many of them had spent years as exiles in foreign countries or as students at foreign universities. Few of them had made a thorough study of the Confucian Classics. Confucianism was something which now belonged to history, and to a political and social order that had been finally swept away. All their energies were bent on fitting China to take its place in the modern world. The founding of the Republic was soon followed by the stirrings of a cultural revolution in which Hu Shih and his colleagues demanded a language and literature of the people which all men and women could hope to learn, and a scholarship based on modern theories of education. The task of a new generation, according to Ch'ên Tu-hsiu, an influential professor in the national university in Peking, is 'to fight Confucianism, the old tradition of virtue and rituals, the old ethics and the old politics, the old learning and the old literature'.[7] In their place he advocated putting the fresh materials of modern democratic political thought and natural science. So strong was Ch'ên's opposition to Confucianism that he referred to it as a fossil, fatal to vitality in the present. Later, in the first decade of Communist rule in China, criticism became vituperation. Professors and students alike joined in the cry, 'Destroy the old curiosity shop of Confucianism.' Effigies of Confucius were burnt. Mao Tsê-tung declared, 'I hated Confucius from the age of eight.' A few lone voices spoke up for Confucius as a defender of the poor and an upholder of democracy, and they referred to Sun Yat-sen, the father of the revolution who himself was honoured by the communists, and who had declared that 'Confucius and Mencius were both exponents of democracy.' The attack on Confucianism was a many-pronged attack. It was pointed out that Confucianism was 'feudalistic'. For centuries it had bolstered up the pre-eminence of a small scholar-class, which had kept to itself all the main privileges of wealth, social prestige, education and the enjoyment of the arts, leaving the masses of the people in poverty, ignorance and degradation. The morality of Confucianism was assailed. It was a slave morality, designed to keep the masses of the people in perpetual subjection. It was a feudalistic morality, which had different laws for the rich and poor, for the governors and the governed, for the scholar and the illiterate peasant. It was a morality which kept women in subjection and confined to the home. It encouraged the rich to have a plurality of wives and concubines. If enforced marriages without the consent of the interested parties. It glorified the past at the expense of the present, and the family at the expense of the individual. It weakened the national consciousness. The spiritual basis of Confucianism was also assailed. Atheistic materialism had no use for the concept of an over-ruling Providence. Man was the arbiter of his own fate and the moulder and controller of his own destiny.

Early in the communist régime, such old Confucian scholars as still remained, and who had been the bulwark of Confucianism, were replaced by young university graduates and army cadres who had had a thorough training in the communist ideology. It looked as though Confucianism had ceased to be a living influence on the mainland of China.

Outside China proper, in Taiwan, Hongkong and other parts of the Chinese Dispersion, there was manifested a revival in Confucian studies, and hopeful signs of an eagerness to enlarge upon the spiritual values of Confucianism and the richness of its ethical and spiritual contribution to the world. Within China itself, however, the period which saw the violent vituperation against Confucius soon passed. The Chinese communists have shown that they are strongly nationalistic, and so are immensely proud of their rich cultural tradition, of which, as we have seen, Confucianism forms an essential part. The preservation of their great cultural heritage is one of the aims of the present government of China. Levenson, in the third volume of his trilogy on *Confucianism and its Modern Fate*,[8] has tried to assess the position of Confucianism in the present communist state of China. He believed that, as 'there was no organized Confucian body whose state could be statistically assessed ... as far as communist policy was concerned, Confucianism as a religion was a dead issue'.[9] But he asked pertinent questions: first as to how far Confucianism has entered into Communism, and secondly, as to the place of Confucius himself in communist thinking.

There is a measure of common ground between Confucianism and Chinese communism. Confucianism taught that the guide-rules for individual conduct and for life's relationships were all to be found in the teachings of Confucius, and so the *Four Books* became the basis of a Confucian education, to be learned, studied, memorized and quoted. In a similar way, in Chinese communism today the *Thoughts of Mao* are extolled and studied in the belief that this book contains all necessary wisdom, providing a solution to every problem both for the individual and the group. Mao Tsê-tung has been exalted to represent in Chinese eyes the ideal sage-ruler of Confucianism, and everyone carries about with him his precious copy of the little Red Book. Like the ideal ruler of Confucian China, Mao's 'virtue' permeates the whole nation, and possesses a dynamic quality to bring about a just and peaceful society. It is true to say that, far more so than in monarchical China, the rulers and those who lead in local affairs today have won their position by their own native ability, proving their adequacy, not by competitive examination in the Confucian Classics, but by their application to Marxist studies and their unswerving devotion to the ideals of the revolution. Furthermore, one finds a similarity between Confucianism and communism in China in their strong emphasis on ethics. Just as Confucianism founded its ethics in the concept of *li*, that is, what is generally considered to be right, proper or fitting, and not in any fiat or revelation of deity, so Chinese communism finds the basis of ethical conduct in what is generally recognized as right and proper within the framework of a Marxist ideology. In both, the social groupings to which an individual belongs mould, determine and, if necessary, correct his conduct to an extent far greater than would be acceptable in Western democracies. The concept of individual freedom, the rights of the individual to decide and choose and act for himself, so precious in the West, never had the same appeal in China, neither under Confucianism nor under communism. Communist

China also resembles Confucianism in the dogmatic assurance that it possesses the blueprint for a politically and socially just society, and consequently regards itself as the standard-bearer for all the oppressed and backward peoples of the world in their fight for a place in the sun.

As soon as the communists gained for themselves an unchallenged supremacy in China, they set about the task of preserving for the people China's cultural heritage, which is, more than anything else, a Confucian heritage. Once they felt assured that Confucius could be relegated to the history books, and that he and his teachings were no longer an effective force in the lives of the people, they ceased from violent criticism and began to accord to Confucius a measure of patronage. They began to encourage the study of the Confucian civilization of the past, much in the same way as Western archaeologists cherish and preserve the relics of the ancient civilizations of Egypt and Mesopotamia, or as historians and classicists study the writings of ancient Greek and Roman authors. But in their case, the communists, just because they are Chinese, take pride in the fact that China's past is their own nation's past, the glories of its civilization something in which they may take legitimate pride, so long as the authors of classical learning and the architects of imperial greatness are kept strictly to their role of sages and heroes of the past. In recent years the communists have restored the beautiful temples, altars and palaces of a Confucian civilization, which had previously been allowed to fall into disrepair and even ruin. They have produced translations of the Confucian Classics in the common and simplified language of the people. They have encouraged research into various aspects of Confucianism – its music, its rituals, its contributions to literature and art – but always they have emphasized that Confucius is a figure of the past, neither to be idolized nor disparaged. He is to be honoured as a great man of his own times, but one who has no real intellectual or moral significance for the twentieth century.

The present régime has been in power for less than twenty-five years, a tiny fraction of the course of history since Confucius was alive. However, changes have taken place during these past few years so drastic and revolutionary that there is no going back, no chance of restoring the pre-revolutionary Confucian civilization. But if the 'hundred flowers'[10] were really allowed to bloom, if there were a return to intellectual freedom and full freedom of expression, there seems no doubt that there would be not only a great revival of Confucian studies, but a renewed emphasis on the Confucian 'way of life' and on the contribution that Confucius can make, not only to China but to the world as a whole. Away from the mainland of China, in Taiwan, Hongkong, Singapore and other parts of the Chinese Dispersion, there is an eagerness on the part of Confucian scholars to enlarge on the spiritual values of Confucianism and the richness of its ethical and spiritual contribution in the realm of thought. No one in these days would wish to try and form a Confucian church organization on a credal or doctrinal basis. That has never been the genius of Confucianism. There is no desire to deify Confucius or to accord to him supernatural wisdom or insight, but there are those who would like to see Confucius honoured in his own birthplace and throughout the Chinese-speaking world with the traditional ceremonies, those time-honoured rituals and music, which not only have an aesthetic appeal but somehow bring to the participants a deep sense of the numinous.

The great ideals of individual perfection and a harmonious social order which Confucius inculcated are as relevant in the modern world as they were nearly 2,500 years ago. Confucius still calls men, through the teachings that bear his name, to seek after a central harmony, a golden mean, the recognition of an inextricable bond between nature and man. He asks men to recognize the benevolent providence of a cosmic power, and the generous and bountiful provisions of mother Earth. He invites men to recognize in themselves a Heaven-born nature, and the capacity to bring that nature to full flower in a rich humanity and devotion to truth. He retains his place, and will retain his place, among the wise ones of the earth who sought after righteousness, and found it to be a thing of great price. Confucius is China's greatest gift to mankind.

Notes

Introduction

1. J. Needham, *Within the Four Seas*, p. 63.
2. The word 'county' is here used to designate the *hsien*, which was the smallest administrative district in Imperial China. It was usually about the size and population of a small English county. A typical *hsien* consisted of a walled city with its surrounding country, in which were several market towns and villages. Its chief officer was a magistrate appointed by the central government. His principal duties were to collect taxes, judge law cases and perform administrative and ritual functions within his district on behalf of the emperor. For a more detailed account of the Chinese administrative system, see S. Couling, *Encyclopaedia Sinica*, pp. 209–14. For the origin of the *hsien* and its place in the administrative system in ancient times, see D. Bodde, *China's First Unifier*, pp. 135, 145, 238–40.
3. *The Historical Records* of Ssŭ-ma Ch'ien state that Confucius selected the 305 poems in the *Book of Poetry* (*Shih Ching*) out of more than 3,000 and suggests that he edited the *Book of History* (*Shu Ching*), studied the *Book of Changes* (*I Ching*) and the ritual material which later went into the composition of the *Book of Rites* (*Li Chi*). Traditionally it has been held that he composed the *Spring and Autumn Classic* (*Ch'un Ch'iu*). This is supported by the studies of G. A. Kennedy, 'Interpretation of the *Ch'un Ch'iu*', *Journal of the American Oriental Society*, LXII (1942), pp. 40–48. But for criticism of Kennedy, see H. G. Creel, *Confucius: the Man and the Myth*, pp. 111–16; a succinct examination of the problem of Confucius's authorship and the conclusion that 'there is no convincing evidence that he wrote or even edited anything at all'.

4. The *Analects* is our earliest and most reliable source, though there is internal evidence of its being a composite work and not all from the same period. Discussions of the authenticity of the *Analects* are to be found in A. Waley, *The Analects of Confucius*, pp. 21 ff., and in Creel, *Confucius: the Man and the Myth*, pp. 313–15. References to Confucius and his teachings are to be found in most extant pre-Han writers. Though many of these references help to supplement our knowledge of Confucius, they need to be used with caution as the work either of detractors or hagiographers.

5. Ssŭ-ma Ch'ien, *Shih Chi* (*Historical Records*), trans. into French by E. Chavannes as *Les Mémoires Historiques de Se-ma Ts'ien*, 5 vols., Paris, 1895–1905; the Life of Confucius is found in Chapter 47 (pp. 282 ff.) and in R. Wilhelm, *Confucius and Confucianism* (English trans. by G. H. and A. P. Danton), pp. 3–70.

6. Waley, *Analects*, p. 21. Arthur Waley suggests that Books 3–9 of the *Analects* represent the oldest stratum, and that Book 19, from which the following quotation is taken, was incorporated later, for it consists entirely of sayings of disciples of Confucius.

7. *Analects*, 19:23–25 (Waley's translation).

8. For a short account of Tzŭ-ch'an see Shigeki Kaizuka, *Confucius*, pp. 74–89.

9. The Duke of Chou, the founder-statesman of the Chou Dynasty: see Kaizuka, *Confucius*, pp. 17–27; W. Eichhorn, *Chinese Civilization*, p. 59; Dun J. Li, *The Ageless Chinese*, pp. 45–6.

10. The Confucian Classics, either attributed to Confucius or believed to have been edited and collated by him, consist of the *Classics of Poetry*, *History*, *Changes*, *Spring and Autumn Annals*, and the *Rites*. These gained a comparatively definitive form during the Former Han Dynasty. To these five were added the three commentaries on the *Spring and Autumn Annals* named Tso, Kung Yang and Ku Liang, the Chou Li and the I Li; the Lun Yü, the *Works of Mencius* and the Erh Ya dictionary, to form a corpus of thirteen classics in all. See R. Wilhelm, *History of Chinese Civilization*, pp. 174 ff.

11. An intellectual Confucian revival beginning in the T'ang

dynasty (A.D. 618–907) became dominant in the Sung (A.D. 960–1279) through the writings and influence of Chou Tun-i (A.D. 1017–73), Shao Yung (1011–77), Chang Tsai (1020–77), Ch'êng Hao (1032–85), Ch'êng I (1033–1108), and Chu Hsi (1130–1200). An excellent account of the Neo-Confucian school of the Sung dynasty is found in Fung Yu-lan, *History of Chinese Philosophy*, Vol. 2, Peking, 1937, Chapters 10–13. Also W. T. Chan, *A Source Book in Chinese Philosophy*, Chapters 28–34.

12. The Manchus were a clan of Nü-chên Tartars, who occupied the territory to the north-east of China, now known as Manchuria. In A.D. 1629, having conquered Korea, they invaded China and, assisted by Chinese rebels, they overthrew the Ming dynasty after a long and bitter struggle. They captured Peking in A.D. 1644, and their ruler, taking the reign title Shun Chih, established himself as emperor of China and founded the Manchu or Ch'ing dynasty (1644–1911).

13. *The Sacred Edict* was published in 1670 and was later expanded and published in colloquial Chinese for the benefit of the general populace.

14. 2 *Corinthians*, 3:6.

Chapter 1

1. Until comparatively modern times the Chinese in general accepted as historical the accounts of the beginnings of Chinese civilization in the *Shu Ching* and the Great Treatise or Third Appendix of the *I Ching*. These accounts refer to the Five Emperors: Pao Hsi, Shên Nung, Huang Ti, Yao and Shun, and the founding of the Hsia dynasty by Yü the Great. See J. Legge, *Sacred Books of the East*, Vol. 3, pp. 31–77; Vol. 16, pp. 382 ff. These are now recognized as mythical or legendary figures, and archaeology has not been able to discover any reliable evidence of a Hsia dynasty. The Shang dynasty is the first dynasty in Chinese history for which there is contemporary documentary evidence in the form of texts inscribed on bones used in divination. These can be assigned to the fourteenth and thirteenth centuries

B.C. According to Chinese traditional dating, the Shang dynasty lasted from 1766 to 1154 B.C. More recently Chinese scholars have advanced cogent arguments for the dates 1558–1102 B.C. The dynasty was often referred to as the Yin dynasty, Yin being the name of the capital city after 1401 B.C. For accounts of the beginnings of Chinese civilization see H. G. Creel, *The Birth of China*; Li Chi, *The Beginnings of Chinese Civilization*, and Chêng Tê-k'un, *Archaeology in China*, Vols. 1–3.

2. The non-Chinese tribes, with which the Chinese of the Shang and early Chou dynasties were in an almost continual state of warfare for hundreds of years, were called by different names. The principal tribes were the *I* to the east, the *Ti* to the north-east, the *Hsien-yün* to the north, the *Jung* to the north-west, the *Man* and the *Miao* to the south. They were distinguished from the Chinese by language and customs. Some were conquered, enslaved and gradually assimilated. Others, like the *Miao* tribes, were driven further and further into the mountainous districts of the south-west. Others, like the *Hsien-yün* and the *Jung* tribes were nomadic inhabitants of the northern steppes, and remained in almost continuous conflict with the Chinese throughout their history.

3. On the origin and significance of the *Ju* the most important essays are in Chinese: Hu Shih, *Lun Hsüeh Chin Chu*, Vol. 1, pp. 3–81, and Fung Yu-lan, *Chung Kuo Chê Hsüeh Shih Pu*, pp. 1–61. See Creel, *Confucius: the Man and the Myth*, p. 182, note 6.

4. Li Chi, *The Beginnings of Chinese Civilization*, p. 20.

5. D. H. Smith, *Chinese Religions*, pp. 6–7.

6. Each day in a sixty-day cycle (and later each year of a sixty-year cycle) was denoted by a combination of two characters: the first, one of ten characters known as *t'ien kan* or 'heavenly stems'; the second, one of twelve characters known as *ti chih* or 'earthly branches'. These latter have the names of animals, and correspond to the twelve signs of the Chinese solar zodiac. The two characters followed a regular sequence to produce the cycle of sixty days (or years). For lists of the ten heavenly stems and the twelve earthly branches, see Mathews, *Chinese English Dictionary*, pp. 1176–7. See also Bredon and Mitrophanow, *The Moon Year*, pp. 9–11.

7. Waley (trans.), *The Book of Songs*, pp. 256–7.
8. Waley, p. 263.
9. Waley, p. 230.
10. Waley, p. 236.
11. These quotations are taken from the *Shu Ching* as follows: *Ta Kao*, 14; *K'ang Kao*, 4; *To Shih*, 3; *Chun Shih*, 2. For J. Legge's translation see *Sacred Books of the East*, Vol. 3, and for Couvreur's see *Chou King*, Hsien-hsien.
12. See Waley, *The Book of Songs*, p. 162.
13. Waley, pp. 146–8.
14. Shigeki Kaizuka, *Confucius*, pp. 87, 141.
15. Shigeki Kaizuka, p. 78.
16. Dun J. Li, *The Ageless Chinese*, p. 62.

Chapter 2

1. For a short account of the ancestry of Confucius see Shigeki Kaizuka, *Confucius*, pp. 49 ff. See also Creel, *Confucius: the Man and the Myth*, p. 29 and note 1.
2. See Creel, *Confucius*, p. 30, note 5. Though caution is necessary towards the traditional accounts, the identification of Confucius's father with the Shu Ho mentioned twice in the *Tso Chuan* may not be wide of the mark, as the Mêng family, which Shu Ho served, certainly seem to have befriended Confucius and probably gave him his education. In manhood Confucius held the rank of *shih* or 'knight' and behaved as though he was descended from people of consequence.
3. Northern League. Throughout most of the seventh and sixth centuries B.C., as the titular king had lost all authority, attempts were made to form the states of northern China into an alliance under the leadership of the most powerful state ruler. These states were pledged to non-aggression among themselves, and to united efforts against the barbarian invasions from the north, and the expansionist policies of semi-barbarian states, such as Ch'u, Wu and Yüeh, in the south. Until the death of Duke Huan of Ch'i in 643 B.C. the leader state was Ch'i. Under Duke Huan the northern states were called to interstate conferences no less than twenty-six

times. After Huan's death, for the next hundred years the state of Tsin assumed the leadership in the north, whilst the state of Ch'u dominated in the south. The formation of the Northern League helped to bring some order in a chaotic situation and was a serious attempt to ensure collective security and mutual non-aggression.

4. A good account of the exploits of Shu-liang Ho is found in Kaizuka, *Confucius*, pp. 51 ff.

5. It is pointless to seek strict accuracy as regards the birth of Confucius, born as he was in humble and inconspicuous circumstances. The *Kung-yang Chuan* places his birth in the eleventh month of the twenty-first year of Duke Hsiang, whilst the *Ku-liang Chuan* places the birth in the tenth month. The *Historical Records* (*Shih Chi*) give the birth in the twenty-second year of Duke Hsiang. Hence the discrepancy.

6. *Analects*, 9:6.

7. *Analects*, 2:4.

8. *Mencius*, 5b:5.4.

9. *Analects*, 5:15.

10. *Analects*, 14:10.

11. *Analects*, 5:16.

12. In ancient China the art of divination was practised by means of the tortoise shell and the stalks of the milfoil (*achillea millefolium*). The tortoise was believed to possess foreknowledge, and to be a source of good fortune. The shell was coated with blood or ink on one side and the other side was placed over a fire. As the ink dried cracks were produced resembling characters, which were then interpreted by the expert diviner. The stalks of the milfoil were manipulated by the diviner to predict what he desired. See L. Wieger, *History of Religious Beliefs and Philosophical Opinions in China*, pp. 73–4.

13. Legge, *Chinese Classics*, Vol. 5, p. 607.

14. *Analects*, 17:21.

15. *Analects*, 11:7. See Waley, *The Analects*, p. 15.

16. *Analects*, 3:1.

17. J. Legge, *The Life and Teaching of Confucius*, 4th ed., pp. 62 ff.

18. *Analects*, 7:13; Waley, *The Analects*, p. 69; Kaizuka, *Confucius*, p. 142.

19. *Analects*, 12:11.
20. R. Wilhelm, *Confucius and Confucianism*, p. 11; Legge, *Life and Teaching of Confucius*, p. 67.
21. *Analects*, 17:1.
22. *Analects*, 17:5.
23. Creel, *Confucius*, p. 43; Y. P. Mei (trans.), *The Ethical and Political Works of Mo Tzŭ*, p. 209; J. Legge, *Chinese Classics*, Vol. 5, p. 745; *Mencius*, 6a:6.6.
24. Legge, *Chinese Classics*, Vol. 5, pp. 776–7.
25. *Mencius*, 5b:4.7.
26. *Analects*, 3:19; 13:15.
27. *Analects*, 18:4.
28. *Mencius*, 5a:8.2.
29. *Mencius*, 5a:8.3. Throughout Chinese history, dress was a means of indicating social position and rank within an elaborate social structure. Confucius, in travelling from one state to another, would wear the dress and insignia to which he was entitled as a scholar-official of the state of Lu, and would be entitled to support and lodging wherever he went in accordance with strict rules of etiquette. In travelling through the state of Sung, however, being made aware that attempts were to be made on his life, Confucius decided to travel incognito, in the plain, simple costume used by the peasantry.
30. *Analects*, 7:30.
31. *Analects*, 5:14; *Mencius*, 5b:4.7.
32. Legge, *Life and Teaching of Confucius*, p. 843.
33. Legge, pp. 824–5.
34. *Analects*, 14:22.
35. *Analects*, 11:16; *Mencius*, 4a:14.
36. *Analects*, 11:7.
37. *Analects*, 11:8.
38. Legge, *Life and Teaching of Confucius*, p. 840.
39. Legge, p. 843.
40. *Analects*, 19:24.
41. *Mencius*, 7b:19.3.
42. Legge, *S.B.E.*, Vol. 27, pp. 138–9.
43. Henri Maspero, *La Chine Antique*, p. 459; Waley, *The Analects*, p. 55; Lin Yü-tʻang, *The Pleasures of a Nonconformist*, Chapter 30; *With Love and Irony*, Chapter 28.

44. *Analects*, 10:2, 11–12.
45. Kuo Mo-jo, *Chin Wên Tsung K'ao*, pp. 16b–17b.
46. *Analects*, 7:7.
47. *Analects*, 6:26; 17:5, 7.
48. *Analects*, 11:8–10.
49. *Analects*, 6:6.
50. *Analects*, 11:16, 23.
51. *Analects*, 19:23, 25; *Mencius*, 3a:4.13.
52. *Mencius*, 3a:4.13.
53. *Analects*, 3:8; 11:2.
54. *Analects*, 19:3, 12.

Chapter 3

1. In this chapter references to the *Analects* are bracketed *in loco* in the text, since the *Analects* is our chief source for the teaching of Confucius. The student will find it useful to have an English translation of the *Analects* available. There are several good translations: A. Waley, *The Analects of Confucius*, is recommended.
2. D. H. Smith, *Chinese Religions*, pp. 36 f.
3. Smith, pp. 40–41.
4. Wu K'ung in *K'ung-tzŭ Lun Chi*, Vol. 1, Peking, 1957, p. 68.
5. Y. P. Mei (trans.), *The Ethical and Political Works of Mo-tzŭ*, chapters 'Against Fate' (*Fei Ming*).
6. Waley, *The Analects of Confucius*, pp. 30–33.
7. Waley, p. 28.
8. Y. P. Mei, *The Ethical and Political Works of Mo-tzŭ*, chapters on 'The Will of Heaven' (*T'ien Chih*) and 'The Exaltation of the Worthy' (*Shang Hsien*).
9. *Mencius*, 6a:10, also 2a:6.
10. Fung Yu-lan, *History of Chinese Philosophy*, Vol. 1, pp. 357 ff.
11. See *Analects* 15:10. '(I) would do away altogether with the tunes of Chêng ... for the tunes of Chêng are licentious.' *Analects*, 17:18. 'I hate to see the tunes of Chêng corrupting court music.'

   In the *Li Chi*, Book 17:8, the disciple Tzŭ-Hsia referred to the music of Chêng and Wei as 'corrupt to excess; there is no end to its vileness'.

12. Smith, *Chinese Religions*, pp. 40–41; W. A. C. H. Dobson, *Mencius*, p. 194, note 37; H. H. Dubs, *Hsüntzŭ : the Moulder of Ancient Confucianism*, Chapter 8.

13. Dubs, p. 113, note.

14. Dubs, p. 25.

15. Dubs, p. 46.

16. Waley, *The Analects of Confucius*, p. 90, note.

17. The authority of the *Ch'un Ch'iu* and Confucius's use of it is highly debatable. There seems no reason to doubt that Confucius had available to him a collection of the documents relative to the State of Lu, but whether or not he was responsible for editing them cannot be proved. It is not mentioned in the *Analects*, yet Confucius shows familiarity with material in it, and one might even conclude that Tso's Commentary was in some measure based on notes left by Confucius. As for the *I Ching*, or the *Book of Divination* on which it is based, in spite of *Analects*, 7:16, it is doubtful if Confucius made any use of it at all in his teaching. See Creel, *Confucius: the Man and the Myth*, pp. 115–16; Waley, *The Analects of Confucius*, p. 126, note 3.

18. *Mencius*, 3b:3.1.

19. Legge, *S.B.E.*, Vol. 3, pp. 481–2.

20. Legge, *Chinese Classics*, Vol. 5, from which numerous examples may be cited.

21. Y. P. Mei, *The Ethical and Political Works of Mo-tzŭ*, chapter on 'Belief in Spirits' (*Ming Kuei*).

22. Legge, *S.B.E.*, Vol. 28, p. 220.

23. H. von Glasenapp, *Buddhism: a non-theistic religion*, pp. 66–7.

Chapter 4

1. Legge, *Chinese Classics*, Vol. 5, p. 846.

2. Legge, *S.B.E.*, Vol. 27, pp. 138–9.

3. Wilhelm, *Confucius and Confucianism*, p. 66.

4. *Analects*, 9:11.

5. *Mencius*, 3a:4.13.

6. L. Wieger, *Textes Historiques*, Hsien-hsien, Vol. 1, p. 303. Wilhelm, *Confucius and Confucianism*, p. 68.

7. Wilhelm, pp. 67, 69.

8. For an account of the 'Burning of the Books' see Fitzgerald, *China: a Short Cultural History*, pp. 144 ff. It has been pointed out that this 'Burning of the Books' by order of the First Emperor was by no means the only occasion on which the ancient literature suffered extensive damage. See Wilhelm, *History of Chinese Civilization*, pp. 22, 53, 169.

9. *Shih Chi*, Chapter 121, 1-2.

10. The period from 403 to 221 B.C. is known in China as the *Chan Kuo* or *Warring States* period, when some seven large states, having conquered and absorbed their smaller neighbours, struggled for mastery. The period ended with the unification of China under the ruler of the state of Ch'in.

11. The Five Elements theory was one of the earliest Chinese attempts to account for the structure of the physical universe. It was believed that five elements, natural forces or powers, represented by wood, fire, earth, metal and water, were the source of everything, and were mutually productive and destructive of each other in rotation. In the period after Confucius, notably with Tsou Yen (*c*. 350–270 B.C.), the theory came to be associated with that of *Yin-Yang*, which attributed all life and phenomena to the interaction of two opposite and complementary creative agents known respectively as *yin* and *yang*. Philosophical schools emerged to develop these theories which exercised a profound influence on Chinese cosmology, philosophy, government and art. See articles in Brandon, *Dictionary of Comparative Religion*, pp. 288, 654, 657, where references to further reading are given.

12. There are many translations of the *Ta Hsüeh* available. Translations with useful commentaries are in Hughes, *The Great Learning and the Mean in Action*, and in W. T. Chan, *A Source Book in Chinese Philosophy*.

13. Chan, p. 84.

14. As Chapter 39.

15. Chapter 28 of the *Li Chi*. Translations in Hughes, *The Great Learning*, and Chan, *Source Book*.

16. Chan, *Source Book*, p. 95.

17. *Analects*, 5:12.

18. Fung Yu-lan, *History of Chinese Philosophy*, Vol. 1, pp. 369–71. Hughes, *The Great Learning*, pp. 86–7.

19. *Chung Yung*, Chapter 20. Hughes, *The Great Learning*, pp, 118–27.
20. *Mencius*, 4b:10.
21. *Analects*, 11:15.
22. *Chung Yung*, Chapters 2–11. Hughes, *The Great Learning*. pp. 106–8.
23. *Chung Yung*, Chapter 6.
24. *Chung Yung*, Chapter 12.
25. *Chung Yung*, Chapter 13.
26. See E. R. Hughes, *The Great Learning and the Mean in Action*, p. 113.
27. Hughes, *The Great Learning*, p. 114.
28. The quotations are taken from Chapters 26, 27, 31 and 32.
29. A recent translation is by W. A. C. H. Dobson, *Mencius*, in which the translator groups the chapters under subject headings. A 'finding list' is appended.
30. Yü the Great was a legendary hero-king who was given the task by his royal predecessor, Shun, of controlling the rivers and draining the marshes so as to make the country inhabitable. After nine years of strenuous toil he succeeded in his task, and was nominated as Shun's successor. To him is attributed the founding of the Hsia dynasty in 2205 B.C.
31. *Mencius*, 3b:9.
32. *Mencius*, 7b:38; 2b:2, 22.
33. *Mencius*, 2a:2, 23.
34. *Mencius*, 6b:6.
35. *Mencius*, 5b:4.7.
36. *Mencius*, 5a:6.
37. *Mencius*, 2a:2; 2a:7; 3a:2; 3a:4; 4a:15; 4a:29; 7b:37.
38. *Mencius*, 1a:4; 2a:1–4; 3b:1, 3, 9; 4a:2, 8, 9; 4b:18, 21; 5a:5, 6, 8; 5b:1, 4, 7; 6a:6, 8; 6b:3, 6; 7a:24; 7b:17, 37.
39. *Mencius*, 4b:19; 6a:7–8, 15.
40. *Mencius*, 6a:12.
41. *Analects*, 13:9.
42. *Mencius*, 1a:7.
43. *Mencius*, 1a:7.
44. *Mencius*, 2a:3.
45. *Mencius*, 3a:3.
46. For the study of Hsün-tzŭ and a translation of his works, see

Dubs, *Hsüntze : the Moulder of Ancient Confucianism*, and *The Works of Hsüntze*.

47. Ssŭ-ma Ch'ien, *Historical Records* (*Shih Chi*), Chapter 74, section 14.
48. Dubs, *Hsüntze : the Moulder of Ancient Confucianism*, p. xxviii.
49. Dubs, p. xxviii.
50. Dubs, *The Works of Hsüntze*, Chapter 17, pp. 173–4; Fung Yu-lan, *History of Chinese Philosophy*, Vol. 1, p. 285.
51. Chan, *A Source Book in Chinese Philosophy*, p. 121.
52. Chapter 17 of *Hsün-tzŭ's Works* : see Dubs, p. 183.
53. This and previous quotations are taken from Chapter 17. See Dubs, *The Works of Hsüntze*, pp. 179–82.
54. Chapter 10: see Dubs, *Works*, p. 151.
55. Dubs, p. 308.
56. Dubs, p. 122. The exaltation of the virtuous had already been emphasized by Mo-tzŭ. See Y. P. Mei, *The Ethical and Political Works of Mo-tzŭ*.
57. Dubs, *The Works of Hsüntze*, pp. 244–5.
58. Dubs, pp. 223–4.
59. Chan, *A Source Book in Chinese Philosophy*, p. 115.
60. Waley, *The Analects of Confucius*, p. 38.
61. *Analects*, 1:2.
62. *Analects*, 2:5.
63. Legge, *S.B.E.*, Vol. 3, pp. 450 f.
64. Fung Yu-lan, *History of Chinese Philosophy*, Vol. 1, p. 361.
65. *Chung Yung*, Chapter 17. Hughes, *The Great Learning*, p. 114.
66. *Mencius*, 1a:1.
67. D. Bodde, *China's First Unifier*, p. 192.
68. *Han Fei Tzŭ*, Chapter 45. A translation into English is by W. K. Liao, *The Complete Works of Han Fei Tzŭ*, 2 vols.

Chapter 5

1. *Mencius*, 3b:9.9. For the teachings and influence of the Mohists see Y. P. Mei: *Mo-tzŭ, the rival of Confucius* and *The Ethical and Political Works of Mo-tzŭ*. Also, Chan, *A Source Book in Chinese Philosophy*, Chapter 9; Fung Yu-lan, *History of Chinese Philosophy*, Vol. 1, Chapters 5 and 11.

2. Accounts of the Shaman-diviners and Taoist practitioners are to be found in Holmes Welch: *The Parting of the Way*, pp. 97 ff.; Waley, *The Nine Songs*, pp. 9 ff.; Mircea Eliade, *Shamanism*, pp. 448 ff.

3. Fung Yu-lan, *History of Chinese Philosophy*, Vol. 2, p. 8. For full discussions of the *Yin-Yang* and Five Elements Theories, see Fung Yu-lan, Vol. 1, pp. 159 ff. and Chan, *A Source Book*, Chapter 11.

4. Fung Yu-lan, Vol. 1, Chapter 13; Chan, Chapter 12.

5. J. J. L. Duyvendak, *The Book of Lord Shang*.

6. D. Bodde, *China's First Unifier*, pp. 170, 178 f.

7. Bodde, pp. 147–61. The large seal script was an elaborate and highly pictographic form of writing, such as is found on inscriptions on early Chou dynasty bronzes. In process of time great variations in the writing arose in the different states which composed ancient China. Li Ssŭ (*c.* 280–208 B.C.), prime minister of the state of Ch'in, was responsible for the simplification and standardization of the script in what is known as the 'small seal' writing. This came into general use for inscriptions and for formal occasions, whereas a still more simplified and abbreviated writing known as the *li* or clerkly script came into common use. By the end of the Han dynasty this *li* script had evolved into a style of writing similar to that used today.

8. Bodde, p. 160.

9. Fitzgerald, *China* (rev. ed. 1950), p. 154.

10. Fitzgerald, *China*, p. 155; R. Grousset, *The Rise and Splendour of the Chinese Empire*, p. 55.

11. Werner Eichhorn, *Chinese Civilization*, p. 136.

12. Creel, *The Birth of China*, p. 247.

13. Fitzgerald, *China*, p. 154.

14. H. H. Dubs (trans.), *History of the Former Han Dynasty*, Vol. 1, p. 115.

15. Because of strong opposition to the reforming measures of Ch'in Shih Huang-ti, and criticisms based on the sacred authority of ancient writings, the emperor, at the instigation of his prime minister, Li Ssŭ, ordered the destruction by burning of all the ancient teaching and all the histories of the Feudal States except that of Ch'in. Exceptions were made as

regards books on medicine, divination, agriculture and arboriculture. Those who possessed copies of the *Shih Ching*, *Shu Ching*, *Ch'un Ch'iu*, and the works of pre-Ch'in scholars had to hand them in to the authorities to be burnt. The penalty for concealing books was death, and some 460 scholars were executed. Copies were, however, preserved in the custody of the central government. See Fitzgerald, *China*, pp. 144–6; R. Wilhelm, *History of Chinese Civilization*, pp. 22, 35, 53, 160.

16. Dubs, Vol. 1, p. 216.
17. Creel, *The Birth of China*, p. 253.
18. Chan, *A Source Book*, p. 273.
19. Tung Chung-shu seems to have regarded the *yin* and the *yang* as two material 'ethers' or 'fluids'.
20. Fung Yu-lan, *History of Chinese Philosophy*, Vol. 2, pp. 16 ff.
21. Tjan Tjoe-som, *Po Hu T'ung*, 2 vols.
22. Fung Yu-lan, *History*, Vol. 2, pp. 20–23, 40–45, 63–5, 70.
23. Creel, *The Birth of China*, p. 264.
24. Sacrifices were offered to five celestial deities who were thought to preside over the five regions of the empire, namely centre, north, south, east and west. These deities were known as the Five Celestial Emperors. A special temple was erected for their worship by the emperor Wên-ti (179–156 B.C.), and from that time, in spite of attempts at suppression, the worship of these five celestial emperors continued. See Werner, *Dictionary of Chinese Mythology*, p. 576; Wieger, *History of Religious Beliefs and Philosophical Opinions in China*, pp. 281 ff.
25. Fitzgerald, *China*, p. 220.
26. Dun J. Li, *The Ageless Chinese*, p. 114.
27. Dun J. Li, p. 125.
28. Dun J. Li, p. 125.
29. Legge, *S.B.E.*, Vol. 28, pp. 207–8.
30. J. Legge, *Life and Teaching of Confucius*, 4th ed., p. 91.
31. J. K. Shryock, *The Origin and Development of the State Cult of Confucianism*, p. 103.
32. Shryock, p. 105.
33. A discussion of this reaction is found in Fung Yu-lan, *History of Chinese Philosophy*, Vol. 2, Chapter 4.
34. Fung Yu-lan, *History*, Vol. 2, Chapter 4, p. 135, note 1.

35. Fitzgerald, *China*, p. 227.
36. Fung Yu-lan, *History*, Vol. 1, Chapter 14. Dubs, *Hsüntze: the Moulder of Ancient Confucianism*, p. 44.
37. A. C. Graham, *The Book of Lieh-tzŭ*, p. 143.
38. Legge, *S.B.E.*, Vol. 28, p. 236; *Li Chi* 22:1.
39. Legge, p. 245; *Li Chi* 22:13.
40. *Lun Hêng*, Chapter 62.

Chapter 6

1. Fitzgerald, *China*, p. 252.
2. Wilhelm, *A Short History of Chinese Civilization*, p. 204. See also S. Couling, *Encyclopaedia Sinica*, p. 447. From very early times the Chinese periodically recorded population statistics. Until A.D. 1712, with very few exceptions, the number of tax-paying households alone was recorded. The estimation of population here given is only approximate, based on a calculation of five persons per household. A similar decrease in population is recorded in the T'ang dynasty after the rebellion of An Lu-shan. In A.D. 754 a census recorded approximately 53 million persons, which in A.D. 764 had been reduced to 17 millions. Of course, as only tax-paying households were recorded, after a period of anarchy many households, through removals, etc., slipped through the official net, and the actual population was probably greater than that recorded.
3. The tribes inhabiting the regions to the north of China were of Turkic, Mongol or Tungus origin, and had connections with the Tu Chüeh, a name given by the Chinese to a nomadic people who, in the sixth century A.D., founded an empire stretching from the northern frontier of China to the Black Sea. In Han times they were known to the Chinese as the Hsiung Nu or Hu barbarians, and several of their tribal groups established kingdoms in North China after the fall of Loyang and Ch'ang-an in A.D. 311 and 316 respectively.
4. Sūtras are Buddhist scriptures which purport to be the discourses of the Buddha himself on a variety of particular subjects. They form an important section of the Buddhist Canon known as the Tripitaka.

5. Shryock, *The Origin and Development of the State Cult of Confucianism*, pp. 118–19. In China, the boundaries of religious faiths have never been sharply delineated as they have been in the West. Confucianism was always an ethico-political doctrine, with a this-worldly orientation, but possessing religious qualities. In so far as Confucianism concerned itself with questions as to the ultimate meaning of life and death, it did so in terms of moral responsibility to men rather than to gods. The Confucian scholars were essentially pragmatists. Whilst they recognized the importance to the state of the ancient religion with its worship of Heaven and a host of subordinate deities, and the value to the family of the worship of ancestors, the Confucians of this period were made increasingly conscious of the religious interpretations of the ultimate meaning of life accepted by Buddhists and Taoists. In respect of the *san-chiao* or 'three religions' of China, there was never any question of an either-or, but each man chose for himself what he considered to be of value. Confucianism, in the pacific and humanistic spirit of Confucius himself, was in the main prepared to tolerate and even assimilate religious expression which was not inimical to morality and the safety of the state.

6. Shryock, p. 119.
7. Shryock, p. 114.
8. Fung Yu-lan, *History of Chinese Philosophy*, Vol. 2, p. 299.
9. Shryock, p. 120.
10. Shryock, p. 121.
11. *Analects*, 7:20.
12. Creel, *Confucius: the Man and the Myth*, p. 223.
13. Fitzgerald, *China*, p. 316.
14. The Six Ministries comprised the ministries of Rites, Finance, Personnel, War, Justice and Public Works. In addition to these there was a Bureau of Censors, with direct access to the emperor, whose duty it was to criticize policy and personnel.
15. K. Ch'en, *Buddhism in China*, pp. 216 ff.
16. Shryock, p. 134.
17. Shryock, p. 137.
18. Chan, *A Source Book*, p. 450.

Chapter 7

1. Fitzgerald, *China*, p. 377. Dun J. Li, *The Ageless Chinese*, p. 190. Wilhelm, *A Short History of Chinese Civilization*, pp. 229 ff.
2. Wilhelm, p. 231.
3. Wu Ching-tzǔ, *The Scholars* (English trans. by H. Y. and Gladys Yang): see Chapter 3 for a satirical account of the effects of passing the state examination on the family of an indigent scholar.
4. J. K. Shryock, *The Origin and Development of the State Cult of Confucianism*, pp. 153–7.
5. Translation bureaus were organized under imperial patronage to carry out the large-scale translation of Buddhist scriptures. They were usually established within the palace precincts or in some famous monastery. According to K. Ch'ên, *Buddhism in China*, p. 368, the translation bureau had an elaborate division of labour among the participants. 'The following divisions were to be found: chief of translation, translator who recited the foreign text and translated it into Chinese, verifier of the meaning of the Sanskrit text, scribe who wrote down the translation in Chinese, verifier of the meaning in the written Chinese, polisher of style, proofreader, and corrector of Chinese characters.'
6. Tripitaka (lit: three baskets) is the name given to the Canon of Buddhist scriptures. It consisted of three divisions: the Vinaya (Buddhist monastic regulations, etc.); the Sūtras (discourses attributed to the Buddha) and the Abhidharma (a collection of attempts to systematize Buddhist doctrines). The Chinese Tripitaka, called *San Tsang*, was printed by order of the first emperor of the Sung dynasty and published in A.D. 973. It consisted of 1,076 items, mainly translated from the Sanskrit, and for the stupendous task of block-printing some 130,000 blocks were cut. See Ch'ên, *Buddhism in China*, pp. 374 ff.
7. K. Ch'ên, *Buddhism in China*, pp. 400–1.
8. Sangha (lit: assembly) is the name given to the order of Buddhist monks. See Brandon, *Dictionary of Comparative Religion*, pp. 555–6.
9. The Doctrine of the Void is the Buddhist doctrine which

asserts that the phenomenal world is void of self-substance, whilst Ultimate Reality is void of all limitations of particularization. The doctrine proclaims the essential Oneness of the phenomenal and the noumenal and is opposed to any form of duality.

10. Carson Chang, *Development of Neo-Confucian Thought*, pp. 153–8.
11. See Chapter 5.
12. The student can consult the relevant chapters in Fung Yu-lan, *History of Chinese Philosophy*, Vol. 2; Chan, *Source Book in Chinese Philosophy*; and C. Burton Day, *The Philosophers of China*.
13. Fung Yu-lan, *History*, Vol. 2, pp. 439, 443 ff., 493 ff. Chan, *Source Book*, pp. 463–5, 497–500. (For translations).
14. Fung Yu-lan, *History*, Vol. 2, pp. 434 ff.
15. W. T. Chan, *Source Book*, p. 460.
16. *Mencius*, 7a:45.
17. Fung Yu-lan, *History*, Vol 2, p. 498.
18. Chan, *Source Book*, pp. 518–19.
19. Chan, *Source Book*, p. 589.
20. J. P. Bruce, *The Philosophy of Human Nature by Chu Hsi*, p. 48.
21. Fung Yu-lan, *History*, Vol. 2, p. 562 note.
22. *Ta Hsüeh*, Chapter 1.
23. This and the following quotations are taken from W. T. Chan's translation of the extant works of Lu Hsiang-shan in *Source Book in Chinese Philosophy*. See p. 574.
24. Chan, *Source Book*, pp. 579–80, 585.
25. Chan, *Source Book*, p. 580.
26. Fung Yu-lan, *History of Chinese Philosophy*, Vol. 2, pp. 601–2.

Chapter 8

1. R. E. Latham (trans.), *The Travels of Marco Polo*, p. 191.
2. J. S. Cummins (ed.), *The Travels and Controversies of Friar Domingo Navarrete (1618–86)*, 2 vols., pp. 137–8.
3. Lin Yü-t'ang, *The Gay Genius*, pp. 184–5; 205–8.

4. See Legge (trans.), *S.B.E.*, Vol. 28; the *Li Chi*, Book 19 (reprinted Delhi, 1966).

5. V. Cronin, *The Wise Man from the West*, pp. 175–6.

6. J. R. Levenson, *Confucianism and its Modern Fate* (3 vols.), Vol. 2, p. 26.

7. Lin Yü-t'ang, *The Gay Genius*, p. 294.

8. *Analects*, 3:1. See also *Analects*, 16:2–3.

9. C. K. Yang, *Religion in Chinese Society*, p. 255.

10. R. E. Latham, *Marco Polo*, pp. 94 ff.

11. When Nurhachi (A.D. 1559–1626) united all the Manchu tribes under his control, he created a politico-military organization by which all Manchus, including their captives and slaves, were required to register in new administrative units called 'banners'. At first there were four and later eight units, and to each unit was assigned a banner of a specified colour. Each banner consisted of a certain number of fighting men under an official who was personally responsible to the emperor. These fighting men were called 'bannermen' and had many special privileges.

12. W. P. Martin, *Hanlin Papers*, p. 44.

13. *Hanlin Papers*, p. 46.

14. Chinese ink was prepared in the form of a solid block. This was rubbed, with the addition of water, on a slab of slate or semi-precious stone such as agate, until a desired consistency of ink was produced. Ink-stones, hollowed to take a small quantity of water, and covered with a lid, were often the work of highly skilled craftsmen, and some of them, artistically carved, were greatly prized by the scholars who owned them.

15. *Hanlin Papers*, p. 46.

16. *Hanlin Papers*, p. 47.

17. Dun J. Li, *The Ageless Chinese*, p. 323.

18. *Lettres édifiantes*, Tome xvii, Letter of Fr. de Fontenoy, pp. 283 ff., quoted in C. Cary-Elwes, *China and the Cross*, pp. 143 ff.

19. H. A. Giles, *History of Chinese Literature*, p. 385.

20. For a fuller and more detailed description of the state religion and the ceremonies appertaining to it, see Bredon and Mitrophanow, *The Moon Year*, and J. Bredon, *Peking*.

21. The main entrance to the Forbidden City in Peking faced south because the Chinese considered the south to be the region in which the *yang* influences, which signified Heaven, light, activity, etc., were most in evidence. For the same reason the principal state temples were sited in areas to the south, south-east and south-west of the Forbidden City. The Altar of Earth, however, which was the antithesis of Heaven, was sited in the northern part of the city where the *yin* influences of darkness, quiescence and absorption were strongest. See articles on Fêng-shui and Yin-yang in Brandon, *Dictionary of Comparative Religion*, pp. 282, 657; and Couling, *Encyclopaedia Sinica*, pp. 175, 615.

22. Bredon, *Peking*, p. 157.

23. The description given here is based on that of J. Edkins, who contributed Chapter 16 to Vol. 2 of A. Williamson, *Journeys in North China*, 2 vols.

24. Bliss Wiant, *The Music of China*, p. 118.

25. Legge, *The Religions of China*, p. 52.

26. Legge, p. 53.

27. Ssŭ-ma Ch'ien, *Shih Chi*, Chapter 47. Quoted from J. K. Shryock, *The Origin and Development of the State Cult of Confucius*, p. 95.

28. Shryock, p. 96.

29. Shryock, p. 98.

30. Shryock, p. 105.

31. Shryock, p, 203.

32. In A.D. 740 the emperor decreed that sacrifices to Confucius should be celebrated on the first *ting* day of spring and autumn, and this continued to be the custom in China till A.D. 1927. *Ting* was the name of the fourth character in a cycle of 'ten stems' which, in combination with 'twelve branches' were used by the Chinese to number the days in a sixty-day cycle. The first *ting* day of spring and autumn came within the second and eighth months respectively. The reason why these particular days were chosen is not known.

33. Shryock, p. 176.

34. See Shryock for a detailed account of the ceremony and also a plan of the main hall of the Confucian temple (pp. 168 ff)., Also Bredon, *Peking*, pp. 192 ff.; Wiant, *The Music of China*,

pp. 120 ff.; Bredon and Mitrophanow, *The Moon Year*, pp. 207 ff.

35. Bredon and Mitrophanow, pp. 210–11.
36. Bredon and Mitrophanow, p. 211.
37. The eight-legged essay or *pa-ku*, developed in the Ming dynasty, was a form of essay which came to be officially approved in the examination system throughout the Ch'ing dynasty (A.D. 1644–1911). It required the rigid observance of a well-defined structural style. The essay was artificially divided under eight headings. Phrases of four and six characters came alternately, and parallel sentences were required to balance antithetically. The emphasis was placed on style rather than content.
38. Martin, *Hanlin Papers*, p. 54. For a critical appraisal of the educational system in China in his own day, see A. H. Smith. *Village Life in China*, Chapters 9 and 10. Smith wrote at a time when the Manchu dynasty was in its last agonies, and the whole Confucian system of education and examination was vitiated by corruption.
39. Martin, *Hanlin Papers*, pp. 1–50 for a full description of the Hanlin Academy.
40. *Hanlin Papers*, p. 116.

Chapter 9

1. Schurmann and Schell, *China Readings*, Vol. 1: *Imperial China*, pp. 123–4.
2. Chan, *Source Book in Chinese Philosophy*, p. 723.
3. The Society of *Righteous and Harmonious Fists* known in English as *Boxers*, was a secret semi-religious organization composed mainly of impoverished peasants and disbanded soldiers. Beginning as a protest against Manchu misgovernment, the rebellion was skilfully directed against the foreigners in China and especially against the Christian missionaries and their converts. The movement, fed on peasant superstitions and resentments, spread with great rapidity throughout north China and came to a head in A.D. 1900 in a virulence born of fanaticism. Initiation into the Society was accompanied by incantations, spells, charms, etc., which were

believed to make the initiate bullet-proof and immune from danger. See Couling, *Encyclopaedia Sinica*, pp. 59 ff.; Dun J. Li, *The Ageless Chinese*, pp. 427 ff.

4. See Fung Yu-lan, *History of Chinese Philosophy*, Vol. 2, p. 690 (trans. note).
5. Levenson, *Confucianism and its Modern Fate*, Vol. 2, p. 15.
6. Shryock, *The Origin and Development of the State Cult of Confucius*, p. 216.
7. Schurmann and Schell, *China Readings*, Vol. 2: *Republican China*, pp. 92–3.
8. Levenson, *Confucianism and its Modern Fate*.
9. Levenson, Vol. 3, p. 62.
10. In February 1957 Mao Tsê-tung gave an important speech in which he said, 'Let a hundred flowers bloom together, and a hundred schools of thought contend.' Thus was initiated a short period, which lasted till the beginning of June in that same year, which was known as the 'hundred flowers period'. So great was the storm of criticism which arose against the government as soon as restraints on free expression were lifted that the communist leaders decided ruthlessly to suppress all 'blooming' and 'contending', and they launched an anti-rightist campaign which shook the country for many months and stamped out 'revisionism'.

Bibliography

Books on Confucius and Confucianism written in Chinese have not been included, nor have numerous articles in journals, general works on comparative religion and encyclopedias. No attempt has been made to produce an exhaustive bibliography. The books listed below have all been consulted, and those starred will be found particularly useful to the reader who wishes to acquire a deeper understanding of Confucian life and thought.

G. G. Alexander, *Confucius, the Great Teacher*, Kegan Paul, Trench, Trübner & Co., London, 1890

J. Bredon, *Peking*, Kelly & Walsh, Shanghai, 1931

J. Bredon and I. Mitrophanow, *The Moon Year*, Kelly & Walsh, Shanghai, 1927

D. Bodde, *China's First Unifier*, E. J. Brill, Leiden, 1938

*J. P. Bruce, *The Philosophy of Human Nature by Chu Hsi*, A. Probsthain, London, 1922

  Chu Hsi and his Masters, A. Probsthain, London, 1923

C. Cary-Elwes, *China and the Cross*, Longmans Green & Co., London, 1957

*W. T. Chan, *Religious Trends in Modern China*, Columbia University Press, New York, 1953

  A Source Book in Chinese Philosophy, Princeton University Press, New York, 1963

Carson Chang, *The Development of Neo-Confucian Thought*, New York Bookman Association, New York, 1957

E. Chavannes, *Les Mémoires Historiques de Se-ma Ts'ien*, 5 vols., Leroux, Paris, 1895–1905

K. Ch'ên, *Buddhism in China*, Princeton University Press, New Jersey, 1964

Chêng Tê-k'un, *Archaeology in China*, Vols. 1–3, Cambridge University Press, Cambridge, 1959 onwards

S. Couling, *Encyclopaedia Sinica*, Kelly & Walsh, Shanghai, 1917; reprinted 1964

F. S. Couvreur, *Chou King*, Textes Chinois avec traduction en Français et en Latin, Catholic Mission Press, Hsien-hsien, China, 1927

    Chou King (as above, 1926)

    Les Quatres Livres (as above, 1930)

H. G. Creel, *The Birth of China*, John Day – Reynel & Hitchcock, New York, 1937

    Confucius: the Man and the Myth, John Day, New York, 1949

    Chinese Thought from Confucius to Mao Tsê-tung, University of Chicago Press, Chicago, 1953

V. Cronin, *The Wise Man from the West*, Rupert Hart-Davis, London, 1955

C. Crow, *Master Kung*, Hamish Hamilton, London, 1937

J. S. Cummins (ed.), *The Travels and Controversies of Friar Domingo Navarrete* (2 vols.), Cambridge University Press for the Hakluyt Society, Cambridge, 1962

R. Dawson (ed.), *The Legacy of China*, Oxford University Press, London, 1964

C. B. Day, *The Philosophers of China*, Peter Owen, London, 1962

W. A. C. H. Dobson, *Mencius*, University of Toronto Press (London: Oxford University Press), 1963

H. H. Dubs, *Hsüntze's Works*, A. Probsthain, London, 1928

    Hsüntze: The Moulder of Ancient Confucianism, A. Probsthain, London, 1927

    History of the Former Han Dynasty (Vol. 1), Waverly, Baltimore, 1938

W. Eichhorn, *Chinese Civilization* (English trans. from the German), Faber and Faber, London, 1969

Mircea Eliade, *Shamanism* (English trans.), Routledge & Kegan Paul, London, 1964. Originally published in French as *Le Chamanisme, et les techniques archaïques de l'extase*, Libraire Payot, Paris, 1951

*C. P. Fitzgerald, *China: a Short Cultural History*, Cresset Press, London, 1935; reprinted 1950

    Revolution in China, Cresset Press, London, 1952

*Fung Yu-lan, *History of Chinese Philosophy* (trans. by D. Bodde), 2 vols. Vol. 1. Henri Vetch, Peking, 1937; Vol. 2, Allen & Unwin, London, 1953

A Short History of Chinese Philosophy, Macmillan Co., New York, 1948

The Spirit of Chinese Philosophy (trans. by E. R. Hughes), Kegan Paul, London, 1947

H. A. Giles, *History of Chinese Literature*, D. Appleton & Co., New York, 1901

Confucianism and its Rivals, Williams & Norgate, London, 1915

L. Giles, *The Sayings of Confucius*, John Murray, London, 1917

H. von Glasenapp, *Buddhism: a non-theistic religion* (trans. from the German by Irmgard Schloegl), Allen & Unwin, London, London, 1970

A. C. Graham, *The Book of Lieh-tzŭ*, John Murray, London, 1960

M. Granet, *La Religion des Chinois*, Presses Universitaires de France, Paris, 1951

La Pensée Chinoise, Albin Michel, Paris, 1934

Chinese Civilization (English trans. by K. E. Innes and M. R. Brailsford), Kegan Paul, London, 1930

J. J. L. de Groot, *The Religious System of China*, 6 vols., Leiden, 1892

R. Grousset, *The Rise and Splendour of the Chinese Empire* (English trans. from the French by A. Watson-Gandy), Geoffrey Bles, London, 1952

*E. R. Hughes, *Chinese Philosophy in Classical Times*, J. M. Dent & Sons, London, 1942

The Great Learning and the Mean in Action, J. M. Dent & Sons, London, 1942

E. R. & K. Hughes, *Religion in China*, Hutchinson's University Library, London, 1950

R. F. Johnston, *Confucianism in Modern China*, Gollancz, London, 1934

*Shigeki Kaizuka, *Confucius* (English trans. by G. Bownas), Allen & Unwin, London, 1956

R. P. Kramers (trans.), *K'ung Tzŭ Chia Yü*, E. J. Brill, Leiden, 1930

R. E. Latham, *The Travels of Marco Polo*, Penguin Books, Harmondsworth, 1958

K. S. Latourette, *The Chinese, their History and Culture*, Macmillan Co., New York, 1946

*J. Legge, *The Chinese Classics* (trans. into English with Chinese text), 5 vols., Hongkong, 1861–72. Also published by Clarendon Press, Oxford.

    The Texts of Confucianism, English trans. in *Sacred Books of the East* (ed. Max Muller), Vols. 3, 16, 27, 28, Clarendon Press, Oxford, 1879, 1888, 1899

    The Religion of China, Hodder & Stoughton, London, 1880

    The Life and Teaching of Confucius, Trübner & Co., London (4th ed.), 1875

    The Life and Works of Mencius, Trübner & Co., London, 1875

J. R. Levenson, *Confucianism and its Modern Fate*, 3 vols., University of California Press, Berkeley, 1964

Li Chi, *The Beginnings of Chinese Civilization*, Seattle, 1957

Dun J. Li, *The Ageless Chinese*, Scribner's, New York, 1965

W. K. Liao (trans.), *The Complete Works of Han Fei Tzǔ*, 2 vols., A. Probsthain, London, 1939

Lin Yü-t'ang, *The Gay Genius*, John Day, New York, 1947

    With Love and Irony, Heinemann, London, 1941

    The Pleasures of a Nonconformist, Heinemann, London, 1962

*Liu Wu-ch'i, *A Short History of Confucian Philosophy*, Penguin Books, Harmondsworth, 1955

W. P. Martin, *Hanlin Papers*, American Presbyterian Press, Shanghai, 1880

H. Maspero, *Melanges Posthumes*, Vol. 1: *Les Religions Chinoises*, Musée Guimet, Paris, 1950

    La Chine Antique, Boccard, Paris, 1927

Y. P. Mei (trans.), *The Ethical and Political Works of Mo-tzǔ*, A. Probsthain, London, 1929

    Mo-tzǔ, the Rival of Confucius, A. Probsthain, London, 1929

J. Needham, *Science and Civilization in China*, Vols. 1–2, Cambridge University Press, Cambridge, 1954–6

    Within the Four Seas, Allen & Unwin, London, 1969

S. J. O'Brière, *Fifty Years of Chinese Philosophy, 1898–1950* (English trans. by L. G. Thompson), Allen & Unwin, London, 1956

K. L. Reichelt, *Religion in Chinese Garment*, Lutterworth Press, London, 1951

F. Schurmann and O. Schell, *China Readings*, 3 vols., Penguin Books, Harmondsworth, 1967

*J. K. Shryock, *The Origin and Development of the State Cult of*

  Confucianism, The Century Co., New York, 1932; reprinted
  1966

A. H. Smith, *Village Life in China*, Oliphant, Anderson & Ferrier,
  Edinburgh and London, 1900

*D. H. Smith, *Chinese Religions*, Weidenfeld & Nicolson,
  London, 1968

W. E. Soothill (trans.), *The Analects of Confucius* (with Chinese
  text), Tokyo, 1910

  The Three Religions of China, Oxford University Press, London, 1923

J. Steele (trans.), *The I Li*, 2 vols., A. Probsthain, London,
  1917

Tjan Tjoe-som (trans.), *The Po Hu T'ung*, 2 vols., E. J. Brill,
  Leiden, 1949, 1952

*A. Waley (trans.), *The Analects of Confucius*, Allen & Unwin,
  London, 1938

  *(trans.), *The Book of Songs*, Allen & Unwin, London, 1937

  Three Ways of Thought in Ancient China, Allen & Unwin,
  London, 1939

J. R. Ware, *The Sayings of Confucius*, Mentor Religious Classics,
  The New American Library, New York, 1955

W. Watson, *China before the Han Dynasty*, Thames & Hudson,
  London, 1961

Holmes Welch, *The Parting of the Way*, Beacon Press, Boston,
  1957

E. T. C. Werner, *Dictionary of Chinese Mythology*, Kelly &
  Walsh, Shanghai, 1932

Bliss Wiant, *The Music of China*, Chung Chi Publications,
  University of Hongkong, Hongkong, N.D. (1968?)

L. Wieger, *History of Religious Beliefs and Philosophical Opinions
  in China* (English trans.), Catholic Mission Press, Hsien-
  hsien, China, 1927

  Textes Historiques (selected texts in Chinese with French
  translation), 2 vols., Hsien-hsien, China, 1929

  Textes Philosophiques (see above), Hsien-hsien, China, 1930

  China Throughout the Ages (English trans.), Hsien-hsien,
  China, 1928

H. Wilhelm, *Change: Eight lectures on the I Ching* (English
  trans.), Routledge & Kegan Paul, London, 1960

R. Wilhelm, *Confucius and Confucianism* (English trans. by G. H.

and A. P. Danton), Kegan Paul, Trench, Trübner & Co.,
London, 1931

History of Chinese Civilization (English trans.), Harrap,
London, 1929

I Ching (English trans.), 2 vols., Routledge & Kegan Paul,
London, 1951

A. Williamson, *Journeys in North China*, 2 vols., Smith, Elder &
Co., London, 1870

Wu Ching-tzŭ, *The Scholars* (English trans. by H. Y. and Gladys
Yang), Foreign Language Press, Peking, 1957

*C. K. Yang, *Religion in Chinese Society*, University of California
Press, Berkeley and Los Angeles, 1961

E. Zürcher, *The Buddhist Conquest of China*, E. J. Brill, Leiden,
1959

A Note on Pronunciation

Chinese names which have an accepted and familiar form in English, as Confucius, Mencius, Kublai Khan, Peking, Nanking, etc., have been retained. In all other cases in which Chinese names or other Chinese characters have been romanized the Wade-Giles system is used. Whatever system is adopted only an approximation to the Chinese pronunciation is possible; the Wade-Giles system has the advantage that it is the most commonly used and accepted by English and American writers on Chinese subjects.

The system makes use of 21 letters of the English alphabet, together with the German ü, a circumflexed ê, and a sign ' after certain letters or combinations of letters to mark a strong aspiration as in K'u = Ktru; p'eng = p-h-e-n-g. The ŭ which follows sz, tz and tz' is used to indicate a kind of buzzing sound by which the initial consonants are vocalized and prolonged. Thus tzŭ is pronounced like dze and adze and tz'ŭ is pronounced like ts in seats.

The following should provide a simple guide to the pronunciation of the Chinese characters romanized in this book:

a	as in father
ai	as in aisle
ao	as ow in cow
ê	as u in us
ei	as in reign
i	as in machine
ih	(only after ch, ch', j and sh) is like r vocalized. Thus ch'ih is like chur in church.
o	as oa in oar
ou	as oe in toe
u	as in rule

ü	as German ü
ch	as j in jug
chʿ	as in church
hs	as sh in sheep
j	is pronounced more like an r vocalized
k	as g in good
kʿ	as k in kind
p	as b in boy
pʿ	as p in pie
ss	as s in simple
t	as d in dare
tʿ	as t in tie
ts and tz	as dz in adze
tsʿ	as in seats
tzʿ	as in quartz

Principal Events in the Life of Confucius

551 B.C. (552?)	Birth of Confucius
548	Death of Confucius's father, Shu Liang-ho
543	Tzǔ-ch'an became Prime Minister of Chêng
537	At 15, Confucius 'set his heart on learning'. The 'Three Huan' (i.e. the three leading families of Lu: Chi-sun, Mêng-sun and Shu-sun) divided the armed forces of Lu into three divisions under their control.
536	Tzǔ-ch'an had the law codified and inscribed on bronze vessels
532?	Confucius married. Accepted minor appointment in Lu
522	Confucius's 30th year. Death of Tzǔ-ch'an
517	The 'Three Huan' force Duke Chao of Lu to flee to the state of Ch'i, where he remained in exile. Chi P'ing-tzǔ took over the supreme authority in Lu. Confucius followed Duke Chao into exile in Ch'i
510	Death in exile of Duke Chao. Confucius returned to Lu
509	Accession of Duke Ling of Lu
505	Death of Chi P'ing-tzǔ
	The principal retainer of the Chi family, Yang Hu, seized power in Lu and sought to persuade Confucius, now aged 48, to join his regime
502	The 'Three Huan' combine to expel Yang Hu and end his reign of tyranny
501	Confucius, aged 52, takes office in Lu as a counsellor to the duke
500	Confucius accompanied Duke Ting to a peace

	conference in Ch'i, and achieved considerable success in diplomacy
	Yen Ying, minister of Ch'i died
498	Confucius persuaded Duke Ting to attempt the demolition of the fortified strongholds of the 'Three Huan'. With the failure of the attempt the influence of Confucius waned
497	Confucius, in his 56th year, left Lu to begin at least ten years of wandering from state to state. He travelled first to Wei, where he was welcomed and given hospitality
494	Accession of Duke Ai of Lu
	Confucius left Wei, and visited Sung, Chêng, Ch'ên and Ts'ai, accompanied by loyal disciples
484	Messengers sent to invite Confucius back to Lu. He returned to his native state, began the training of a younger group of students, and engaged in literary work
483?	Death of Confucius's favourite disciple, Yen Hui, and of Confucius's only son, Po Yü
480	Confucius's oldest disciple, Tzǔ-lu, died
479	Death of Confucius in his 74th year

Table of Dynasties

PERIOD	DYNASTY	CONFUCIAN PERSONALITIES	EVENTS, etc.
Semi-legendary	SHANG (YIN) (1766–1122 B.C.)		Names of Yin rulers preserved on Oracle Bone inscriptions. In 1402 B.C. capital city moved to YIN. Rise of Chou in the West
Feudal	CHOU (1122–249 B.C.) (W. Chou 1122–771; E. Chou 770–249; Anarchy 249–221)	Kings Wên and Wu defeat the Yin and found the Chou dynasty (11th century B.C.) Duke of Chou (?) Confucius (551–479) Mo-tzŭ (c. 479–438) Mencius (371–289) Hsün-tzŭ (c. 298–238)	Ch'un Ch'iu Period (722–489 B.C.) Warring States period (403–221 B.C.) 255 B.C. the state of Ch'in rises to power
Unification	CH'IN (221–206 B.C.)		Building of Great Wall
Empire Building	HAN (206 B.C.–A.D. 220) Former Han (206 B.C.–A.D. 25) Later Han (A.D. 25–220)	Tung Chung-shu (c. 179–104 B.C.) Ssŭ-ma Ch'ien (c. 136–84 B.C.)	Burning of the Books (213 B.C.) Emperor Wu-ti (140–87 B.C.) Confucianism accepted as State Orthodoxy Expansion of Chinese Empire into central Asia Introduction of Buddhism c. 65 A.D.

Disunity	North and South China divided under several short-lived dynasties		North ruled by Tartar kings (A.D. 220–589) Buddhism flourishes
Restoration of Chinese Empire	SUI (A.D. 589–618)		Block printing invented
	T'ANG (A.D. 618–907)	Han Yü (A.D. 768–824)	Hsüan-tsang – pilgrim to India A.D. 629 Creative period for arts
Disunity	THE FIVE DYNASTIES (A.D. 907–960)		Printing of Confucian classics
Unity restored but from A.D. 1127 North China under Mongol rule	SUNG (A.D. 960–1279)	Chou Tun-i (A.D. 1017–1073) Chu Hsi (A.D. 1130–1200) Lu Hsiang-shan (A.D. 1139–1193)	Revival of Confucianism as Neo-Confucianism Age of cultural strength but political weakness
Mongol empire	YUAN (A.D. 1280–1368)		Kublai Khan (d. A.D. 1294) Marco Polo (c. 1253–1324)
Chinese rule restored	MING (A.D. 1368–1644)	Wang Yang-ming (A.D. 1472–1529)	Emperor Yung Lo (A.D. 1403–25) rebuilds Peking and makes it his capital
Manchu Empire	CH'ING (A.D. 1644–1911)	K'ang Yu-wei (A.D. 1858–1927)	K'ang Hsi (A.D. 1661–1722) Ch'ien Lung (1736–1796) Boxer Uprising (1900)
Republic	People's Republic of China		

Index

Agronomists, 112

Ai, Duke of Lu, 54–5, 89

Alchemy, 140

Almanac, 118

Altar of Heaven, 184–7, 188, 189

An Lu-shan, 144

Analects, 13, 41, 46, 48–52, 54–8, 64, 67–74, 76–87, 90–1, 97–8, 100–1, 111, 124–5, 143, 161

Ancestor(tral) spirits, 63, 64, 174; worship, 26, 33, 46–7, 175, 182–3

Ancestors, cult of, 31, 128–9, 174

Ancestral tablets, 183, 187–8, 193

Arrow War, 201

Astrology, 140

August Heaven (*Hao T'ien*) cult, 129

Board of Rites (*Li Pu*), 174, 177, 180–1

Bodde, Derk, 113, 120, 204

Book of Changes (*I Ching*), 25, 122, 132, 157–9, 162

Book of Genealogies (*Shih Pên*), 41

Book of Poetry (*Shih Ching*), 24, 34–5, 41, 146

Book of Rites (*Li Chi*), 55, 56, 74–5, 85, 89, 96, 106, 124, 131, 133–4, 170, 180

Bouvet, Father, 178

Boxer Rebellion, 201–2

Brotherly love (*t'i*), 72–3

Buddha, 63, 140–3, 144–5, 156; Amida, 169

Buddhism, 15, 131, 133, 135, 137–43, 145–8, 153, 157, 160, 162, 168, 170, 173–4, 182, 194, 202; rivalry with Taoism, 140; rapid expansion of, 139–40; doctrine of *karma*, 142; reason for flourishing, 143; flourish-ing of, 144; reaches peak of popularity, 147; regarded as chief rival to Confucianism, 154; *Tripitaka*, 155; Tibetan or Lama, 168

Burning of the Books, 123, 132

Chan, Professor, W. T., 96, 106–7, 110, 148, 160–1, 202

Ch'an (Zen) school, 149

Ch'ang-an (city), 128, 130, 140, 144, 148, 175

Chang Tsai, 157, 158–62; teach-ing, 160; Works, *The Western Inscription*, 158

Chao, Duke of Lu, 49–51, 54

Chao, state, 104

Chao Kuang-yin, 151, 154–5; in-augurates period of unprece-dented cultural advancement, 151; reorganizes civil service examination system, 151–2

Chao-tzǔ, 49

Chê Tsung, Emperor, 171

Ch'ên, state, 53–4

Ch'ên Tu-hsiu, 206; opposition to Confucianism, 206

Ch'êng, King, 24, 32

Ch'êng (sincerity), 97, 164

Chêng, state, 14, 47, 75

Ch'êng Hao, 157, 160–2; fore-runner of idealistic school of Neo-Confucianism, 160–1

Ch'êng I, 157, 160–1; forerunner of Rationalist school, 161

Chêng K'ao-fu, 41

Chêng Tsai, 42

Ch'i dynasty, 142

Ch'i state, 37, 44, 49–50, 91

Ch'i, substance, 159, 162, 164

Chi Huan-tzǔ, 51–2

Chi K'ang-tzǔ, 52, 54, 58, 82

Chi Ping-tzŭ, 49–51
Chi-sun family, 44–5, 49
Chieh, 101
Ch'ien Lung, Emperor, 176 180, 186, 189, 191
Chih (wisdom), 102, 163
Ch'in dynasty, 114, 120–1, 124, 139
Ch'in, state, 24, 36, 113, 119
Ch'in Shih-Huang-ti, Emperor, 97, 104, 119, 120, 125
China, 30, 169–70; prosperity of, 124–5; introduction into of foreign ideas and practice, 156; reaches level of civilized living, 200; preservation of cultural heritage, 209
Chinese civilization and religion, early evidences of, 22
Ching, Duke of Ch'i, 50
Ch'ing T'an ('Pure Conservations'), 138
Ching-tzŭ, 54
Chou, Duke of, 14, 26–7, 32, 44, 50, 64, 100, 191
Chou dynasty, 22–4, 26–34, 83, 101, 104, 112, 117, 127, 129; four elements of civilization of, 64–6
Chou Kung, 87
Chou Li, 75, 124
Chou Tun-i, 157, 158–60, 162; foundation of Neo-Confucianism, 160; Works, *Diagram of the Supreme Ultimate and its Explanations*, 158–9
Christianity, 62, 202
Chu, Duke, 54
Ch'u, state, 35–6, 123, 127, 132
Ch'ü-fu, 32, 42–3, 131–2, 189–93, 204
Chu Hsi, 59, 157, 161–5, 179, 200; beliefs, 162–4
Chuang-tzŭ, 92, 118, 135
Ch'un Ch'iu Fan Lu, 125
Chun-tzŭ, 68, 70, 81
Ch'un, Ch'iu period, 35–6
Ch'un Ch'iu text, 124, 127, 132
Chung Yung, 85, 92–100, 111, 133, 148–9, 158; as philosophical development of Confucian beliefs, 97
Cities, life in, 38–9
City states, founding of, 32

Classic Feasts, 198
Classic of Filial Piety, *see* Hsiao Ching
Classic of History, *see* Shu Ching
Clerk script, 120
Code of law, concept, 113
Communism, 206–9
Confucian Classics, 93, 124, 128, 136, 140, 142–4, 147–8, 150, 152–3, 155–8, 167, 170, 180, 191, 195, 198–200, 204–5, 209
Confucianism: regarded as ethico-political system, 11; agnosticism of, 11, 109, 117; as religion, 11–12; pervasive moral and spiritual teaching of, 11; accepted as orthodox doctrine, 12, 15; receives state recognition, 13; unassailable orthodoxy of, 16; as dominant ideology of China, 17–18; as state cult, 25; vital principles as integral part of, 29–30; distinctive traits of, 29–30; schools of, 59; education as one of supreme aims of, 81; development of, 91; fundamental principles of, 93; acceptance of universe theory, 118; conception of universe, 122; gradual triumph of, 122; factors contributing to growing influence of, 123–4; theology of Heaven, 129–30; unassailable position and influence of, 131, 152; as ideal system suited to empire administration, 135; challenged by Buddhism, 135; main function, 136; rapid decline of, 137; becomes religious cult, 145; control of education and examination system, 154; Buddhism as chief rival to, 154; no firm philosophical basis to counter Buddhist universe theories, 155; re-emphasis on fundamental teaching of Confucius, 157; domination of, 168; glories and weaknesses of, 172; reaches maturity, 180; emergence as principal buttress of tradition, 191; attempt made to establish Confucianism as

China's national religion, 204; similarity with Communism, 208; relevance today of, 210

Confucius: regarded as China's greatest sage and teacher, 13–14, 135, 143, 205; birth, 21, 42; keen interest in ritual, 24; ancestry, 41; early education, 43; career, 43, 48; interest in music, 43, 56, 79–80; marriage, 43; influenced by interstate relationships, 45; fundamentally religious, 48, 63, 85, 87–8, 98–9; deep affection felt for mother, 48; ambitiousness of, 48; receives first official appointment, 51; in office, 52; resigns office, 53; tribulations encountered, 55; death, 55, 89–90; physical appearance, 55; character and personality, 55–7; number of disciples, 58; adverse opinions of, 60; philosophy, 62; ethical concepts of thinking, 68–76; definition of righteousness, 70–2; teaching of value of study and search for knowledge, 75–7; chief aim of teaching, 76–7; emphasis on study and search for knowledge, 76–7, 194; principles of education, 78–9, 80–1; moral emphasis in teaching, 78, 194; genius as teacher, 80; proposes careful attention to word-usage, 83; observation on financial and economic aspects of government, 83–4; humanism as ethical philosophy, 84; moderation in all things as one of chief aims, 97; belief in graded hierarchy as ideal system, 114; emphasis on principles, 114; posthumous honorary titles conferred on, 132; development in cult of, 147, 190–1; stresses virtues of filial piety and loyalty, 172; belief in autocracy, 173; worship of, 189–91, 205; growing fame of, 190

Creel, Professor H. G., 124, 128, 143

Culture, standard of material, 34

Decree of Heaven, *see Tien Ming*

Democracy, 108

Divination, 24–5, 47, 107, 117–18, 158

Doctrine of the Mean, *see Chung Yung*

Dubs, Professor H. H., 76, 105, 106, 123, 124

Dynastic Histories, 198

Dynasties, 200

Earth, worship of, 184

Education and educational system: chief concerns of, 95; failings of, 194–5; powerful influence of Confucian, 199

Eichhorn, Werner, 121–2

Erh Ya dictionary, 124

Eunuchs, 137–8, 170–1

Examination system, 114, 195–8

Fan Chên, 142

Fan Ch'ih, 54

Fang, 42, 48

Fang Shu, 41

Fate (*ming*), 85–6, 97

Fêng (sacrifice), 128

Fêng Tao, 150

Fertility cults, 25

Feudalism(tic), 30–4, 36, 37–8, 60, 65, 66–7, 92, 112–13, 119, 120–1, 183, 207; destruction of, 121

Filial piety (*hsiao*) as basis of Confucian morality, 32, 65, 72–4, 99, 111–12, 140, 143

Fitzgerald, C. P., 130

Five Dynasties period, 150

Five Elements theory and school, 94, 118, 125–6, 132, 158–9, 174–5

Five grains, 38

Four Books, 179, 208

Fu Fu Ho, 41

Fung Yu-lan, 111, 118, 160, 164

Gerbillon, Father, 178

Glasenapp, Helmuth von, 88

God, 62, 187

Great Learning, *see Ta Hsüeh*

Han dynasty, 12, 15–16, 23–4, 90–3, 100–1, 110–14, 117, 120, 123, 129–30, 134, 136–9, 173,

184, 190; Former, 130, 148; Later, 130-1

Han Fei Tzu, 113

Han Fei-tzŭ, 59

Han Huan Ti, Emperor, 138

Hanlin Academy, 177, 192, 195, 196-9

Han Ming Ti, 132

Han P'ing Ti, 132

Han Wu-ti, Emperor, 12, 125, 132

Han Yü, 147-9; beliefs regarding Buddhism and Taoism, 148-9

Hangchou, 168

Hao, 35

Heaven (*T'ien*), 26, 47-8, 63-4, 117; *see also* Altar, and Temple, of Heaven

Hedonists, 112

Hinduism, 204

Hong Kong, 207, 210

Hou Chi, 31

Hsia dynasty, 21, 83

Hsiao, Duke of Wei, 101

Hsiao Ching (*Classic of Filial Piety*), 59, 74, 83, 92, 94, 111-12, 124, 142

Hsien, Prince of Ho-chien, 132

Hsing (nature), 163-4

Hsüan Hsüeh ('Dark or Mysterious Learning'), 138-9

Hsüan-tsang, 145-6

Hsün-tzŭ, 13, 92-4, 104-10, 126, 133, 149; emphasizes external authority and *li* exalted as basis of morality, 105; interpretation of Confucianism, 106; develops humanistic philosophy of history, 107; disbelief in democracy, 108; exalts *li*, 109; purpose of *li*, 109-10; influence on Han dynasty Confucianism, 133; rationalism of, 133

Hu Shih, 206

Hua Yen school, 149

Huan, Duke of Ch'i, 36-7, 44

Huan T'ui, 53-4

Huang Ti (Yellow Emperor), 31

Hughes, E. R., 99

Human history and laws of nature, theory regarding links between, 126

Human nature, estimate of, 95, 102-3, 126

I (righteousness), 65, 70-2, 102, 105, 163, 165

I Ching (Book of Changes), 25, 122, 132, 157-9, 162

I Li, 75, 124

I-yin, 101

Immortality, 63, 133-5, 140

India, 26, 204

Islam, 62, 204

Jan Ch'iu, 54-5, 58, 74

Japan, 157, 202, 204

Jên (love), 65, 68-70, 73, 81, 95, 96, 102, 105, 160, 163, 165-6

Jên Tao (Way of Man), 63, 97

Jesuits, 171, 178

Ju Chiao, 22

Judaism, 62

K'ang Hsi, Emperor, 16-17, 125, 156, 175-80, 181-2, 186, 191, 194; *Sacred Edict* of, 17

K'ang Hsi Tzŭ Tien, 178-9, 198

K'ang Yu-wei, 203-5; advocates reformation of monarchy in China, 203; advocates acceptance of Confucianism as China's national religion, 203; Works, *Ta T'ung Shu* (*Book of the Great Concord*), 203-4

Kao Tsu, *see* Liu Pang

Korea, 16, 157

Ku Liang, 124

Kuan Chung, 37, 50

Kuang-Hsü, Emperor, 203-5

Kuang Wu, Emperor, 130-1

Kuangtung, 148

Kublai, Emperor, 175, 192

K'ung (surname of Confucius), 190-1, 193

K'ung, Duke, 193

K'ung Fu-chia, 41

K'ung Yu, 54

Kung, Prince of Lu, 132

Kung-Shan Fu-jao, 51

Kung Yang, 124

Kuo-tsŭ-chien, 176, 195, 199

Lama (Buddhism), 168

Lao-tzŭ, 50, 92, 135, 141, 143, 145; Works, *Tao Tê Ching*, 50

Legalism(ts), 92, 94, 112, 113, 124, 128; advocate single law,

119; doctrine, 119; Legalist school (*Fa Chia*), 119
Legge, James, 111, 188
Levenson, J., 171, 207–8; Works, *Confucianism and its Modern Fate*, 207
Li, Duke, 41
Li (rules and rituals), 66, 69, 73–6, 79, 102, 105–11, 113, 208
Li (principle), 159, 162–4
Li Ao, 147–9
Li Chi, Professor, 22–3
Li Chi (Record of Rites), 55, 56, 74–5, 85, 89, 96, 106, 124, 131, 133–4, 170, 180
Li Pu (Board of Rites), 174, 177, 180–1
Li Shih-min, 144–5, 147; seeks to include religion in Confucianism system, 145
Li Ssŭ, 104, 120
Li Yüan, 144
Li Yüan-kuan, 146
Liang Wu-ti, 142
Lieh-tzŭ book, 134
Lin-tzê, 50
Ling, Duke, 53–4, 101
Liŭ Hsiang, 105, 133
Liu Hsin, 133
Liu Pang, Emperor, 120, 122–3
Liu Tsung-yüan, 147
Logicians, 92
Loyalty and consideration as basis of Confucian morality, 32, 64, 74, 140
Loyang, 35, 50, 139, 175
Lu, state, 32, 41, 44, 48–9, 79, 91, 190
Lu Hsiang-Shan, 157, 164–5; founder of Neo-Confucianism school of Hsin-hsüeh, 164
Lun Yü, 13

Magical practices, 140
Mahāyāna Buddhism, 141, 156
Manchu dynasty, 125, 181, 195, 200–2, 205
Mao Tsê-tung, 206, 208
Marco Polo, 168–9, 175
Maspero, Henry, 56
Medicine, 140
Mencius, 13, 29, 43, 52, 59, 70, 82, 90, 93, 97, 100–4, 106, 110, 111, 126, 133, 148, 154, 160,

179; demonstrates superiority of Confucianism, 101–2; expounds virtues, 102–4
Mencius, 92, 94, 149, 158
Mêng family, 41–3, 50–2
Mêng Hsi-tzŭ, 50
Mêng Hsien-tzŭ, General, 42
Mêng I-tzŭ, 50, 58
Min, Duke of Sung, 41
Ming dynasty, 165, 175, 188, 192–3
Ming (fate), 85–6, 97
Ming Ti, Emperor, 131–2, 191
Mo-tzŭ, 52, 55–6, 64, 70, 85–6, 92–4, 102, 117; preaches universal altruistic love, 117
Mohists, 112, 117
Mongolia, 16
Monotheism, 174, 188
Music, Confucius' emphasis on, 75

Nanking, 139, 175
Nan-kung Ching-shu, 50, 58
Nature, interrelation with man, 122, 126, 135
Navarrete, Friar Domingo, 169
Needham, Joseph, 11
Neo-Confucianism, 148, 156–67; Ch'êng-Chu school, 161
New Text school of Confucianism, 125–6, 131–2, 135; production of pseudo-science of numerology, 126; theories, 127; attacks made on by Wang Ch'ung, 134–5
Nobility: life of, 39; training of, 68–9
Numerology, 135

'Old Learning' or Old Text school, 132–3; rationalistic attitude of, 134
Omens, 107
Opium War, 201

Pa (rule of the tyrant), 104
Peasantry: animistic beliefs of, 22–3; life of, 39–40
P'ei Wên Yün Fu, 179
Peking, 175–6, 191–3, 196, 199, 201, 205–6
Period of Disunity, 139, 140, 143
Philosophy of Change, 118

Pi-yang, 42
P'ing Ti, Emperor, 191
Po Ch'in, 32
Po-i, 101
Primogeniture, law of, 33
Principles, establishment of vital, 29–30
Propriety, study of, 75

Religion, growth of scepticism in, 46–7
Ritual, 50, 66, 82–3, 109, 128, 133–4, 136, 184–9, 192–4, 205; see also Li

Sacred Edict, 17, 179
Sacrifice(s), 109, 128, 133–4, 141–3, 145–6, 174–5, 180–93, 204–5; Small, 180–1; Medium, 181; Great, 181–8, 204–5
Sages, 68, 71, 98–103, 108, 110, 112, 136, 160, 165, 178, 192–3
Schools, establishment of, 57
Shan (sacrifice), 128
Shang dynasty, 21–6, 28–30, 33, 41; religious structure of, 22–3; divination as important element in Shang religion, 25
Shang Ti, god, 23, 28–9, 47–8, 129, 186–8
Shang Yang, 119
Shang-Yin dynasty, 32
Shansi, 38
Shantung, 32, 38, 43, 128, 189, 204
Shao Yung, 157, 161, 162
Shê-chi t'an (altar of spirits of soil and grain), 33, 183–4
Shên Nung, 181
Shên-tsung, Emperor, 153–4
Shêng Jên, 68
Shih, priest-scribes, 24, 37, 42, 58
Shih-Chi (Historical Records), 55, 89
Shih Ching (Book of Poetry), 24, 34–5, 41, 146
Shih Pên (Book of Genealogies), 41
Shinto, 204
Shryock, J. K., 190
Shu Ching (Classic of History), 43, 79, 123
Shu Hsiang, 45

Shu-liang Ho, 42
Shu-sun family, 44, 55
Shun, legendary emperor, 79, 98–9, 101, 103, 111, 129
Sian, 35
Singapore, 210
Single-mindedness and sincerity, 99–100
Sino-Japanese War, 202
Six Disciplines, 123–4
Spirit-tablets, 146, 183, 186–8
Ssŭ-ma Ch'ien, 12–13, 41–2, 55, 89–90, 92, 106, 190; Works, Historical Records, 12
Ssŭ-ma Kuang, 153–4, 171–2
Ssŭ-ma Niu, 53–5, 58
State cult, 12, 25, 121–2, 127–9, 156, 174, 180–3, 188–9, 191
State rituals, 12
Su Tung-p'o, 169
Sui dynasty, 141–2, 144
Sun Yat-sen, 206
Sung dynasty, 16, 150–6, 168, 173–5, 195
Sung, state, 37, 41, 45, 53–4
Syncretism, 118, 132, 158
Szechuan, 38

Ta Hsüeh (Great Learning), 59, 92–6, 148–9, 158, 164; concerned with education and social and political matters, 96
Ta T'ung Shu (Book of the Great Concord), 203
T'ai I (supreme unity), 118, 128
T'ai Lao, sacrifice, 141, 146
T'ai Miao or Great Temple, 183
T'ai Shan, 128
Tai Shêng, 131
Tai Tê, 131
T'ai-tsu, Emperor, 154–5
Taiping Rebellion, 201
Taiwan, 16, 207, 210
T'ang dynasty, 131, 144–6, 151, 156, 168, 193, 195; final extinction of, 150
T'ang legendary king, 129
T'ang T'ai Tsung, see Li Shih-min
Tao, 'The Way', 67–8, 71, 147–9, 159, 165
Taoism(ts), 15, 92, 94, 112, 128, 131–5, 137–43, 146, 152–3,

155–6, 158, 160, 162, 170, 173–4, 182, 194; rivalry with Buddhism, 140; reasons for flourishing, 143; flourishing of, 144; mysticism of, 147

Tao Tê Ching, 50, 118

Tê (power of virtue and personality), 63, 82, 103, 113

Temple, ancestral, as most important building, 23

Temple of Confucius, 192–3

Temple of Heaven, 185–7

Temples to Confucius, establishment of, 145–6

Three Religions, 141

Tibet, 16, 168

T'ien (Heaven), 26, 47–8, 63–4, 117

T'ien chih (Will of Heaven), 86

T'ien Li, Principle of Nature or Heavenly Principle, 161, 163–4

T'ien ming (Decree of Heaven), 86

T'ien Tao (Way of Heaven), 63, 67–8, 77–8, 81, 84–6, 97, 99, 118

Ting, Duke, 51, 52

Toba Tatars, 139

Ts'ai, state, 54

Tsai Wo, 85

Tsai Yü, 48

Tsêng, tzŭ, 59, 71–2, 95, 111

Tsin, state, 42, 44–5

Tso, 124

Tso Chuan, 42, 47, 52, 85, 89

Tsou, 41, 42–3

T'u Shu Chi Ch'êng, 179, 198

Tung Chung-shu, 125–7, 131, 158; theories, 125–7; Works, *Luxuriant Gems of the Spring and Autumn Annals* (*Ch'un Ch'iu Fan Lu*), 125

Tzŭ-ch'an, 14, 45–7

Tzŭ-chang, 59

Tzŭ-hsia, 59, 79

Tzŭ-kung, 13, 53, 54, 58–9, 74, 77, 79, 90

Tzŭ-lu, 51, 53, 55, 58, 85, 89–90

Tzŭ-ssŭ, 97, 98–9

Tzŭ-yu, 59

Universe, questions regarding nature and origin of, 117–18

Vedic religion, 26

Waley, A., 56, 69

Wan Li, 170–1

Wang An-shih, 153–4; reappraises civil service examination system, 153

Wang Ch'ung, 134–5

Wang Yang-ming, 165–6, 200; his fundamental doctrine, 165–6

Warring States period, 92–5, 111–12, 117, 158

Way of Heaven, see *T'ien Tao*

Wei dynasty, 139

Wei, state, 53, 75

Wên, legendary king, 27–9, 87, 101, 104, 129

Wên, Marquis of Wei, 59

Wên Ti, Emperor, 124–5

White Tiger Hall (*Po Hu T'ung*), 127

Wilhelm, R., 150

Will of Heaven, see *T'ien chih*

Wood-block printing, invention of, 150

Wu, divination experts, 24–5

Wu, legendary king, 26–7, 127–9

Wu, state, 36–7, 42, 54

Wu San-kuei rebellion, 178

Wu-ti, Han Emperor, 130, 141; proclaims Confucianism as recognized state cult, 127–8

Yang, 107, 118, 122, 126, 129, 159, 184

Yang, C. K., 175

Yang Chu, 92, 102

Yang Hsiung, 134

Yang Huo, 51

Yang-tzŭ River, 36, 139

Yao, legendary king, 87, 103, 129

Yellow River, 21, 36

Yen family, 42

Yen Ch'ou-yü, 53

Yen Hui, 53, 55, 58, 84, 143, 145, 146, 154

Yen-ying, 45–6, 50

Yin, 76, 107, 118, 122, 126, 129, 159, 184

Yin dynasty, 21, 83

Yin-yang school, 94, 112, 118, 125–7, 133, 158, 174–5
Yu-jo, 59
Yu, King, 35, 100–1
Yüan Shih-k'ai, 205–6
Yüeh, state, 36

Yung Chêng, Emperor, 176, 179–80, 191
Yung Lo, Emperor, 17, 175, 181–2
Yung Lo Ta Tien, 198

The End of Atlantis
New Light on an Old Legend

J. V. Luce

In the fifteenth century B.C., a volcanic eruption of exceptional violence occurred on the island of Thera (Santorin), 75 miles north of Crete.

Did this mark the destruction of Atlantis, the story of which Plato gave to the world eleven centuries later?

Was there ever, in fact, such an island as he described, the home of an advanced culture and the centre of a great empire?

If so, where was it, when did its civilisation flourish, and why did it disappear?

Mr Luce, with the help of archaeologists, vulcanologists, seismologists and oceanographers, suggests the real truth. It is a double story – of a legend, Atlantis; and of a cataclysm.

'The evidence is here fully mustered for the first time . . . we must be grateful to him for a most stimulating book.'

DAILY TELEGRAPH

'An exciting controversy.'

SUNDAY TIMES

'It needs a book like *The End of Atlantis* to put the archaeological evidence in perspective.'

GUARDIAN